I WANT TO TELL YOU HOW I FEEL

*How to Know What You Feel,
Express How You Feel,
And, How to Listen to Others*

Ron Johnson, Ph.D., Deb Brock, Ph.D.

I Want To Tell You How I Feel
How to Know What You Feel, Express How You Feel, And, How to Listen to Others

Copyright © 2020 by Ron Johnson, Ph.D., Deb Brock, Ph.D.

All rights reserved. No part of this book may be reproduced or transmitted in any form or by any means without written permission of the author.

ISBN 978-1-7354289-0-1

Published by Midlands Psychological Associates,
Lodi, Wisconsin.

Midlandspsychological.com
brockandjohnson@gmail.com

Cover photo by Deb Brock, "Sweet Secrets" found on West Frisian Island, Ameland, Netherlands.

Other works by the authors available through Midlands Psychological Associates:

The Positive Power of Sadness:

How Good Grief Prevents and Cures Anxiety, Depression, and Anger

Friendly Diagnosis: What is Right With Me!

Watch Your Temperament: Discovering Your Natural Personality

Seen and Not Heard: Effective Parenting with Fewer Words and more Action

Mantalk: How Men Express their Feelings

Balls: Men Finding Courage to be Honest

4-8-12: Managing Difficult Children

Contents

Foreword 1
Introduction. 5
1   What Are Feelings? 9
2   What are Emotions? 33
3   Personality Factors in Feelings. 59
4   Expressing Feelings 95
5   Hearing Feelings 129
6   Rules of Engagement. 153
7   It's All About Hurt 171
8   Temperamental Conversations. 197
9   Scripts for Successful Feeling Communication 229
About the Authors 247
Annotated References. 251

Foreword

Seventeen years ago, I walked into the office of Midlands Psychological Office. I was unaware that I was about to begin a journey of seeking truth and meaning, a journey that has helped me discover myself, other people, and the world around me. I have taken advantage of visiting with Dr. Johnson, and occasionally his wife, Dr. Deb Brock, as I have progressed on this journey. What Dr. Johnson and Dr. Brock have taught me, and what you will learn in this book, made the quality of my life deeper and richer. Most specifically they taught me how to know what I feel, value how I feel, and communicate how I feel, none of which I had ever done before despite the fact that I come from a good family and am reasonably intelligent. Drs. Johnson and Brock have dared to write this book about "feelings," a term that represents a profound concept that is at the heart of human experience and essential in human relationships. The ability to understand feelings, which is the heart of experiencing life, has empowered me, and it has helped me empower the people I live with and work with. Drs. Brock and Johnson have given you an opportunity to do the same.

Johnson and Brock's previous book, *The Positive Power of Sadness*, dealt primarily with the centrality of the emotion of sadness. The present work has broadened the concept of emotion to include the other basic emotions of joy, fear and anger. Furthermore, this present book suggests a deeper understanding of emotions by seeing that emotions are a subset of *feelings*. The most profound idea in their earlier book is that sadness is not only necessary but good because sadness comes having lost something you love. The present book takes this concept a step beyond the importance of sadness to encompass the other emotions and highlights the essentiality of knowing how to communicate feelings, our most basic relational transaction.

This book will show you how to feel in a way that is insightful, useful, powerful, and beautiful. The format that Drs. Johnson and Brock have presented gives us the ability to *feel feelings*, which means to understand them and gain greater clarity on what we feel and how we can utilize these feelings in daily life. Beyond this self-knowledge lies the equally important aspect of understanding how others feel. The idea of understanding one's own feelings leading to understanding others' feelings suggests that this book is not just about yourself, but also about other people, and ultimately about deepening relationships.

This book is about mastering feelings. Mastering feelings is not controlling them and it is not repressing them, nor is it forcing what you feel on someone else. Mastering feelings is valuing them and carefully utilizing them to make a better life for yourself and for others. Mastering feelings also leads to such significant social elements in life as forgiveness, gratitude, encouragement, and challenge. You can only do these things if you know what you feel, know how to communicate what you feel and be patient when others are speaking their feelings. If you read this book with an open heart and an open mind, you will feel deeply, feel better, communicate your feelings, and understand other people's feelings. You will then begin a lifelong journey that will enhance your life as you simultaneously enhance others' lives.

—Joseph Hastreiter, Vice President,
EWH Small Business Accounting. Milwaukee, WI. 2020.

***

As you look into this book, *I Want To Tell You How I Feel,* you are being brave. Before I read this book, when someone said those words, I was prone to run. In my mind, those were fighting words. However, as a pastor, a service professional and a married person, I cannot and should not ignore feelings. Ron and Deb provide a thoughtful construct and an entertaining dialogue for understanding emotions and articulating feelings.

Let Me Tell You How I Feel has many well researched and insightful observations with a significant annotated bibliography. One great truth discussed here is that dark emotions are derivatives of love. Ron and Deb point out that fear and anger arises because something loved is threatened. This includes introspective things, like a sense of security, belonging, ego or self-image all which can be threatened. The anticipation of losing these things creates a defensive position from which many of us have tried to present our feelings. Deb and Ron instruct us on how to manage our defenses so we can explore the love in all we experience and then adequately communicate our feelings. Connecting people back to the foundation of love is revelatory and restorative, provides a gateway to healing, and is the basis of all feelings. Accepting fear and anger and moving from there to sadness is what releases us to love again. These ideas are transformative for me, I hope they will be for you.

Deb and Ron remind us that how people express feelings greatly surpasses the use of words. In fact, these authors suggest that verbal expression of feelings usually fail, mostly because people don't really understand the depth of their feelings. Understanding our feelings and the feelings of others is needed by all, whether personally, interpersonally or professionally.

I commend this book to you, to expand and empower you to help others identify emotions and express their feelings. The words "let me tell you how I feel" can be a gateway to more love, more understanding, and more community. Thank you, Ron and Deb, for this labor of love.

—David Michael, River Hills Church
Connections Pastor. Sauk City, Wisconsin, 2020

Introduction

WHAT DOES IT MEAN when someone says, "I have to tell you my feelings" or "I need to tell you my feelings"? How do you feel when you hear such statements? You feel defensive. But why should you feel "defensive" when someone says to you that they want to tell you how they feel? When someone says, "I want to tell you how I feel," this statement *seemingly should* mean that your friend simply wants you to listen, understand, and learn about him or her. Shouldn't this be a time where you listen intently to what your friend has to say? Shouldn't you be all ears given this apparent opportunity to know, understand, and maybe even love your friend more? When people say that they want to tell you how they feel, this should be a wonderful opportunity for you to learn about your friend. It should be such a time, but it usually isn't.

The statement, "I just have to tell you my feelings" almost always is a precursor to telling you what *you have done wrong*. Often, that statement will be followed up with telling you that you *did* something wrong, *said* something wrong, or *failed* to do or say something. In most cases the statement, "I need to tell you my feelings" will not be about me whatsoever. It will be about you. Tragically, we have transformed this most valuable experience, *how I feel*, into a criticism of *what you did*. How did the conversational expression "I need to tell you how I feel" evolve into a statement about *you* rather than *me*? We hope to make sense of this conundrum. We want to help people come back to the real meaning of "I need to tell you how I feel", which should be about *me*, not about *you*. Our task in this book is to get back to what it means for people to express their feelings. But this is a huge task, an almost impossible task because most of us simply don't know how to tell each other how *we feel*. The key word in the statement, "I need to tell you how I feel" is the word *feel*. But what does *feel* mean? If we can help you understand this central word... feel...we will have laid the groundwork of speaking your feelings.

In order to understand the word "feel" we have to start by saying that we cannot define this word. We begin Chapter 1 with a discussion of how some of the most important concepts in life and are undefined, like love, and wisdom. Furthermore, science does not define such basic concepts as time and distance. To understand such things as love, time, and feelings we have to see the effects of these things. Granting that we can't define feelings with exact words, we can see how feelings *erupt,* how they are *felt* and how they are *expressed*. In Chapter 1 we make a case for the fact that feelings are experienced and expressed in four ways: physically, emotionally, cognitively, and in action. We suggest that emotions are but a subset of feelings, not the entirety of feelings. We discuss how different people experience their feelings and express their feelings predominantly in one of these four ways. Do you immediately see how people might fail to communicate their feelings if they are using different expressions of feelings?

If it is a challenge to express our feelings because we have different avenues to do so, we suggest the process is made even more difficult when it comes to the emotional aspect of feelings. In Chapter 2 we examine the four basic emotions of *joy, sorrow, fear,* and *anger* as well as combinations of these emotions. We propose that these emotions always occur in pairs: the "love-based" pair of joy and sorrow, and the "defense-based" pair of fear and anger. When emotions dominate one's expression of feelings things go wrong in human communication. But emotions are so central to who we are that we need to find ways to effectively incorporate emotions into our communication. In order to understand emotions, we examine how, why, and when these four basic emotions develop in childhood. We discuss what it means to be emotionally *mature*, and how emotional maturity always leads to *social maturity*.

Beyond understanding the process of experiencing feelings and the nature of emotions, we suggest that there are differences in *temperament* that significantly influence how people experience and express their feelings. We discuss temperament in Chapter 3 where we identify four different styles of life based on the temperaments of players, caretakers, analysts, and lovers. Players' orientation to life is experienced-based in life, whereas caretakers are property-based, analysts are meaning-based, and lovers are connection-based. Because people have these significantly different orientations to life, the means by which they experience feelings, express feelings, and understand others' feelings can be profoundly different.

Having laid the groundwork of an understanding of feelings, emotions, and temperament, we come to the heart of this book: expressing feelings in Chapter 4 and hearing feelings in Chapter 5. In Chapter 4 we discuss the challenges of expressing feelings, and how particularly hard it is to manage emotions in our expression of feelings. We suggest that there needs to be "license" in expression of feelings just as we give poetic license, musical license, and grammatical license to people who communicate in those modalities. We discuss how much feeling expression can appear to be negative and offend our listeners which then cause negative emotional reactions. We talk about how it is particularly important to avoid questions when expressing feelings, how any expression of feelings makes you feel vulnerable, and how the whole business of feeling expression is imperfect.

Granting that expressing feelings is fraught with imperfection, hearing feelings is even harder, which we discuss in Chapter 5. Hearing someone else express their feelings is a challenge not only because you will have your own emotions and thoughts while hearing your friends speak their feelings. Additionally, you will have to wade through the murky waters of someone doing this very imperfect thing of expressing feelings. Hearing others' feelings is difficult because of the temperamental differences we discuss in Chapter 3 but also because people speak in "circles," or cycles as we prefer to call them, when they express their feelings. We propose that the hardest task in hearing someone's feelings is to govern your own emotional reaction and cognitive thoughts in order to give your friend room to express their feelings. In Chapter 6 we suggest some "rules of engagement" when people are expressing and hearing one another's feelings. A central rule that we suggest is perhaps the hardest to follow: "One at a Time," which means that one person talks about feelings and the other person listens. This is extremely hard to do and relates to the emotional reaction you have to your friend's expressed feelings.

The reason that hearing someone's feelings is so hard is that he or she will often be expressing some kind of *hurt* that they felt, perhaps even something that you said or did that hurt them. We devote the whole of Chapter 7 to this central concept of hurt while admitting that hurt is centrally important but also undefinable. We discuss how hurt comes to different people from different quarters and experiences but also from their different temperaments and value systems. The beauty of hurt is that it is always about love in some way. The challenge of hurt is that it usually leads to fear, anger, and resentment as well as stirring up by old hurts in your life. We propose that hurt can be resolved and *finished* rather than remaining in the fear-anger-resentment stage, but finishing hurt is a real challenging task.

In Chapters 8 and 9 we present theoretical conversations between people in various kinds of relationships that involve the expression and the understanding of feelings. Feelings are not only a central element of human relationships, but feeling-based conversations can be a wonderful addition to your interpersonal life.

Chapter 1

What Are Feelings?

FEELINGS ARE A CENTRAL element of human existence and even more central in human relationships. If we can understand feelings and value feelings, we can learn to communicate this central ingredient to improve both our personal lives and our interpersonal relationships. We will be happier with ourselves and most certainly be happier in our relationships. The task we have in this book is to find ways to *feel* feelings, *express* feelings, *communicate* feelings, and ultimately understand *other people's* feelings. Note that expressing feelings is not the same as communicating feelings. Expressing feelings is hard for everyone, but truly communicating feelings is nearly impossible. Nevertheless, we are endeavoring to help you succeed in this task of communicating what you feel. This is no easy task because feelings are difficult to identify, difficult to communicate, and difficult to understand. How can something so fundamental to our lives and our relationships be so difficult to do? It is difficult to communicate feelings because feelings are *undefined*.

FEELINGS ARE REAL BUT UNDEFINED
People talk about their feelings all the time, and yet there is no universally agreed upon definition of this term "feelings." People say things like, "I just have this feeling," or "I have a gut level feeling," or, "I have a deep feeling"

about something that might be very important to them. We all have said "I just feel…," but what does "just feel" really mean? When people say this kind of thing, they think that the words they use to convey their feelings will adequately communicate. Seldom is this the case. Rather, when people truly feel something, they are never as truly able to perfectly communicate this feeling in words. Feelings are simply too important, too central to our sense of self, and too pure to be able to put into words perfectly. In fact, the more important the feeling is, the more difficult it is to communicate this feeling. At best, most of what we attempt to communicate with words about our feelings pales in comparison to what this feeling really is. Most words simply don't do justice to what we feel, which makes this endeavor of communicating our feelings a huge dilemma. There are at least three things that contribute to this dilemma: (1) feelings are central to our human existence, (2) feelings are not definable, and (3) using words to communicate feelings is fraught with potential problems. We *feel* things all the time and we *feel* compelled to try to communicate what we *feel*. But do we ever really successfully communicate our *feelings*? Rarely.

We all have feelings, we all know that our feelings are very important to us, and we all make some attempt to communicate our feelings. We believe that there is nothing more important than our feelings. Yet, none of us is able to find adequate words to communicate this central ingredient of human existence. The challenge at hand is to describe, and ultimately understand feelings even though we can't exactly define feelings. This is the essence of this chapter, to discuss the nature of feelings.

If feelings are not definable, and words do not do justice to communicating feelings, how are we to proceed with this endeavor of learning how to adequately speak our feelings? Furthermore, even if we think we have successfully communicated our feelings, how can we trust that if people have truly understood what we have said about our feelings? The undefinable nature of feelings is at the core of this dilemma. Just because feelings are undefined does not mean that they are not real. *The things that are most important in life are all undefinable.* We know this to be true in the science of physics. For example, the three basic ingredients of the physical universe, time, distance, and mass, are all undefinable. Think of it this way: we know what time is and we know what distance is. We really know what mass is because mass is something like stuff or things. Even though physicists don't define time, distance, and mass, we know these things exist because we have observed and *experienced* these things. We have experienced time; we have experienced distance, and we have experienced mass.

The undefinable nature of important things is not solely the domain of physics. The central ingredient of the biological sciences is *life*, and yet we do not actually define life; we just know it because we observe life and experience it. Neuroscientists, together with philosophers and theologians are jointly examining the nature of consciousness, but we cannot yet define consciousness, this central ingredient of human functioning (Foreman, 1999). Life, this central ingredient of the human existence cannot be defined. It has to be *experienced*.

Perhaps the most important ingredient of our personal and interpersonal lives is *love*, but who can adequately define love? Poets and composers might be the best at describing love but they can't define it. Many authors have spoken of love. Two thousand years ago the Apostle Paul wrote what might be one of the most fundamental "definitions" we have of love. He said that "love is patient and kind" by nature and that it "protects, trusts, hopes, and preserves" in action. Paul then told us what love is not: "love lacks envy, avoids boasting, isn't arrogant, isn't rude, and is never self-seeking or angry." While these qualifiers might go a long way to clarify the behavior of love, or the manifestation of love, they still do not adequately *define* love. Love is something to be *experienced*, not defined. Some authors have suggested that there are two, four, or many "kinds" of love, while others think that love is a unitary concept not to be broken down. Is there a difference between the experience of someone truly loving her child and someone truly loving a football team? You might love that football game until you see that it is your child who fell of her bike and needs your help. In the very moment of loving something, we know what we feel, even if we can't really perfectly define what we feel. It isn't terribly important that we can't define the experience of loving something because it is just good to love something. We simply experience the exhilaration of our team winning, or we experience a joyful love when our child speaks her first words or makes her first steps while she cautiously walks towards us with open arms. We spend a quiet moment appreciating the sunset, a favorite piece of music or the scent of a rose and declare that we love it. While love is central to life, and we know lots of loves, we just can't really pin down an exact definition of love. We highlight the significance of love because as we go on throughout this book, we will see that *love is the basis of all feelings and emotions.*

Most importantly, we put *feelings* into this group of undefinable, important elements of life. If we try to define feelings and the concept that this word represents, we will be hopelessly abstract or unduly concrete. Abstract definitions of feelings only provide yet other undefined or ill-defined phraseology, like "having a sense of," "having a reaction to," or even an intuitive "just knowing." These vague definitions are all tautological or repetitive. Concrete definitions are no better in helping us understand feelings, like "the act of self-expression," "the physical feeling you have in your chest," or "emotional response" to such and such. The all too common expression of "I just feel" doesn't define what it is we are experiencing. There is value to all of these attempts at describing feelings or putting them into a context to illustrate them, but none of them definitive, and none is particularly helpful in our pursuit of understanding what it means when you say "I feel something."

There are three important elements to the statement, "I feel something": 1) this is an expression erupting from your core self; 2) this core self is of a spiritual nature, and 3) this expression is the most important means of making a connection with another person. Having identified these three central ingredients of feelings, we have now introduced three other elements that we have to define, or at least understand: *core self, spiritual,* and *connection* to another human being.

We need to discuss this concept of "core self" because it is central to what we think about feelings. We think that core self and feelings are both *spiritual* in nature. Unfortunately, we have again introduced a word, spiritual, that we are not able to define. We can only experience spiritual matters; we cannot define spirituality. In the fields of psychology and theology, we read such words as mind, spirit, soul, inner self, and core self, all of which have about the same connotation. They all refer to a significant inner part of what it means to be a human being.

David Claus (1981) provided a thorough study of the word *psyche* in early Greek literature concluding that it means "inner self" but noted that at least seven other Greek words were also related to *psyche*, all of which provided different aspects of the idea of core self.

We will discuss how our feelings emanate from our own core selves. These feelings may be drawn out by external circumstances, like people, places, and experiences, but the feelings themselves come from deep inside of us. Our own preference among these words that describe the inner workings of a person is "core self," but we find ourselves using the other words occasionally, like mind, spirit, or soul but we are always referring to this undefinable, yet very real, part of ourselves.

The core self is not the brain. We can locate the brain and we can locate various mechanisms of the brain, but we can't locate the core self. We need to be content, at least somewhat content, in considering that the core self exists as we experience it. Because of this indefinability and nonmaterial nature of core self some theorists (Damasio, 1996, LaDoux, 1996, for example) think there is no inner self or core self, but rather just a physical brain. We are content to suggest that a core self exists in every human being on the basis of experience, just as we do with time, love, life, and the other basic ingredients of life.

Instead of vainly trying to define core self, we suggest that we observe this part of a human being, and see how a person engages the world and experiences life so we can understand this core self by observation and experience rather than by definition. We understand love not by having an exact definition of love but falling in love, being loved, seeing love in action, or even by reading and seeing love in poetry and art. We know how to define love only through experience. We believe we come to a meaningful understanding of core self in the same way, by observing the *effects* of these undefinable elements of existence. These most important ingredients of existence that are so significant to us humans can only be experienced, not defined. There is value to all of these attempts at defining feelings, but none of them is definitive, and none is particularly helpful in our pursuit of understanding what it means when you say "I feel something." We believe that feeling is the first and foremost expression of core self, and that these undefinable terms represent something that is spiritual in nature which contributes to them being undefinable.

You will note above that we used the term "spiritual" to describe the core self, but with great caution. It is too easy to use the term spiritual loosely, which then can mean any number of things including religious, mystical, or even magical things. We have heard from many good people, and have read many of their works where the term spiritual is used too loosely as if everyone understands what this term means. We believe our spiritual core is not mystical, not even essentially religious, and most certainly not magical. We have chosen to use the term spiritual to suggest that there is a godlike, or good and pure quality to every person and hence to every person's feelings. We acknowledge that we have a theistic philosophy, but we are not suggesting that one has to believe in God as we do in order to accept the term *spiritual* when we talk about feelings. In using the term spiritual, we are suggesting that every person has a nonmaterial element at their deepest level of existence. This core self exists but it is undefinable, just as feelings are undefinable.

Feelings are not core self. Feelings are an emanation from core self. What we feel is what tethers us to our core. Feelings define us as our own unique persons. Feelings could be called "soul strings" that reverberate when we are affected by some experience, whether an internal experience or an external one. When we have this "feeling" that emanates from our core self, we feel compelled to acknowledge this feeling to ourselves and often feel compelled to communicate this feeling to another person. The trouble with feelings, however, is that they are so basic to our existence that it is impossible to intellectually understand what this feeling is, much less communicate it to someone else. If there were a way to access feelings directly from core self, we would feel a kind of perfection, or purity that could be called one's *soul*. We frequently say to our clients, "Your feelings are never wrong." They are never wrong because your feelings emanate from your core self, which is most certainly not wrong. This understanding of feelings is basic to how we try to help people understand themselves, value themselves, and ultimately communicate themselves. It is helpful for people to have this concept of the purity of feelings or even the godlike quality of feelings so they can begin the process of communicating their feelings. Looking at feelings as spiritual, nonmaterial, and nonverbal by nature helps people go through the very difficult process of communicating their feelings.

Some would challenge our proposition that "all feelings are pure and never wrong." Our suggestion that "feelings are never wrong" can easily be misunderstood, so we often add, "the words you use to express your feelings might be wrong, and imprecise at the best, but the feelings themselves are never wrong." Thus, we make an important distinction between you and what you communicate. What you say or do may be hurtful, harmful, or dangerous, but the feelings that are being expressed are not wrong. An important matter related to this discussion of core self, core feelings, and words that are used to express them relates to the difference between feelings and *emotions*. Certainly, we understand that many emotions, particularly, anger and fear, are difficult to manage, and that these emotions can lead to harmful words and dangerous actions but we contend that both words and actions are approximate manifestations of feelings, not feelings themselves. We shall shortly discuss the important difference between emotions and feelings, which should assist in our proposal that feelings are never wrong. We leave a larger discussion of emotions to the next chapter.

If our contention is right that feelings are spiritual and never wrong, what makes it so difficult to understand feelings, communicate them, and be understood by other people? The difficulty is in the transition from feelings into words, or we might say the *translation* of feelings into words. Think of it this way: we experience a feeling at our core self; then we experience that feeling in a physical or emotional way; then we might think about how to talk about that feeling; and finally, we say something that approximates what we feel. This rather complex process is fraught with danger, the danger of miscommunicating. If we use the idea of feelings being "soul strings" from our core selves, we could conceive of this soul string going through the physical, emotional, cognitive, and active experiences before we actually say something. This complex operation of feeling something and saying something about the feeling is difficult because most of us are not yet fully aware of the purity of our core selves, much less cognizant of the challenge of finding words to express this feeling. We will shortly discuss these physical, emotional, cognitive, and active elements of feelings.

Hard as it is for people to understand what they feel, it is even harder to adequately communicate feelings in words. The task of this present work is to provide a framework for understanding what feelings are, how to notice when you are having a feeling, how to become fluent in communicating this feeling, and then the really hard task of understanding other people's feelings. This is a dreadfully important task because our whole lives are involved in our feelings, certainly daily and usually hourly. If we can understand our own feelings, and eventually understand other people's feelings, we will be able to improve our lives and our relationships. We don't have to define "feelings" to in order to communicate them any more than we need to define swimming in order to learn to swim. Nor do we need to define walking, talking, laughing, crying, and loving. We know them by experiencing them. Our intention in this book is to help you experience your feelings first, understand them second, and communicate them third.

Over the five-plus decades of our work with people we have put together several formulas to help explain certain components of human functioning, components that are centralized around feelings. Each of these components has four parts: (1) there are four primary means of experiencing and expressing feelings; (2) there are four basic emotions; and (3) people operate primarily out of one of four different temperaments. In this chapter we will start with the four basic elements of feelings. We will shortly discuss how there may be a difference between how we *experience* feelings and how we *express* them. A person may primarily experience feeling through one component yet have a preference for expressing feelings through a different component. You will also see that sometimes there is a very fine line between the experience and the expression of feelings.

In Chapter 2 we will discuss the four basic emotions which, we will explain, are not the same as feelings, but rather a subset of feelings. Then in Chapter 3 we will discuss the four temperaments. We use the term "temperament" to describe how a person engages life at large. You will see that there are many intrinsic connections between feelings, emotions, and temperaments but that these three components of human functioning are relatively distinct. We hope these four-part formulas will be of value in answering the question, "How can I tell you my feelings?" We will begin this endeavor by examining the four elements of feelings.

THE FOUR ELEMENTS OF FEELINGS

Simplified, the four elements of feelings are *physical, emotional, cognitive*, and *active*. These four components occur sequentially from the core outward. When I *feel* something, my first experience is a physical one. Secondly, I experience some emotion. Thirdly, I experience some thought about what I feel, and finally I experience some action that reflects this feeling. I always feel something in this succession: first physical, then emotional, then cognitive, and then active. These four elements of feelings are really the avenues or modalities through which we both *access* our feelings, *experience* our feelings and ultimately *express* our feelings.

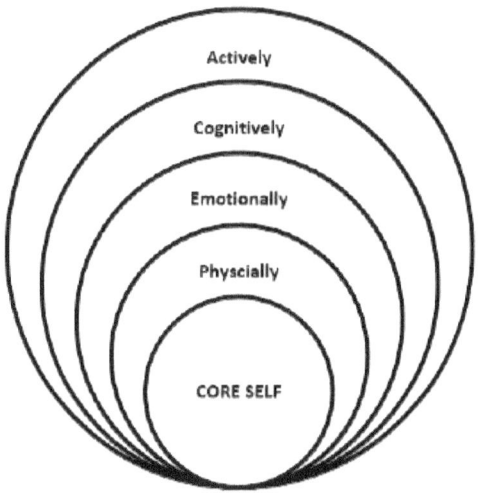

Everyone accesses these four elements of feelings in sequence but people tend to experience feelings predominately in one of these four ways, which then leads to how they express their feelings. Consider how you might experience or express your feelings as we discuss how these four expressions of feelings come to all of us sequentially.

- *I experience feelings physically.* This means that I have some kind of physical sensation in some part of my body and that I am keenly aware of it as it occurs. Gestalt therapists (Perls et al., 1971) often ask patients to "note how you feel physically" when they are helping someone become self-aware. Furthermore, therapists who do "body work" of some sort focus primarily on one's physical experience as a representation of one's inner feelings (Reich, 1975; Lowen, 1967). More recently, neuropsychologist Lisa Barrett (2017) has made a point of how any emotional experience is first physical. Most dramatically, this could be the feeling "in the pit of my stomach" or a "gut level feeling." These gut reactions are quite prevalent for some people. For others, the physical sensation is barely noticed or quickly over run with one of the other three elements. People who primarily experience feeling physically tend to have strong visceral reactions to their inner feelings as well as being very aware of their physical senses. Things visual, auditory, tactile and even gustatory and olfactory are heightened. Some of these folks will easily tear up although this is not true for all people who are physical in their experience of feelings. Some people will simply adjust their body posture, present a facial reaction or other physical mannerisms. Frequently, someone will find it necessary to put his hand to his chest and say, "I just feel" this or that. There are milder feeling-based physical expressions of feelings that could affect any part of the body from head to toe including a "tingling" in your fingers to a feeling that you need to step backward or forward. People who experience or express their feelings physically often move their arms, legs, or their whole bodies in their expression of their feelings. Physical movement often includes hand gestures or full body gestures, like turning away, bowing down, holding one's head, or arching one's back. When we discuss how people express feelings physically, we will find that physical expressions very closely mirror the physical experience of feelings. While many people experience their feelings primarily in some physical form, many people race right through the physical experience into having an emotional reaction.

- *I experience feelings emotionally.* This means that someone immediately recognizes some kind of emotion like fear, anger, sadness, joy or a compilation of these emotions. Often people with this inclination are unable to identify exactly which emotion they feel but they know that they *feel* "emotional." Emotionally-experiencing people often simply report that they are "moved" or "affected" by saying something simple like "that really makes me feel happy (or disappointed)". It is important to note here, while introducing the four elements of feelings, that the emotional element is not the same as feelings. The emotional element is but one way of experiencing and expressing feelings. This is an important distinction, namely that emotion is a subset of feelings. People who tend to experience feelings emotionally are not necessarily more aware or expressive of their *feelings*. Rather, they are more aware and expressive of their emotions. We will examine more carefully emotions in the next chapter as well as explaining the difference between emotions and feelings. Once you have traveled through the physical and emotional aspects of feelings, you will then tend to have some kind of thought, which is the third element of feelings.

- *I experience feelings cognitively.* This statement must seem like a contradiction in terms but it is not. People almost always think something after they have felt something emotionally. Some people "feel" cognitively and think about their feelings as their best way of experiencing them. Cognitive people sometimes will fast forward over their physical and emotional experience without awareness of those sensations and move right into their cognitive experience of feelings. It is in this element, as well as the next one, activity, that is more easily explained when we get to the expression of feelings. Cognitive-based feelings take the forms of ideas, possibilities, intuitions, abstractions, calculations, and explanations. When people experience their emotions cognitively, they may simply ruminate on the sequence of events that brought forth their feelings.
- *I experience feelings through activity.* Of all the four elements of experiencing feelings, this is the hardest to explain because action doesn't seem like a feeling in our culture. Rather, activity is considered to be the *result* of a feeling, not an experience of feeling. People who experience their feelings through activity have some similarity to the people who experience their feelings cognitively in that they pass through the physical and the emotional aspects of feelings quickly. You don't

hear these folks talking about how they "feel." You have to watch them do something or talk about doing something. "Activity" comes in two forms: verbal or physical, and sometimes both. Activity-based people tend to be busy doing something physically, but they also talk about what they have done, what they will do, what they should do, and what other people should do. More often than not, this "doing" is in the form of work, whether simple work or complicated work, physical work or intellectual work. When people express their feelings actively, this expression is very often with some kind of *production*, but an active expression of feeling could also be in *play*.

Everyone goes through all four of these feeling elements when they experience feelings. This sequence of the elements of feelings happens in such rapid succession that people do not usually recognize the transition from one modality of feeling to another. Notice the people in your life and you will see all four elements of the experience of feelings. It is easiest to see how people who express themselves emotionally, but it harder to see how people express feelings physically, cognitively, or actively. Note also how you tend to experience your feelings and note which of the four elements seems to be your preference.

EXPERIENCING AND EXPRESSING FEELINGS

Everyone experiences feelings physically, emotionally, cognitively, and then actively in that sequence, but people have a tendency to *notice* their feelings in one of these four ways. Likewise, people have a preference for expression of their feelings in one of these four ways. Recognizing these four elements of feelings and how they are experienced and then expressed will help you better understand yourself and other people, and ultimately help you articulate how you feel.

We suggest that you consider how you first experience feelings. Are you inclined to identify your feelings through your body, through your emotions, your thoughts or your activity? Perhaps, you experience your feelings primarily in one way but secondarily in another way. Try to identify which feeling element you are more inclined to experience. Then, identify how you prefer to express the feeling you have experienced. Remember that we all experience feelings first physically, then emotionally, then cognitively, and then productively, but we tend to strongly favor one of these modalities in the way we display of our feelings. Some of you might be intrigued that you intrinsically experience your feelings through one element but prefer to express your feelings through a different one. You might, for instance be someone who experiences feelings cognitively and then expresses them in action. Because of the sequential nature of the four elements of feelings, however a person experiences feeling their expression of feeling will most likely be through one of the elements that follows it. For instance, a person who experiences feelings cognitively will probably express these feeling either cognitively or through activity. People who experience their feelings physically would most likely express feeling emotionally, cognitively, or through activity. If you can get a handle on how you first recognize what you feel, you might then see how you tend to proceed in expression. It is also possible that your experience and expression of feeling is in the very same arena. In other words, you might be someone who both experiences and expresses feelings emotionally.

Allow us tell to you how we both experience and express our feelings. Ron experiences his feelings first emotionally and primarily expresses his feelings actively, mostly through production of some kind. Deb experiences her feelings primarily physically and expresses her feelings cognitively. These differences in the experiencing and expressing feelings have led to many-a misunderstanding over our 40-some years together, and we have slowly accommodated to these rather profound differences in the experience and expression of our most central core selves. A recent experience in our lives revealed how we differ in the feeling experience, and how these differences resulted in miscommunication. Deb told me that she had had a random thought that we might be called upon to take over primary care of our grandchildren, and then added that she didn't think we had the capacity to do that important task given the intensity of our psychological work. At this point Deb was *expressing her feelings cognitively,* true to her nature. Not realizing that she was speaking her feelings, I responded with *my feelings*: I suggested that we could care for the grandchildren by hiring a nanny. I missed the point. I missed the fact that Deb was speaking her *feelings*. I thought she was just considering a *possibility*. My attempt to "resolve the potential problem" was to offer a solution, but

Deb wasn't presenting a "problem;" she was presenting her feelings. In that instance, so fresh after our daughter's death, Deb was feeling deeply about loving our grandchildren and feeling a potential sadness if we could not care for them adequately. I jumped into my doing mode and completely overrode her feelings. When she told me about this later, I could clearly see how she expressed her deep feelings of love for our grandchildren albeit in a way that sounded to me like facts that needed an active solution. In fact, once we had both clarified ourselves in this example, Deb later told me that when I first suggested we could "just hire a nanny" that she literally felt like slapping me. As we have mused about this experience, actually in the course of our writing this book, we have considered that when she was assaulted by my suggestion of action, she *felt* something physically, which then might have led to her *feeling* of slapping me. I am grateful that she didn't slap me as it would have been the first time such a thing has happened. But it is notable that she *felt* like slapping me, an obvious indicator of the depth of her feeling experience. I apologized for my intrusion, which was an intrusion into the expression of her feelings. This event and all the feelings involved is an example of the complexity of expressing feelings, which we will discuss in Chapter 4 and the hearing of feeling, which we will discuss in Chapter 5.

Consider the challenges implicit in both the experiencing and the expressing of feelings that occur between good people who don't know their feeling expression preferences. Frequently, we both encounter men and women in our offices who do not adequately hear their partners' feeling expressions, often about the relationship, which are laden with emotion. When people hear their partner's feelings, they hear "problems" that seem to call for "solutions" where, in fact, the other person is simply trying to express their feelings through their emotions. Likewise, some people who are deeply emotion-based in their experience and expression of feelings might gravely miscommunicate their feelings by crying or laughing, which might cause a cognitive response in the person listening to these feelings. A man whom I see in my office experiences his feelings cognitively and expresses them in activity. Somewhat as a result of this combination he has been very successful in his independent business, which often requires this thinking/doing process. His wife, however, experiences and expresses her feelings emotionally. Another couple I see have the same combination but the gender roles are reversed: the man is the emotion-based person while his wife *thinks her feelings*. It is a slow process to help them see that they are all trying heartily to express their feelings but seldom succeed in that endeavor. How sad is it to see people who love each other but do not really know how their partners feel.

THE FOUR MEANS OF EXPRESSING FEELINGS

Our intent for the rest of this chapter, as well as for the rest of this book, is to elaborate on how people express their feelings. We will refer occasionally to how people have initially experienced their feelings in our attempt to focus on improving communication of feelings. Importantly, the first two elements of feeling, physical and emotional, occur on a subconscious level. We call these two elements of feelings "reactional" because we have no conscious control over these two events. When people have a feeling, they react to that feeling almost immediately, first physically and then emotionally. Then people think their feelings or act on their feelings. Following the four-part process that occurs with feeling, they may express those feelings verbally. As we discuss how people tend to express their feelings, keep in mind our proposition that feelings themselves are both spiritual and pure. So, when our minds get involved in expressing these feelings, we do so without being entirely conscious of what we feel. Our bodies and emotions have a greater sense of the purity of our feelings, but when we begin to think about these feelings, or take action on these feelings, we tend to lose track of this pure spiritual nature. For this reason, it is dreadfully important that we learn to take great care in what we think, do, or say when we feel something because we want our thoughts, actions, and words to reflect this spiritual purity as much as possible.

Feelings expressed physically

There are at least three ways that people express their feelings physically: they report their physical experiences, they use body metaphors in their speech, and they are often very physically active. English language is replete with references to the body in some way to describe feelings, and physically expressive people use them frequently. These metaphors can be central for expression of feelings. Consider the following phrases and see if you identify with them as expressions of feeling that you might use:

> Oh! That just makes my heart hurt.
> I can't stomach hearing any more.
> That just doubles me over.
> I am sick with the grief of it.
> That makes my heart smile.
> I could just jump for joy!
> That washed over me like a warm breeze.

Some people use such expressions more than others, but we have all heard these body metaphors as expressions of people's feelings. All of these expressions refer to feelings being represented in one's body. People who regularly use such body metaphors may actually be closer to the spiritual purity of feelings. For them this kind of feeling expression is essential for communication.

Beyond the use of body metaphors there is another means of both experiencing and expressing feelings physically, namely being aware of one's physical sensations. People who are particularly aware of their physical sensations will usually speak of how they feel physically, which take the forms of feeling physically good or not so good. These expressions can be of a simple goose-bump joy feeling that one has hearing a child giggle or a more profound feeling of grief that "tears at one's soul." Physical awareness is particularly acute in these people in any kind of physical distress, and it serves notice to them that they have an important feeling. People with this means of feeling expression are more attuned to their physical needs than people without this ability. Since a physical representation of feeling is the first experience that we have when we have a feeling, people with this ability can notice their feelings sooner than people who have a different preference for feeling expression. This awareness of one's feelings can take the form of saying, "something in my body says that what I am hearing is wrong (or right)." Just recently, a patient of mine, Jake, spoke of having a sense of "a kind of crawling" inside his body when he was considering accepting a certain job promotion. He had no thought or emotion associated with this physical feeling, but as we explored his consideration of this new position, it became obvious that it would not be good for him. He came to a decision of what to do in his work not so much with thought or with emotion but with noting how his body was talking to him. Evidently, his body was saying, "this new position is not good for you" (at least at the present time). It is interesting that Jake's preference for experiencing feelings is cognitive, while his expression of feelings is in activity. But in my office, where hopefully he is learning more about the whole of his feelings, his prominent feeling was physical.

In addition to the use of body metaphors and being aware of physical sensations, a third way of experiencing and expressing feelings physically is to be physically active in some creative, athletic or otherwise energized manner. This activity could be gardening, creating sculpture, working out, running, or just bubbling about in the kitchen. We are reminded of the matron of a bed and breakfast in south England where we stayed who, while cooking the typical English breakfast for her residents, danced about in the kitchen singing and literally poking fun at her employees with her spatula. Active people can be like the B & B matron dancing around the kitchen, running a marathon, playing the air guitar to music playing in the background, or just bouncing in their chair while they are working at the computer. Because of their need for physical activity, body-expressing people can get caught in excessive activity, frivolous activity, fidgeting, or even dangerous activity, but for the most part their physical activity is either playful and harmless, or productive and life changing. Physical movement is good for people of this nature because it suits their natural orientation to physically expressing their feelings.

Having a good sense of one's bodily experience of feelings is a gift that not all people have. While the experience and expression of feelings physically is natural and good, people who tend to be first physical in their expression of feelings can become hypersensitive to these physical experiences. Hypersensitivity to any experience can block a person from moving into the other three dimensions of experiencing feelings. As a result, people with this gift of physical experience of feeling can be inclined to talk about their aches and pains and fail to proceed to the place where they carefully say something or do something about their physical experiences. In other words, such people can be physically aware of their feelings *to a fault*. The "fault" is failing to move through the emotional and cognitive expressions of feelings so they can do something about what they feel physically.

Feelings expressed emotionally

There is no conscious choice in feeling something physically nor is there a conscious choice in feeling something emotionally. There is, however, a conscious choice to express these feelings. People who are inclined towards expressing their feelings emotionally might say that they have "a feeling in their gut," but their focus is more on their emotion than on the physical experience. It is particularly important to be reminded that emotion is part of the feeling process but not the entirety of feelings. Feelings and emotions are too often equated. People who express their feelings emotionally are usually more aware of their emotions, attentive to them, and expressive of them. They are not necessarily better at expressing *feelings*; they are better at expressing *emotions* because they are more attuned to emotional experience.

There are several characteristics of people who favor the expression of feelings emotionally. They display their emotional expression physically and verbally, sometimes simultaneously. If you happen to be a person with a preference for emotional expression of feeling, you will note that when you feel something emotionally you will be inclined to speak about your emotions when you feel them while simultaneously demonstrating your feeling physically. A classic example would be someone placing hand to chest while taking a gasp of air and voicing an exclamation of joy or sorrow. In those instances, there is no question that the person is expressing feeling through the emotional element. These are the folks who "wear their hearts on their sleeves". People with this persuasion cry more easily than other people, but they could also laugh, yell, or scream without reservation.

People who have an emotion-based expression of feelings use emotional words frequently, particularly words that represent some form of sadness, like being hurt, disappointed, discouraged, distraught, or just "feeling down." Of all these words the most prominent is *hurt*. People who are emotion-based in feelings use the word hurt for a variety of feelings including sadness, but also for anger and fear. They are particularly aware of their own emotional hurt but they can be equally aware of other people's hurt. When they say something like, "I am so hurt," they are suggesting that something is terribly wrong with what someone said or did. The experience of hurt is so important in our discussion of feelings that we devote the entirety of Chapter 7 to the phenomenon. People of all persuasions experience emotions in the same amount and the same frequency, but they do not stay in this genre of feelings as long as emotion-based people do. It is remarkable how emotion-expressing people can know how they feel emotionally, express how they feel emotionally, and even act on their emotions without reference to anything else in the environment. They truly know the centrality of emotion in human life and relationships.

People who express their feelings with emotion are truly gifted because it is in the realm of emotion that people can dramatically improve their personal lives and their relationships. That having been said, emotion-driven people can move so quickly into emotion that the emotion begins to dominate them, and may quickly dominate the people around them. There is no ignoring someone who is crying, yelling, or laughing. Furthermore, as with all four gifts of feelings, emotion-based people can become so overwhelmed with their emotion, particularly sadness, fear, and anger, that they lose control of what they say and do. More harmful things have been said out of emotion than have been said out of the physical, cognitive, or active experiences of feelings.

Feelings expressed cognitively

As we noted before, expression of feelings cognitively (or intellectually) seems to be a contradiction of terms, yet many people are compelled to express their feelings in cognitive or intellectual ways. More often than not, cognitively-expressive people use the term *think* when they express their feelings like, "I really think you're wrong about that" or "I just think that this is really important." They tend to be good at expressing their *opinions* and ask for others' opinions often not knowing that their opinions and thoughts are eruptions of their feelings.

As we noted previously, Deb is more inclined to express feelings cognitively than I am. Deb and others like her tend to talk about their feelings through the use of facts and reasons and tend to "explain" feelings more than emote feelings. Cognitively-expressive people will be inclined to explain *why* they feel cognitively more than to explain *what* they feel emotionally. This cognitive expression of feelings can be very misleading because, like all four elements of feelings, the essence beneath the expression is not the expression itself. Cognitive expression of feelings is perhaps the most misunderstood because it is not emotional, and thus does not appear to be a feeling expression.

People who express their feelings cognitively often don't seem to be expressing feelings. Rather, they seem to be "just talking about their thoughts." In fact, "just talking about their thoughts" *is* talking about their feelings.

I am reminded of a patient, Robert, I saw recently who is almost unable to come out of his cognitive style of expressing his feelings, so much so that the other elements of feeling-expression, like physical, emotional, and productive are almost absent in his daily operation. Robert's expressions are so replete with data, information, justice, fairness, and reason that he is quite unaware of the other three means of expression of feelings, particularly emotional expression of feelings. He is so strong in the matters of justice and reason that he is quite unable to understand why anyone would ever have an emotional reaction. While assisting Robert recently, I pointed out how his "logical" expression of his feelings caused emotional hurt and disappointment in the people in his life, particularly his family members. His response was, "how can I explain to them so they won't be hurt when I am just trying to tell them what I *feel*?" He thought if people would see the facts that he was presenting, they wouldn't be hurt by what he said. I think that it is interesting Robert used the term "feel" when talking about how he was expressing himself with fact and logic. I am reminded of a time when I told a colleague that he had hurt me with what he had said. He immediately said that I could not possibly be hurt because he had not intended to hurt me. The operative word is *intended*. Because he had not intended to hurt me, he could not conceive that I had been hurt. Cognitively-expressing people tend to equate the intention of their expression with the effect of their expression.

People who express feelings cognitively tend to know more facts than people of other feeling persuasions. For these folks knowledge itself is used as an expression of feeling. A cognitive-expressive person could simply say, "The maple leaves have all dropped from the trees" while privately having a deeply felt emotion of joy or sorrow that is not stated. Such a person might feel quite deeply about how the seasons change, how death always follows life, or how beautiful the falling of maple leaves is but never say such things. It would be enough for him to "just feel" the feeling associated with leaves falling and state this feeling as a matter of information, not so much emotion, and certainly not of activity.

People who are more inclined to express their feeling cognitively can easily tell you what they think as a way of telling you how they feel. This form of feeling expression can be quite confusing and interpreted as a lack of feeling, but a statement of fact might truly be profoundly felt even though it is not emotionalized. If you are in the room with someone of this nature, you can sit back and listen to her expound on history, science, politics, or religion and note that she is truly alive when she gets a chance to tell you who she is by telling you what she knows and what she think*s as a way of telling you how she feels.*

People with a cognitive expression of feeling have their challenges in life as do all people. These challenges are essentially related to causing misunderstanding and offense. If, for instance, you present a challenging situation in your life, your cognitive friend might be inclined to tell you what you should do even though you might just want to talk about your feelings. It is quite a dilemma for these people to be giving their best to their friend and then to see that this best gift offends. How many times have you heard from such a person, "I was just trying to help, I was just trying to explain what was wrong!" when you just wanted your feelings heard, not solved. Cognitive people can easily get lost in their ideation, philosophy, theory, or facts and neglect the reaction of their audience and not come around to adequately expressing themselves and not understand why someone didn't understand their feelings.

Feelings expressed with activity

People who express themselves though activity have a similarity to people who display their feelings physically in that both types of people move a lot. The difference is that people who are active in their expression of feelings are more task oriented where people who express themselves though their physicality are more in tune to their bodily responses.

People with this inclination tend to be action-prone in their expression. They are busy doing something. They do something that will lead to accomplishment of a task, produce something, or finish something. This "something" could be swinging a hammer, turning a wrench, writing a book, cleaning house, running errands, or doing chores around the house that other people might think are menial. The expression "I just need to do something" is a sure sign that a person is looking to express his feelings through an activity that will result in some level of productivity. "Production" comes in the two forms of verbal activity or physical activity, and sometimes both. Such people talk about what they *have* done, what they *will* do, what they *should* do, and what *other people* should do, which are all expressions of their feelings. This "doing" is usually in the form of work, whether simple work or complicated work, physical work or intellectual work, but expressing one's feelings in activity can even be in play, like sports, video games, or word games, or in artistic productions.

The notion of production is quite specific to this group of people because it is in the actual doing something and producing something concretely that they communicate what is important to them. People who express their feelings in their doings tend to view activity itself as alive, and it is this aliveness of doing and producing that is at the heart of people with this mode of feeling-expression. We have sometimes used the term "doers" to describe such people, but it is more than doing that displays their feelings. As I (Ron) sit at my desk looking out at a snowy February day in Wisconsin where I live, I can physically feel the desire to push the snow. It will be great to be done with the snow plowing later this afternoon, but it will be better to actually be on the tractor doing the plowing or to have the shovel in hand and to be doing the shoveling. At this very same minute I am fully involved in writing this very paragraph, which is truly a reflection of how I *feel*: I want to get this book finished, edited, and published as if my life depended on it. Yes, this is an intellectual project and certainly an emotional matter for me, but more than these factors, it is a life force that drives me to write, now competing with my desire to push snow. Both of these projects call forth from my feelings, both of them being productive albeit in very different ways. I recall a statement that an actor said in a movie I recently saw, a man who was in a hurry to get something done: "We can *explain* or we can *do*." People who experience their feelings through production need to "do."

People who express their feelings with activity often do not appear to be expressing their feelings, any more than the people who express their feelings cognitively or physically. It is difficult for people who do not have this persuasion to understand that doing and producing is an expression of feeling just as much as it is for those who express their feelings in one of the other three ways. When you hear these people talk about their productive activity, perhaps to a fault, consider that they are trying to communicate their feelings from their core self. Someone who is activity-based in expression would say things like, "It felt so good to get the garage cleaned out", "It is a relief to have finished that project for the pastoral committee", "I am glad that the chapter is finished and ready for review", or "if I can just finish up the rest of the reports on my desk, I think I will be okay". "It felt so good to get the garage cleaned out" could represent a sense great personal joy, a joy in knowing that tools and space are well utilized.

People who are activity-based in their expression of feelings have just as much an inclination to difficulties as the other ways of expressing feelings. Such people tend to be less articulate in the other three expressions of feelings, and as such, can be so busy doing things that they are without evidence of any physical, emotional, or cognitive expression. As with people of all feeling persuasions, they think that their way of expressing feelings should be sufficient for people to understand them. The feelings of activity-based people are usually understood only by other activity-based people. Folks with other feeling expressions might see them as simply busy, or even unemotional, thoughtless, or generally unaware of life around them. Activity-based people know that it is important to do something for life to be meaningful. People who have a minimum of activity and production in their lives can get stuck with their physical experiences, their emotions, or their thoughts. What active-expressing people do not know is that their productive activity may not be meaningful to the world around them. They can, as philosopher/theologian Soren Kierkegaard said, "Do everything but lack meaning in what they do."

SUMMARY:

1. Feelings are *central* to life, and ultimately central to work, play, and relationships.
2. We *cannot define feelings* but we can know what we feel even if we can't find words to express perfectly these feelings.
3. *Feeling* are always experienced as physical, emotional, cognitively, and in activity, with these phenomena occurring in sequence.
4. People tend to experience their feelings in one of these four genres.
5. They may express their feelings in a different genre.
6. Emotions are just one part of experiencing and expressing feelings.

Chapter 2

What are Emotions?

IF WE CAN HELP you understand your emotions, not only will you have a better ability to engage in the other three aspects of feelings, but you will be better able to communicate your emotions while not being governed by the immense power of emotions. While emotions can certainly bring the most joy to us, they are the most dangerous aspect of what it means to express our feelings. What is most remarkable about the potentially joyful and dangerous aspects of emotions is that they are all *love-based*. Every time we feel some emotion, we have encountered something that is important to us. In other words, when we feel something emotionally, the emotion is somehow related to what we love. Before we discuss this central understanding of emotions, we need to discuss the different emotions that we have.

Having spent the last chapter describing our conception of "feelings," we now engage in the process of understanding one of the "elements" of feelings: emotions. While feelings are so important as to be undefined, we can define emotions to some degree, or at least identify different emotions. We know this: emotions have a very significant neurological component and emotions always have some physical demonstration. Some theorists have suggested that emotions are first physical, and then cognitive, but there is yet much debate in the psychological community as to how we feel emotions and what they are.

There are other words that are sometimes chosen to describe emotions, namely *affect*, which is what Jungians prefer rather than the term emotions. We will defer to writers we have noted in the References to describe the neurological and physical elements that are related to emotions.

We propose that emotions are a subset of feelings, that we all experience emotions, and that some people are inclined to experience and express their feelings through emotions more than others. The distinction between feelings, as we have described them in the previous chapter, and emotions as we will describe in this chapter is a delicate matter because we yet find ourselves using the term "feelings" for the deeper sense of who we are as persons and the emotional expressions that are so uniquely human. We hope you will bear with us as we continue to unpack this difference between feelings and emotions, but this distinction is challenging because no words adequately explain these dreadfully important concepts of feelings and emotions.

Feelings are the most basic *reflection* of our inner selves, but they are *not our inner selves* as such. One's inner self is simply too profound, too spiritual, too basic to our existence, and too undefined to be communicated in words, especially emotional words or rational words that tend to overly emotionalize or overly intellectualize. One's inner self can only be *felt*. In this chapter we will describe the nature of emotions as we conceive this phenomenon of human existence. In all the forthcoming chapters we will continue to focus primarily on emotions as they impact how we communicate our feelings. Emotions are not more important than the physical, cognitive, and active elements of feelings, but they are the most problematic.

There are hundreds of words that can be used to describe feelings and emotions although none of them does complete justice to either of these concepts. There is great debate on just how many feelings we humans experience as well as what types of emotions we experience. Some psychologists (e.g. Seligman, 2002) think there are "positive emotions," like joy and surprise, and "negative emotions," like anger and fear. One theorist (Ekman, 2003) thinks there are nine emotions while other theorists think that there are scores of emotions. We have the further complication of using the word "feeling" when people are really talking about emotions or intuition. The vocabulary that has developed for describing emotions has become so complicated that most of us have a limited awareness of emotions, much less ways of effectively using our emotions. We have noted that feelings are almost impossible to define. Not so with emotions. We can define emotions even amidst the challenges as to how many emotions actually exist in the human experience. We believe that we have four primary emotions. These four emotions all have to do with *having* something we love or *losing* something we love.

THE FOUR EMOTIONS

We will first remind you that in the larger concept of *feelings* we first experience feelings physically and then emotionally, and that both the physical and the emotional aspects of feelings are unconscious. In other words, emotions come to us unbidden: they just occur. We do not have any control over the experience of feeling an emotion. We have control over the eruption of our cognition and our activity but not over our physical reactions and emotions. We use the paradigm that we have four basic emotions: *fear, anger, joy and sadness*. Furthermore, we usually experience these emotions in pairs. We experience anger and fear on some occasions, while we experience joy and sadness on other occasions. Too often people are unable to identify exactly what they feel emotionally, and end up using terms like "frustrated," "upset," "disheartened," or even just "emotional." We have found it helpful to assist people identify the essence of what they feel emotionally by using the paradigm of four feelings coming in pairs: *fear and anger* as one pair and *joy and sadness* as the other pair. Being able to identify a relatively exact nature of what one feels emotionally is of great benefit in being able to value emotions, express emotions, and contain emotions when wise to do so. In the current atmosphere of the world there is an increasing experience of anxiety that confuses people as to how they actually feel in general, and certainly how they feel emotionally. When people find meaningful ways of identifying what they feel emotionally, their anxiety decreases, their inclination towards anger decreases, and they are better able to manage their lives. We discussed in *The Positive Power of Sadness* (Johnson and Brock, 2017) that people are much less inclined towards anxiety and anger when they allow themselves to experience the combination of joy and sadness more readily.

Following the four-part paradigm of feelings that we proposed in Chapter 1, emotions erupt from our core selves as the second experience of feelings after the earlier physical experience of feelings. This eruption of feelings and its four components, physical, emotional, cognitive, and productive, is a reflection of something important to our inner self. We believe that this "something that is important" can be simply stated as what we *value* or *love*. Thus, the whole experience of feelings, including the emotional experience of feelings, has to do with valuing something, or as we prefer to say, loving something. It is from this perspective that we propose that the couplets of fear/anger and joy/sadness are experiences that have to do with what we love. We need to explain this simple, but also profound understanding of emotions as it is extremely helpful to see that when we experience, express, and contain emotions, we are always dealing with things that we love. We will unpack what we love and how we love differently according to what we call "temperament" in Chapter 3, but for our current purposes we will simply state that when we experience any emotion, we are experiencing a reaction to something that has erupted from our core selves and from the fact that we love something. The joy/sad pair of emotions has to do with the present experience of having something or losing something. If I love something and have it in the present, I will experience the emotion of joy. If I lose something in the present, I will experience the emotion of sadness. The fear/anger pair of emotions are emotions that have to do with the past or the future. I am angry because I have lost something in the past. If I am afraid, I fear that I will lose something in the future.

While all emotions erupt from our inner core selves and have to do with things that we love, we refer to fear and anger as *defense-based* emotions and joy and sadness as *love-based* emotions. When we experience the joy of having something or losing something in the present, we are living in the present: the joy of having or the sadness of losing. If I have a perfect espresso in the present, I experience this simple emotion of joy. If I spill my espresso, I feel the simple emotion of sadness. Both of these emotions relate to the present moment, namely of having or losing my espresso. I love something that is real and present or I lose something that is real and present. For this reason, we call joy and sadness love-based emotions.

We call the emotions of fear and anger defense-based emotions because these emotions assist us in defending against loss, whether that loss is in the past or in the future. I get angry because I *have lost* something in the past and feel the necessity to prepare myself for any future loss. Anger may be necessary if I am in immediate danger, if for instance, I am attacked by someone while I'm walking on the street. I get angry at my attacker as a means of defense. Most anger, however, is not about a real danger in the present; rather, it is about some loss that occurred in the past. I feel anger now because it is safe to feel anger where it wasn't safe or possible to feel anger when I was attacked in the past. One time in high school I was brutally attacked by someone much bigger and stronger than I was. I did what was *reasonable* to do at the time: avoid being angry at my attacker because I could have been hurt even more had I done so. I recall feeling anger for years afterward every time I thought of having been attacked. I felt anger after this event because it was *safe* to feel anger now, while it was not safe to feel it in high school. My anger about this past event often took the form of my thinking of some kind of revengeful action I might have taken out on him. Anger that is associated with a past loss usually leads to feelings of hostility and revenge.

Fear is also a defense-based emotion because when I am afraid, I am thinking of the necessity of defending myself from potential loss. Fear may also be necessary in some circumstances, like when I may be in some genuine immediate danger. The operative phrase is *immediate* danger. Most fear, however, is not about immediate danger but rather about potential danger in the distant future. I can become overcome with fear, which then leads to anxiety, about this potential loss and thus continue to the emotion of fear in the present. I could be overcome with anxiety if I think about that nasty bully who *just might* attack me again.

We suggest that most anger is about loss that occurred in the past even though we "feel" the anger in the present. Likewise, most fear is about some potential future loss but we "feel" it in the present. When I am angry, the fact of the loss is in the past but the emotion of anger is experienced in the present. When I am anxious, the possibility of the loss is in the future but the emotion of fear is in the present. This is not an easy concept to understand because humankind has an undue tendency to remember losses in the past and stay angry over these losses, or consider things that they might lose in the future and become overcome with anxiety. This tendency to be angry about past losses or afraid of possible future losses is different from actual defensive needs of fear and anger when we might be in real life present danger.

Fear and anger can be experienced in the present if we are in a real-life threat. We need to be able to be afraid and/or angry when there is a *present* possibility of personal harm. But most anger that people carry around with them is about past losses and anxiety is always about potential losses. I can also feel joy or sadness about past experiences or potential future experiences. When I feel the love-based feeling of joy about some past experience, I simply smile or laugh at the memory while recalling something that I loved. This something might be a person, an event, a place, a thing, or any other experience that I had in the past. Likewise, I can experience the sadness associated with something that I loved in the past but lost in the past. Remembering something that I loved in the past can easily bring me to tears, tears that are generated by my remembering this thing that I loved then and still love now. We call this experience of looking nostalgically at something lost in the past *retroactive sadness*. We have both been experiencing this retroactive sadness in the recent months since our daughter Krissie died. Sometimes tears that erupt when I think about something that I loved in the past are not distinguishable into joy or sadness. In such cases I am simply experiencing the love that I had for something. There is a profound difference between allowing myself to feel joy and sadness about something that I have lost compared to feeling angry, and ultimately resentful and revengeful of this loss.

I can also feel joy or sadness about future events, where I might have something or where I might lose something. If I find myself looking forward to a promotion at work or a good game of golf, I will feel a smile coming over my face as I anticipate some kind of success. I could also feel what we call *anticipatory sadness* about some future experience of potential loss. In such cases I would anticipate feeling sad about the loss of a promotion or a bad golf game. We have elsewhere recommended that it can be valuable to anticipate loss and feel anticipatory sadness as a way of forestalling anxiety about potential loss. Feeling anticipatory sadness is a process of *feeling sad in the present for some loss that I might have in the future*. If I am afraid of failing to secure a job I apply for, I can cure the fear by allowing myself to actually imagine this failure and allowing myself to feel sad for this failure that hasn't actually occurred, and may never occur. Think about it right now: consider that what you would feel if you lose, say, an important person in your life. Really think about it and see if you can develop a picture of where you might be and what you might do. You will notice that you will tear up just thinking about losing this person. You are experiencing anticipatory loss, which is tantamount to saying that you love this person very much and want to have this person in your life. You might even decide that it is about time to tell him/her that.

Before we examine these four emotions more fully, allow us to explain briefly the concept of love being the core of all emotions:

Love-based emotions: I feel

- *Joy* when I *have* something that I love *(in the present)*.
- *Sadness* when I *am losing* something that I love *(in the present)*.

Defense -based emotions: I feel

- *Anger* when I *have lost* something that I loved *(in the past.)*
- *Fear* when I *might lose* something that I love *(in the future)*.

Note that all four of these emotions have something to do with loving something, or valuing something. There are degrees of valuing or loving, but the concept that emotions has to do with loving or valuing is a central theme in our understanding emotions as well as the larger concept of feelings. When we express our feelings emotionally, we are expressing something about love. All four elements of the feeling process are experiences of my loving something, and all four emotions are expressions of love. Our focus in this chapter, as well as in much of this book, is on the emotional element of feeling because of the immense danger of miscommunication that can occur when emotion is not understood, valued, and governed. I can govern my physical experience, my thinking, and my activity somewhat easily, but it is not so easy to govern my emotions. Ungoverned emotion can cause immense harm to people and ultimately to their relationships. The English language and perhaps many languages do not do great justice to verbal expressions of emotion. It is our concerted hope that we can be of some assistance to you in finding ways for you to *feel* emotion, *value* your emotion, and *communicate* your emotion so that your *feelings* and *love* will be even more understood. Before we get into the meat of how to express emotion and the underlying feeling, we need to make note of the obvious fact that there are many faces to the act of loving something.

DEGREES, DIFFERENCES, & COMBINATIONS IN LOVE

How much do I love my spouse? Very much. How much do I love my work? Much. How much do I love my car? Some. How much do I love reading a manual for my new cell phone? Not much. I love all these things but I love them with differing degrees: my spouse very much, my cell phone manual not very much. Note however, that even though I don't particularly love the manual, I value it because it just might help me use the cell phone. We admit that we are forcing the issue here to say that I "love" the cell phone manual, but we do this on purpose because we do *value* this little booklet. In fact, if my dog chews the dreaded thing up, I might actually feel a good deal of emotion. I would undoubtedly feel anger at the dog but at a deeper level I would feel sadness at the loss. We might suggest that on a scale of 1 to 10, I love my spouse at a 10 level and my cell phone manual at a 1 level. There are different *degrees* of loving something.

Not only are there different degrees of loving, there are many *combinations* of emotions within the concept of loving something. Some theorists suggest that there are more than the four emotions of joy, sadness, fear, and anger. Ekman (2003) suggests that humans have distinct emotions of surprise and disgust in addition to the basic four that we propose. We understand surprise to be a form of joy with an amalgam of fear resulting out of a startled response, and we conceive of disgust as a form of anger with an element of sadness mixed in. When we are truly disgusted, we feel sad that something is violating our sense of rightness plus feeling anger as a means of defense against something that disgusts us. People frequently say that they are "frustrated" with something or someone. We find the word frustration to be a cognate of anger, with some element of sadness added to the anger. Much frustration is a sense of feeling helpless in a situation of loss (sadness) with a desire to change the situation (anger). When we feel excited about some coming event that "excitement" is a combination of joy associated with (joy) a mild amount of fear that the event might not happen, or might not happen soon enough. We are currently planning a trip to Malta, a bucket list element that has long been waiting to be ticked off. Our excitement about this forthcoming trip is palatable, especially for Deb, in the anticipation of viewing the goddess temples on Malta. But this excitement has an element of fear of some yet unknown impediment, like getting stuck on our New York layover because of a February snow storm. We can even have competing feelings about an event as when you might feel sad at your mother's death but happy that she no longer suffers from Alzheimer's disease. These are but a few examples of how the emotional experience is a complex one that does not lend itself to an exact definition. Let's look more carefully at *degrees* of loving, *differences* of what people love, and the *combinations* of emotions that occur when we love something:

Degrees of emotions in love

We noted how we might love a spouse, work, car, or an activity with different amounts of love. Now consider how these different degrees of loving something might cause difficulties in communication:

- Margaret really loves the color green. As a result, she has many words that she might use for green, like fern, avocado, forest, lime, olive, emerald, Hunter, Kelly green, and teal among others. Her husband, John, is not so fluent with green and it is certainly not his favorite color. Knowing that Margaret loves green, John buys a brand-new green Corvette for Margaret. Unfortunately, the Kelly green of the Corvette is one of the very few shades of green that Margaret actually cannot tolerate. How will Margaret respond to this generous gift of something that she hates… just because of its color? Certainly, nothing is wrong with Margaret liking some shades of green and not others. Equally certain, nothing is wrong with John failing to distinguish green shades. Just as certain, this scenario is ripe for disagreement, hurt, offense, and anger when it starts out with Margaret liking green and John not caring much about green. We discuss such challenges in a later chapter.

- We live in "Packer country," namely Wisconsin where the Green Bay Packer football team plays. Fair to say, while many Wisconsonians love the Wisconsin Badgers, the Milwaukee Bucks, the Marquette Warriors, and other sports teams that play in Wisconsin, the love for the Packers is pretty universal save a few transplants from Minnesota or Illinois who might favor the Vikings or the Bears. Ron cares a bit about the Packers, just enough to read about a Packer game on Monday morning. Deb, on the other hand, truly has no interest in the Packers whatsoever. There are in Wisconsin many millions of T-shirts and sweatshirts with the Packer logo, and many thousands of houses, living rooms, and cars that are decorated with the Green and Gold colors of the Packers. How easily it would be for an unsuspecting person, like Deb, to easily offend someone by dismissing a Packer game as "only a game"?
- Loving in degrees does not necessarily have to do with colors and sports. One can love a person deeply, another modestly, and yet another with little or no love. How hard would it be for Sam to appreciate the fact that he loves one of his boys more than the other, but never actually say that to anyone? Animal lovers have an ability to love certain animals more than they love people, sometimes so deeply that the loss of a pet is tantamount to a tragic life loss. These degrees of love are often hard for others to comprehend.
- We can love things mildly at first and then modestly later on, and finally with such passion that we almost cannot live without this thing that we love. We think that we have come to love our 100- plus year-old house more each year that we have had it. We certainly have come to love our children and grandchildren more than when they were born. Furthermore, there are things, people, and events that we used to love with great zeal but now find ourselves less impassioned by. We have current friends and past friends that have been moderately important to us, then dear to us, and then less important to us as we have traversed our way through life. These changes in the degrees of loving a person could easily cause hurt or cause offense to a person who might retain a love for us that is not particularly returned to the same degree.

Differences in emotions in love

Degrees of loving and differences in loving often merge. However difficult it might be to understand how *deeply* someone might love something; it can be even more challenging to see *what* someone actually loves. We will discuss differences in loving more in the next chapter as they relate to our differences in temperament. Depending on one's temperament some people love property, some people, some ideas, and some experience. First, let us consider some challenges that might occur when people simply love different things:

- Audrey loves cooking. She really, really loves cooking. To watch Audrey in her kitchen cooking up some new recipe is to watch someone enjoying every moment of life, from the flour in her face to the disarray of pots and pans on the counter; from the joy of her tasting her masterpiece to the disappointment of the cheese cake that fell. Audrey tends to lose a sense of time when she is cooking, so much so that her guests are often a bit disappointed that dinner didn't actually begin until an hour or more than the stated time. In such a case we have someone truly loving what she is doing but this very act of doing what she loves causes disappointment, hurt, and possibly resentment in other people.
- Mack loves to work. His work, whatever it is and whenever it occurs, is always with his hands. He works as a mechanic in a shop in town and is well respected for his quality of work, so much so that he has received raises every year for 15 years running. But Mack's tendency to hands-on work does not stop with his turning a wrench 8 to 5. When he comes home, he grabs a quick sandwich and eats it on his way to his shed to work on his own little business of lawn care, landscaping, and snow-plowing. When he drops in bed at night for a quick 6 hours of sleep, he usually has put in some 14 hours of work. He just loves it. His wife, however, doesn't love it so much. They have had words about his "working all the time," but his answer is always, "so I can make a good living for the family." Nothing wrong with Mack working and enjoying working. Nothing wrong with his wife wanting to have conversation. But it's hard for them to really understand what each other loves.

- Julie loves here kids like no tomorrow. She was made to be a mother and thought about being a mother since she was 12 or perhaps younger. She always loved kids, loved to babysit as a teenager, and even loved taking care of her younger siblings. She got married to a guy who said that he was just as interested in kids as she was. Indeed, he wanted kids and loved his kids but not like Julie. In a 24-hour day, likely 16 of those hours were devoted to her kids. She put her time in at her "day job" but only so she could provide food and fun for her kids. Julie's value system is like many mothers: kids first, house second, marriage third, and herself last. Sadly, Julie died young and at her celebration of life most people sang her praises as a mother more than anything else. Unfortunately, she was divorced some years before her untimely death perhaps largely because it was always "kids first, everything else last."

Combinations of emotions in love

Degrees of emotion and differences in emotion associated with love are hard to understand, but when emotions are complex and combined, we have to work even harder to understand what we feel emotionally. In fact, when we love something, it is likely that we will experience all four emotions to some degree in the process of loving. What parent has not experienced this range of emotions when trying heartily to survive the terrible twos or the terrorizing teens? There is nothing like a screaming two-year old boy or an overly dramatic 13-year old girl to cause a full range of emotions with a parent. This range always starts with love because, certainly, we love our children. But it is nearly impossible to avoid feeling fear that our children will come to harm, and equally impossible to avoid feeling anger if they cause harm to someone else. The joy of watching a child perform his first concert is perhaps equaled in intensity to the sadness we might feel when his sister breaks her leg in a cross-country race. Parents who know how to value their emotions and manage these emotions teach their children how to feel and manage emotions.

I have a 14-year old patient who is hardest on his mother, so much so that he yells and screams at her but has none of these explosions at school or with his friends. In fact, he is quite the opposite with friends: he is quite passive, usually going along with whatever they want, but at home he is demanding, yelling, and reacting all the time to his mother. What is happening with this young man, who by the way, is quite bright? He is allowing himself the privilege to have the feeling of anger with his mother that he can't seem to allow himself to have in any other circumstance. What has become clear to me is that his mother is by far the most important person in his life; he loves her far more than anyone else. He could not conceive of living without her, and yet at the same time he is almost vicious with her at times. The dilemma Max has is that he loves his mother so deeply and so dearly that she is the only person with whom he can dare express the feelings of anger that he represses elsewhere. So, Max experiences the joy of loving his mother and the anger that she is not the savior of his life giving him everything he wants in life.

A mixture of emotions is not solely in the arena of child rearing. It occurs in all aspects of life, specifically work, play, relationships, and even in times of solitude. We used to think that it was sufficient to identify the one emotion that we had at a particularly point in time. We no longer think that life is that easy, feelings are that easy to express, and emotions are that simply displayed. A typical day of work for us brings a great variety of emotions, mixed emotions and changing emotions. We have found that we run the full gamut of emotions every day even though we have worked diligently to highlight our "love-based" emotions of joy and sorrow and decrease our "defense-based" emotions of fear and anger. We have come to realize that everything we love we will eventually lose, so when we have lost something, we are quite a bit better at avoiding the tendency to be angry. Likewise, we have worked diligently at avoiding the tendency to think about the future and end up feeling anxious about some possible loss in the future. In the work we do, which is largely one-to-one therapy, we experience the joys and sorrows of our patients on a daily basis as we laugh and cry rather frequently as we hear the successes and failures that people encounter in their daily lives.

While our particular profession allows us to experience and express our emotions as we deem appropriate, as well as assisting our patients to do the same, not all professions allow for such an experience. How difficult would it be for a dentist to allow herself to feel all that she might feel in the process of extracting a tooth? She might experience the fear of damage to the gum structure or she might experience anger that the tooth broke while it was halfway out. She might experience sadness in bringing her patient pain in the process of the extraction. Hopefully, she would also experience joy at having completed such an important process successfully. Whatever she feels emotionally, it is important for her to know what she feels, and eventually learn to express these emotional feelings when appropriate, or sometimes, keep them to herself. This is no easy task for people who are working diligently to do good work while frequently experiencing a variety of emotions.

Emotional experiences at work

Working people are often asked to do four things in the time it takes to do one. This causes an individual to choose between feeling his emotions, repressing his emotions, or expressing his emotions. Most supervisors prefer repression, which may be the best thing to do at the time but repression comes at a cost because repressed emotions always surface later. I currently am seeing a patient who has been thoroughly responsible all his life from the time he took a leading role in his dysfunctional family through a time when he was the primary caregiver for his children, and throughout all his very successful career as a store manager. Unfortunately, he did not acknowledge all of his emotions, particularly the emotion of sadness that occurred through his 55 years of life. When Peter came to me, he was so exhausted that he was on disability leave for six months, barely enough time to recover from the years and decades of failing to recognize all of his emotions.

It is hard enough to feel one emotion, like sadness that Peter experienced for these decades, and he is now making progress in finding ways to simply feel sad for all the losses he experienced in life. It is quite another thing to have a combination of emotions that often occurs in various life situations. How would you feel if you had just made a great sale at work, and just as the sale was completed, you were challenged by your supervisor to make three more sales before quitting time? What would you feel? Probably joy and anger. More accurately, you would feel joy at having succeeded and sadness at having to triple your success over the next two hours. Work particularly can cause these combinations of emotions, often with little room to experience them, much less appropriately express them. The best you can do in situations where you experience a mixture of emotions is to note what these emotions are. Then you can see that whatever emotion you feel, it always has to do with love in some way. This assessing of your emotions won't necessarily make work better, but it will help you to manage your feelings in the moment and possibly keep you from ending up on disability because of being depressed or being fired because you blew up at your employer.

Combinations of emotions that occur in the loving process stretch beyond love for our children and work. The combinations of emotions that we have in our relationships is perhaps the hardest of all to manage. We usually feel more emotion and express more emotion with the people we truly love than with anyone else. Why is that? It is because we trust that our friends or partners will allow us to have these expressions of emotions. After all, shouldn't these people be the ones that we can turn to when we are emotional? Unfortunately, because we tend to store up anger and fear in other circumstances, these can be the dominant emotions expressed with our loved ones because of our mistaken assumption that a loved one can hear any manner of emotions however harsh or confusing the emotion might be. How easy is it for us to keep our emotions to ourselves when we are at work, at some social outing, or with an acquaintance, and then come home with a combination of emotions like frustration and excitement. We may act the controlled adult outside the house but be uncontrolled emotionally in the house.

CHILDHOOD EMOTIONAL DEVELOPMENT: A REVIEW

Let's go back to the basic four emotions: fear, anger, joy and sadness. We can understand the necessity of all four of these basic emotions by understanding how they develop in children. It is with very young children that we see the purpose of all four of these emotions. In fact, the difficulty adults have with understanding and expressing their emotions, and the even harder task of hearing other people's emotions, is that they have not had the opportunity to feel these four emotions deeply, express them, and ultimately come to appreciate emotions.

Children are not born with the capacity to express all four emotions, much less the feelings that underlie all emotions. Rather, each of these four basic emotions is developed at a certain stage of life. The process is developmental. It is important for us to understand how and when these emotions actually erupt in order to make some sense of how emotions can get out of control or be unduly repressed thus leaving adults with an inadequate capacity to engage their own emotions. Let us look at how each of the emotions comes into the life of a child. The first emotion an infant feels is fear.

- **Fear**: this is the first and only emotion a newborn has. *An infant feels fear or no emotion at all*, an experience that we might call contentment. The infant feels fear when she is hungry, alone, or physically uncomfortable. Fear shows itself in crying, which is her only means of expressing a need. The infant needs to rely on this most important feeling of fear because she is literally helpless to care for her most basic needs, which are primarily eating, sleeping, and comfort. Infants' crying is 100% fear-based and need-based. The infant is understandably scared because she has no way to satisfy her felt need, whether relief from hunger, relief from physical discomfort, or securing physical comfort. The fear that an infant displays in crying is akin to the fear of dying. Rightly so, because she is helpless in meeting her own needs, so she would die if she did not cry when she feels some kind of basic human need. The only love that an infant has is *for herself*, and ultimately for her safety although certainly she is not capable of expressing this love. She just *feels* it. This early self-love is important because it is quite natural and central to every human being. Natural self-love is also central to how we conceive of a person's core self, a matter that we will discuss later. An infant is not capable of loving anything outside of herself. Fear should begin to subside in dominance as the infant approaches toddlerhood and begins to experience other emotions. Children who did not have a safe and nurturing environment retain an undue amount of fear in their later years, often stretching into their adult years.
- **Joy**: this is the next emotion an infant begins to feel in later infancy and further developing in toddlerhood. *A toddler feels joy when he has something*. This might be the comfort of a parent's arms, the

pleasantness of something to eat that is satisfying, a favorite blanket, or some toy that is interesting. The emotion of joy that we see in toddlers is a wonderful thing to observe. From the first smile that we see on a baby through the many times of adventure and fascination that can be the heart of the toddler years, about the first two years of life. While the year of infancy where a child is cared for, nurtured, and protected are essential for the child to find basic security, the toddler years should be times where the child *wants* something, *has* something, *values* (pleasures in) something, and, very soon, begins to recognize the *loving* of something. This "something" can be a candy bar, a new toy, a father's arms, a mother's kiss, or just the freedom to run around and pick up everything that fits into their little hands.

When the toddler begins to walk and talk, his capacity for loving extends beyond himself into the environment. He now loves more than himself. He loves things, exploration, people, and the rudiments of a relationship. The freedom of walking and talking increases the possibility of new things to love, sometimes toys, sometimes people, and sometimes simply walking, talking, and running. Correctly experienced, the emotion of joy then continues to deepen and broaden in the rest of the toddler's life. He learns the joy of loving something other than himself. Children who are limited too much during early toddlerhood fail to develop enough joy in their core and can remain "stuck" in feeling the necessity of being afraid.

- **Anger**: this is the third emotion that naturally develops in childhood primarily beginning at about the age of two. These are the preschool years of about ages two to five. If a child has successfully incorporated the emotion of fear into her emotional system, she will be able to be appropriately afraid when there is danger. Likewise, if she has had sufficient experiences of having and loving things, she will have the feeling of joy in the having and loving something. While anger may not be the dominant emotion expressed by preschoolers, it is the most important. *Anger erupts naturally when a toddler can't have what she wants.* As a child transforms from sitting, smiling, and crawling into walking, talking, and running, she simultaneously experiences more freedom but also more limitation, something that hasn't particularly occurred much during infancy and early toddlerhood. Her natural reaction to any kind of limitation is anger, and rightly so because she used to get pretty much everything she wanted, and now things have changed. While we see some anger early in toddlerhood, it really accelerates during the ages three to five. Children at these ages get more limitation than they had in infancy and toddlerhood because they want so much more than they did when they were infants. At these crucial ages of 2-5 children's wants multiply 100–fold because they can now walk and talk, grasp and grab, throw and hit. Furthermore, as these crucial years of childhood unfold, children continue to see more and want more, but at the same time they get a smaller percentage of what they want. The more they want, the less they get. Importantly, this time of life is filled with seeing new things, having things, loving things, and losing things. They love more and lose more, so they get angry more.

- **Sadness**: this is the fourth and last emotion a child develops. Some infants experience what appears to be sadness, especially in environments where they are not properly nurtured and comforted. When such deprivation occurs, the result is often called "infantile depression," but more accurately, this condition is a lack of interpersonal development, which then leads to a lack of engagement with people, often called "attachment disorder." Infants do not experience true sadness because they have not experienced true joy. Toddlers (ages 1-2) experience some sadness, but their emotional experience is largely in the realm of feeling less fear and more joy. Preschool kids (ages 2-5) experience a great deal of sadness, but this sadness is normally expressed in anger. At least ideally, they should experience a lot of sadness, but we usually see a lot more anger than sadness because kids this age are faced with frequent limitation and loss. The central theme of a preschool child is the experience of *not* getting what he wants and learning to simply be sad about that loss. Children of this age *love* more, so they *lose* more, and then should be *sad* more. Ideally, a child who at 5 or 6 and entering school has come to realize that he can't have everything he wants. If a child has learned this very important lesson, i.e. that he won't get most of what he wants, he will then be able to spend the next few years of elementary school learning the give-and-take of relationships. School can be a tough time for kids, and especially difficult for kids who have been indulged during the toddler years by parents who did not limit their children sufficiently. If, during these preschool years, a child does not experience enough limitation, and the sadness that results from being limited, he will not be emotionally mature, something that will hamper him for the rest of his life.

Ideally, if children are raised in environments that are primarily nurturing and comforting in infancy, primarily freedom-oriented and exploratory in the toddler years, and primarily limiting in the preschool years, they are ready to engage the challenges of school and early relationships, which are the heart of the elementary school years. During these early school years, children should then be able to discover and develop their abilities and interests, which will become some of their best expression of their core selves. If children successfully learn to experience and express a breadth of emotions during these first six years of life, they then have the necessary ingredients of "core self" from which the rest of life can now evolve: school, friendships, ultimately work, and intimate relationships in adulthood. The concept of our core self is central to all things that are feelings related. We want to begin a discussion of the core self here and continue it as we go along throughout the rest of the book.

DEVELOPMENT OF CORE SELF

What is most central to successful living is to have a good sense of what we call "core self," from which our feelings erupt as we discussed in Chapter 1. One's core self is a spiritual entity and is, in itself, reflected in the expression of feelings as we defined them: physical, emotional, cognitive, or active. Most importantly, however, our core selves are developed through all of these feeling *experiences* and *expressions* including emotion. Ideally, children have the opportunity to go through the stages of early childhood development and have the experiences and expressions of all four emotions as we have outlined them: fear in the first year, joy in the second year, anger in the next few years, and ultimately the emotion of sadness. We all suffer in feeling awareness and expression to some degree because none of us has progressed perfectly through these first six years of life. Until we become fluent with our emotions our core selves remain undeveloped. Emotional maturity, which is essentially knowing how I feel emotionally and being able to express how I feel emotionally, is the first best way of experiencing what I feel at my central core. If people achieve a modicum of emotional maturity, they can better develop and utilize their cognitive maturity and productive maturity as experiences and expressions of their feelings. The problem with most people, however, and certainly the difficulty with most relationships, does not belong with deficiencies in cognitive maturity and productive maturity, but with lack of emotional maturity. We will see how emotional maturity is the central ingredient in the effective communication of one's feelings, and even more so in the understanding of other people's feelings, which is the heart of social maturity.

Because the core self is such a central ingredient of personhood, we might say that core self *exists* in every human being beginning in infancy, where we ideally have a foundation of safety, comfort, and nurturance. But core self is really developed in preschool years when children have experiences of loving and losing. Core self begins to really take shape during these years, which is based upon this wanting, having, valuing, and ultimately losing things. This is when personal expressions begin to really surface. Children of this age begin to "talk their feelings", they become much more prolific in verbal expression, and it is that combination of experience and expression that begins to formulate a child's personal identification. The "security blanket" is an example of something that helps a child develop a sense of self because the child feels that the blanket is "mine." This feeling that something is *mine* helps a child develop a sense of *my* and eventually a sense of *me*. When children are deprived of having such things, including the expression of emotions, they can fail to develop a true sense of self, which is the central ingredient of engaging life. One's core self develops primarily by having many experiences of wanting, having, and losing, which all have an "I" component: I want something; I love something; I lose something. It is the combination of the experience and the expression of emotions associated with wanting, loving, and losing that begins to shape the child's self. This is why the toddler's saying "no" is so important. When a toddler says "No," he is stating that he *exists*. It is the wonderful joy of having something that assists a child in having a sense of self. The experiences of wanting, having, and losing solidify a child's sense of what it means to be a human being.

Hard as it is for toddlers to want and not have, it is even harder for them to hear the limiting "No" from a guardian. The more a child can *want and not have* because her guardian has simply limited her, the more she will develop an ability to simply feel sad about not having something. The wanting and not having experience that ideally occurs thousands of times during the pre-school years is essential for a child to develop a skill at simply being sad for the loss of something: sad, not angry and not afraid. Just sad. Sadness is the most important building block for the core self. It is here where we all begin to identify the love and loss sequence we talked about at the beginning of this chapter. It is this ultimate paradox of wanting, losing, and learning to trust that you still *exist,* you still are *safe*, and you still can *love* something even though you lost something else.

We are focusing on these early years of a child's life because the development of core self is so dependent on proper development during these years. The "I" component develops through wanting, having, and ultimately losing things, whether these things are physical, emotional, or relational. Core self is constellated around "I want," "I have," and "I lost." If kids are not allowed to have these three experiences, together with the emotions attached to these experiences, they will forever be *narcissistic*. Preschool kids are quite demanding, often unhappy, often angry, and actually, quite narcissistic. Adult narcissism is the feeling that I need something from the outside world and that I deserve to have it, together with attempts to get what I think I deserve to have. We are not inclined to use such terms as narcissism because the term is too frequently used, often as some kind of an attack against someone. What we have in a child of 3-5 is *natural narcissism*. We might do better too call these 3-5 years being naturally greedy. These years are meant to be ones where children are *selfish* so that they can develop a sense of *self*. Personal maturity, emotional maturity, and social maturity are demonstrated in kindness and generosity, but we cannot have this kind of maturity without first being selfish, where we focus on having and losing what we want. The selfishness of the preschool years, if properly fostered and limited, ultimately leads to a maturity shown in generosity and kindness.

The real phenomenon of narcissism begins during the preschool years, and it should be experienced to its fullest. The surface of narcissism, whether we see it in a preschooler, or an adult is essentially selfishness. When we see selfishness in adolescents and adults, we are seeing people who still think that they should have everything they want and the subsequent expression of those demands. This thinking that I should have everything I want is normal for preschoolers, but not normal for adults. Or perhaps instead of "not normal" we should say that selfishness, which is called narcissism in adults, is *emotional immaturity*. We have written about normal childhood narcissism and pathological adult narcissism elsewhere (Brock and Johnson, 2011). Emotional immaturity is what keeps us from truly identifying our feelings and having the ability to communicate what we feel though the four different elements of emotion. We should expect our preschoolers to be emotionally demanding while at the same time guarding against the tendency to give in to their demands or chastise them for having demands. If we do that, we help our children recognize that their emotions are normal and acceptable, and ultimately representations of our deeper feelings.

The purpose of this present work is to help people mature emotionally so they can mature socially. Our society is dependent on this process of development of self first, others second. We spend countless hours with people being with them while they *emote* so they can come to respect what they *feel*. Emoting is part of the process of emotional maturity, but it is not the same as feeling. It is accessing our deep feelings that leads to personal and social maturity. This overall general maturity has to occur sequentially, first through emotional maturity and then social maturity. Emotional maturity is best developed in early childhood, while social maturity is best developed in the school years that are so intrinsically social. Sadly, most people have some gaps in both emotional and social realms.

EMOTIONAL MATURITY

It would make our work easier if people came to our office knowing what they feel emotionally and knowing how and when to express these emotions. But very few people know what they feel emotionally in these simple terms of anger, fear, sadness, and joy. *If people are to learn how to express their **feelings**, they must start with knowing how they feel physically, emotionally, cognitively, and actively.* This is true whether one expresses feelings primarily emotionally or through the other three means of feeling-expression. If we are successful at helping people understand their basic four *emotions*, we then have a chance to help them understand their *feelings* that lie deeper in their core selves. Good therapy always begins with self-awareness, but many people are so tied up in their emotional experiences that they cannot reach into their deeper feelings. We often tell patients that the initial task of therapy is understanding their emotional feelings, namely:

- *Knowing* what you feel emotionally.
- *Valuing* what you feel emotionally.
- *Expressing* what you feel emotionally.
- *Communicating* what you feel emotionally.

Emotional maturity is based on being aware of your emotions so that your emotions do not control what you say or what you do. Emotions can *motivate* you to say something or do something, and they can enhance what you say or do, but emotions themselves should not be the substance of what one says, nor of what one does. Emotional awareness prevents emotional outbursts and emotional repression, both of which prevent people from knowing what they really feel at their deepest level of core self. Emotional outbursts do not successfully communicate to the people around them what they feel. Rather, they cause their listeners to have equally uncontrolled emotions. We want people to learn to know, value, express, and communicate their deepest feelings, which include emotions, without being dominated by their emotions. In our work with people we attempt to help them understand that emotions are but a reflection of their feelings, not their feelings themselves. Our usual focus with people is to help them understand their emotions and value them so that their emotions do not dominate in the expression of feelings, but rather augment their feeling expression.

The task, as we see it, is to help people find ways to understand, value, express, and ultimately communicate their emotions as a first and necessary step towards communicating their deeper feelings. But the story of communicating emotions and deeper feelings doesn't stop with self-awareness and self-expression. In fact, the story of communicating doesn't end with *self*. If this were the case, we would be suggesting that psychology in general and communication in specific were for a narcissistic self-centered goal. The process of successful communication with emotional expression and deeper self-expression leads to being loved. The process that leads to being loved is as follows:

- I successfully communicate how I feel.
- I am heard by someone important to me.
- I am understood by this person.
- I am valued by this person.
- I am loved by this person.

Emotional maturity is first about knowing how I feel and communicating how I feel, which eventually gains me the thing that I most want: to be loved. It is in the emotional part of the feeling process where people get lost because they have not understood and accepted their emotions. You don't have to be a person who prefers emotional expression of feelings to be emotionally mature. You just have to know what you feel emotionally and value those emotions. Hopefully now, you are more familiar with recognizing what you feel and can begin to distinguish between what emotion you experience and the underlying deeper feelings that you have.

An important element that erupts out one's developing emotional maturity is *social maturity*, which we will address more in Chapter 5 where we discuss the challenges of hearing other people's feelings. Once you begin to master the fine art of communicating your feelings, which include emotion but is not dominated by emotion, you will have established meaningful connections with other people. Accompanying the knowledge that you have communicated your feelings to the people around you, you will find yourself increasingly interested in other people's feelings. Social maturity is knowing what someone else feels emotionally, which is a window into how they feel at their deeper feeling level. You can develop social maturity only after you have first succeeded in having people understand you. A truly beautiful thing happens when you have succeeded in communicating your core feelings: you become more interested in other people and their feelings than you are in yourself. When you know someone's deeper self, you will unavoidably love that person. True self-esteem leads to true expression of self, which in turn leads to a true interest in other people. In essence, genuine self-esteem leads to humility.

Before we leave this discussion of emotional expression and emotional maturity, let's review how people experience their emotions. You may feel the defense-based emotions of anger or fear in the presence of danger, you may feel the love-based emotions of joy and sadness, or you may feel a combination of these emotions. The key of emotional maturity is to know what you feel emotionally, value your emotion, govern your emotion and express your emotion at the right time. Becoming emotionally mature is hard work.

THE HARD WORK OF UNDERSTANDING EMOTIONS

- It's hard work to know that I really enjoy something that is unimportant to someone else.
- It's hard work to know someone else really enjoys something that is unimportant to me.
- It's hard work to know that I am afraid that I might lose something that I love that may not be valuable to anyone else.
- It's hard work to know that someone else might be afraid of losing something that I don't think is valuable.
- It's hard work to admit to being angry at having lost something in the past that was very important to me.
- It's hard work to understand how someone else can be so angry at having lost something that was important to that person when it isn't important to me.

- It's real hard work to allow someone else to simply be sad at having lost something that was important to that person when it wasn't important to me at all.
- It's hard work to allow myself to be sad at losing something and keep with the feeling of sadness and thus forestalling the emotion of anger.

The business of knowing, valuing, expressing, governing and hearing emotions is hard work. We will discuss the specifics of how we can effectively express emotions, as well as the larger concept of feelings, in Chapter 4.

SUMMARY:

1. Feelings are comprised of physical, emotional, cognitive, and active experiences. The most potentially valuable and potentially dangerous experience of feelings lies in the emotional experience and expression.
2. There are four basic emotions:
   - *Joy* when I have something I love; *sadness* when I lose it.
   - *Fear* when might lose something I love; *anger* when I have lost it.
3. Emotions are developed sequentially in children:
   - Fear during the first year of life.
   - Joy approximately during the second year of life.
   - Anger during the approximate ages 3-5.
   - Sadness begins to develop at about age three but significantly develops at about age six.
   - All emotions continue to develop through the span of life
4. Children normally express emotions without restraint.
   - Repression of their emotions leads to undue fear.
   - Indulgence of emotions leads to undue anger.
   - Effective parenting allows for anger until the child feels sadness and allows this feeling to finish by expressing sadness.
5. There are differences, degrees, and combinations of what we love.
6. Emotional maturity is knowing what you feel emotionally and successfully communicating what you feel emotionally.
7. Developing emotional maturity is hard work.

Chapter 3

Personality Factors in Feelings

NOW THAT WE HAVE made our best attempt to explain the challenging notions of feelings and emotions, we tackle a third important element in this section of "I want to tell you how I feel." This is how personality factors influence how we feel feelings, how we express feelings, and how we hear other people's feelings. Before we deal with the whole communication process, which is expressing feelings and hearing feelings, we need to take note of how our personalities are similar in some ways and different in some ways. These differences in personality profoundly affect how people feel, understand, communicate, and hear feelings. We all feel feelings that emanate from our core selves. We all experience physical and emotional reactions to our feelings and we all think about our feeling experiences and eventually do things and say things that are resultant of our feelings. At a core self level we are all alike in the sense that this core self is spiritual, pure, and godly. Furthermore, we all have feelings that erupt from our core selves. But as similar as we are at the level of core self, our expressions of our feelings can be profoundly different depending on how our personalities are constructed. Our primary way of understanding these personality differences is seeing differences in *temperament*.

One's "temperament" is the way he or she perceives, evaluates, and engages the world. My temperament affects all of what I see, value, say, and do. We propose that there are four primary temperaments that are displayed in humankind.

We will demonstrate how these four temperaments have correlations with the four feeling expressions and the four emotions, but that temperament is more than feelings and emotion. Temperament is an orientation to the world that drives people to communication, and ultimately to achievement and success in the world. Consider that one's temperament serves as a lens through which one sees the world and has a feeling reaction to the world, and a microphone to communicate about what is seen and felt.

There have been theories of personality construction for more than 2000 years beginning at least with the Greek philosopher Galen who described four different personalities related to the "four body fluids". Since Galen there have been various theories of personality differences and personality characteristics, most often using a four-part system and sometimes using more complicated systems. For example, the enneagram identifies nine different personality structures, a system that is popular in religious genres (e.g. Riso and Hudson, 2003). The Five Love Languages system (Chapman, 1992), also used in religious circles is a recently popular way of understanding how people interact with one another. The DISC system (Hedge, 2015) and the StrengthsFinder (Buckingham and Clifton, 2001) are most often used in business. Certainly, the most popularly used system of understanding personality differences is based on the Myers-Briggs Type Indicator (MBTI) (Myers and Myers, 1992), which itself is largely based on Carl Jung's theory of psychological types (Jung, 1974). Keirsey and Bates (1984) proposed a system of "temperament" based on the MBTI that is substantially different from what we propose. We developed the Johnson Temperament Indicator (JTI, Johnson and Brock, 1982) as a way of identifying the different overall patterns that people use to engage the world. Understanding an individual's temperament helps us understand people better, particularly as this most basic way they engage the world. It is through the JTI analysis that we have been of assistance to people to first understand themselves and then to understand others with the goal of successful communication.

THE FOUR TEMPERAMENTS

The term temperament has been variously used to describe personality characteristics as well as personality problems. Our perspective of personality analysis is focused on one's natural abilities, successful use of these abilities, and the dangers implicit in any use of these abilities. Thus, we do not look at what is wrong with an individual but what is right with that person seeing that abilities can be used successfully or used to a fault, and hence unsuccessfully. We use the term temperament to mean one's *primary means of engaging the world*. It is important for us to note that no system of understanding of personality and no psychological test yields an exact and absolute definition of one's personality. We know that no person fits perfectly into one category of personality because people are too complex and too unique to be just one thing. We use the JTI along other means of examining personality as a beginning step in understanding people. The terms that we have used for temperament over these many years have helped us understand people and helped people understand themselves. These four temperaments reflect the value system the person has, and the means of engaging the world including connection with other people. The four temperaments in our terminology are as follows:

- *Player*: a person who seeks experience in life, and often seeks excitement.
- *Caretaker*: a person who seeks to care for property, and often produces things.
- *Lover*: a person who seeks connections with people, and often shares feelings.
- *Analyst*: a person who seeks meaning in life, and often develops understanding of life.

Intrinsic in temperament analysis is how people of different temperaments experience feelings and express feelings. Note how these differences in experiencing feelings incline people towards a particular way of expressing their feelings and that these differences are based on differences in what people value and love.

Players

Players look to experience as much of life as possible. They do not look to understand life, or even necessarily improve upon their lives but rather simply engage as much as life as possible. Their mantra is something like, "Engage in something, disengage, and then engage in something else." This "engagement" could be in any of the four feeling elements: physical, emotional, intellectual, or active. They are excited and enticed by the new and different and gravitate towards the unknown possibilities that might occur if they engage in something new. They might think something or feel something in their quest for the new and different, but more likely, they would say something or do something as a way of engaging the world.

Players are most obvious in their physicality, namely how they actually engage activity and physically move. They certainly use the other elements, but as this diagram illustrates, the physical element is central to them.

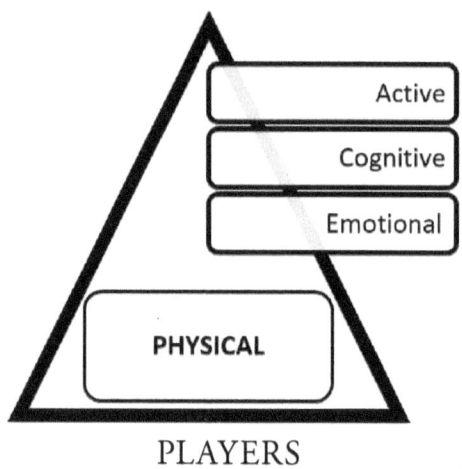

PLAYERS

To watch a player is to watch her move. She might move her arms or legs as a way of engaging the physical world around her; she might move the muscles of her face with a grimace, a smile, a frown, or a laugh; she might move her whole body in a unique way or in a spontaneous dance. This physical engagement is a way that players feel connected to the world. That "world," by the way, could be the physical world around them, the relational world around them, the emotional world around them, or the intellectual world around them. They want to engage the world, in all of its glory, not just observe the world. In a social situation a player could easily hug, grab, tickle, or otherwise touch someone if they feel so inclined because they are compelled to have physical contact with people just as they are compelled to have physical contact with objects and environments. Players love the physical element of life, whether something they feel in their own bodies, see in someone else's body, or what might occur if two bodies experience something together. Physical engagement with other people, physical engagement with the environment, or just physicality itself creates a sense of connection for players.

As their name implies, players tend to *play* at everything that they do. They play at work, play at recreation, play in relationships, play with ideas, play with emotions, play with property, and play with dreams. They can even play while they are alone but their distinct preference is to play with someone. This playing with something or someone is an attempt to find some kind of stimulation or excitement. Players have a sense of potential excitement in their bodies and souls and seek ways to express their internal excitement with anything or anyone in their environment.

Several people come to mind in our thinking about players, the most dramatic of which is our older daughter. Krissie moved more in utero than her younger sister, and that movement continued from her first breaths until her last breaths. She went from crawling to running, skipping the whole walking part of development. In fact, some of our dearest recall of her as a child was her skipping from room to room. She worked hard, played hard, and otherwise engaged the physical, emotional, relational, professional, and recreational world with gusto. As a toddler she found great excitement in taking out every tissue from the 200-tissue box. As a kid in school she engaged every person, every book, and every teacher with an equal amount of zest. You can only imagine what she was like during the teenager years. Suffice it to say that she was engaged with all the good and bad that engagement can bring teenagers. She said things she shouldn't have said and did things that she shouldn't have done but with no malice of heart or mind, always seeking to engage rather than to watch and listen. She swam naked at the Outer Banks, flirted with every available boy in school, tried to run off with the toothless cowboy she met when she worked at a dude ranch in Wyoming, and got married at 17 before divorcing a year later. In all of this she engaged, had fun, and experienced life as much as possible and never meant anyone any harm.

We have known many players in our days, some of whom were friends but many more as patients. One particular friend, Jason, was actually the primary person who helped us conceptualize the whole idea of the player temperament. Jason did all that players do with play: work, words, relationships, thoughts, emotions, and of course play. He would say something just because it seemed to come to him, do something for the same reason always engaging the world in all of its aspects with an intention of finding new and different experience. While well trained professionally in accounting, his profession did not really serve him well, so he found ways to play at his work. He had a myriad of admirers who were fascinated with his engaging nature and his experience-seeking nature, our daughter Krissie among them. Once he volunteered to do a video school project about players and was glad to do it. He was an expert basketball player, an accomplished flutist, and played a mean air guitar, but he took all these activities in stride as his real interest was not so much excellence as it was experience. We have both seen many young players in our offices brought in by distraught parents thoroughly frustrated with how to manage, encourage, and limit their player children. Players themselves have come in when their spouses threaten divorce, or when they have once again been dismissed by an employer, or who just don't understand why all work can't be fun and exciting. Players present a challenge to any therapist who wants to help them succeed in work, relationships, and life in general.

Recall that we look primarily at what is right with people, rather than what is wrong about people. So, when we present someone as having predominantly a player temperament, we are suggesting that this individual first and foremost has positive characteristics that help him engage the world and make a positive contribution to the world. Players primarily find joy in the world and bring joy to the world through their experienced-based nature. This good thing about players inclines them to difficulties in life just as the good things about people of all temperaments incline them to difficulties. We understand these difficulties as "strengths to a fault." The strength to a fault with players is that they can seek experience and excitement so passionately that they are usually not good at listening, observing, working, producing, and just waiting. They'd rather just jump into saying something or doing something because it seemed exciting. A player might be on a bridge over a river and "just want" to jump off the bridge without thinking of the consequences of such an action. Such a person needs to accept his desire to experience the fall and the water below but govern his tendency to just jump right in. Later we will discuss the notion of *governance* of one's nature, one's actions, and one's words.

Caretakers

Caretakers see property as if it were alive. The key to understanding caretakers is to know that they view property as having a spiritual essence. As a result of this view of physical property, they tend to care for property as if property is just as alive as plants, animals, and people. In their care of property caretakers are, in their minds, caring for people because they see the necessity for people to have property that is properly cared for. They feel an intrinsic responsibility for the care and protection of things physical. When caretakers speak, they usually speak about property, namely how it can be appreciated, repaired, saved, or even given away. They abhor the ill use of property as much as other people abhor the ill use of people or ideas. Being a caretaker, Ron often has seen me roll my eyes when he is intensely caring for property, like keeping an outdated phone system which might still be useable even though it has already been replaced or a plastic tarp that he thinks should be duck taped instead of being replaced.

As a result of their distinctive property orientation, caretakers tend to be busy doing things, often repairing, restoring, or restructuring the things in their environments. The operative word is "busy," usually busy in doing something, usually physically, but this busyness can be intellectual, or less likely, emotional. The central element of expression for Caretakers is Activity.

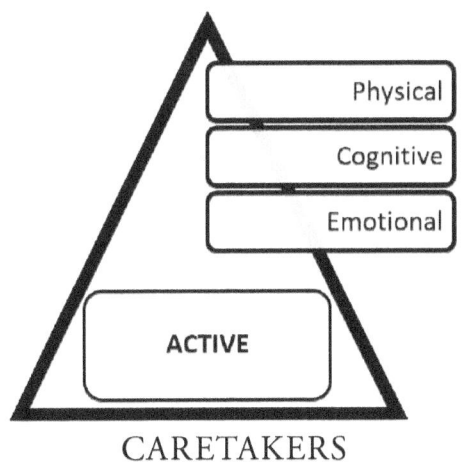

CARETAKERS

Many caretakers enjoy the care of people, especially if they have a combined temperament of caretaker and lover, the next temperament to be discussed. The busyness that typifies caretakers is the expression of their energy form, which is primarily engagement of property, quite different from players who engage for the purpose of experience. The action of caretakers is doing something productive, as the term "doers" certainly applies to them. The doer label fits caretakers because you can see them at their best when they are busy doing something. This "something" might not be meaningful to you, and may even seem to be wholly a waste of time, but to caretakers it is first important to do something, usually physical in nature.

The caretakers we have known in our lives are often successful tradesmen, like our neighbor, Lonnie, who is skilled at all kinds of construction crafts and has helped us out numerous times with the upkeep and repair of our old farm house. He is never bored, always enjoying the challenge of doing something, often with expert skill, and loves to stand back and see the product of his work, like the metal roof he installed, the chimney he repaired, or Deb's greenhouse he glazed. You don't have to be an expert tradesman to enjoy the trades as many a successful householder has thoroughly enjoyed repairing the roof, refinishing the hardwood floors, or painted the barn as we have done over our years together. People who seem to be the most natural mothers are those who have no trouble getting up four times a night to feed the baby and change the diapers, the father who works hard to make the playhouse for the kids in the back yard, the child who just loves to shovel snow for anyone on the block, or the man who prefers to split wood by hand rather than by machine. Always busy, always fixing, never bored, and never tired until he or she drops in bed.

It is the busyness that typifies caretakers that causes difficulties for people who try to relate to them. Because they are usually working all the time, they tend to become irritated with people who don't seem to want to work as much as they do. Work is foremost and there is always work to do. They don't give enough time to things other than producing and protecting things. Hence, they don't play enough for players, analyze enough for analysts, and don't connect enough for lovers. Caretakers play by doing, analyze by doing, and love by doing. They do this all by themselves. They don't need someone else to go about taking care of things. They are usually too busy working to do such things as play, analyze, or connect the way players, analysts, and lovers go about life.

Lovers

Lovers have a special ability for emotional connection with other people. As all four temperaments have some special gift, people with this ability seek, find, and magnify this emotional connection.

Lovers first and foremost desire is to feel *with* someone else, i.e. feel what someone else feels emotionally and have other people feel what they feel emotionally. They are in heaven, of a sort, when they find this connection, so much so that time itself passes quickly, events come and go, words are spoken and heard all without their particular notice because their attention is on how they feel emotionally. Specifically, they want to feel the joy that occurs when two people find a deep commonality of feeling. They want to like what you like and want you to like what they like. If they have the opportunity to maximize this emotional connection, there is no distinction between the other person and them. This connection can be physical, cognitive, or active, but their primary goal is to have a fusion of hearts with other people. They know that at our deepest core selves, we are all spiritual and we are all alike, so there should be no good reason for any kind of disparity or difference in what we feel.

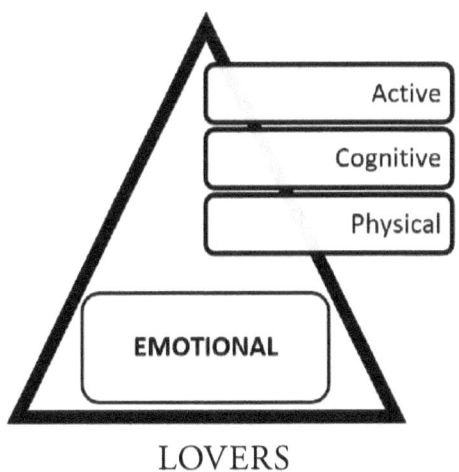

LOVERS

Lovers do not so much think of "you and me" as they think of "us." You can hear their feeling and desire for connection with their frequent use of the pronouns we and us as in statements like, "We really like...," "We really dislike...," or other such statements that reflect a desire to be in agreement in all things. We often chuckle when we recall a time with my sister, Cookie, years ago when we were negotiating where we might go for Mexican food. We thought a favorite restaurant, Carlos O'Kelly's, would be good and put forth the idea to Cookie. Without missing a beat Cookie responded, "Oh, but *we* don't like Carlos O'Kelly's. We like Pedro's." Note the pronoun *we* when my sister spoke of *her* preference. The psychological operation with Cookie was that "she loved Pedro's, so we must certainly love Pedro's because we love each other." Since we value our love for Cookie more than our preference for some particular restaurant, we acknowledged that we most certainly would enjoy Pedro's.

Because of their desire for connection and their ability to love without reservation lovers tend to be quite generous. If they own something that you might need, they would immediately be willing to give you that something. They seem to have the understanding of property that Native Americans reportedly had, namely that "everything belongs to the tribe, and whoever needs it, should have it." This means that if you need money and the lover has money, she will offer it to you or even put it in your mailbox anonymously. Likewise, if you need a particular recipe for a special pie, she might not only give you the recipe but bake the pie for you. It is not only with property that lovers are generous: they give their emotions generously and share your emotions just as generously. While recovering from the death of our daughter over the last few months, many people shared our grief in some way and many were exceedingly generous in their love and concern for us. We encountered people of all temperaments during this difficult time of life, but we have been most taken by the lovers that we encountered who often immediately cried when hearing of our loss, insisted on hugging us, and otherwise sharing our grief. Their sharing our grief has not been a burden to them because they are intrinsically better at grieving. Lovers have been a precious gift to us.

The lovers that we have seen in our life come in the form of family, friends, and patients. Our younger daughter, Jenny, displays all the characteristics of the lover temperament, most specifically seeking emotional connection and being generous. Jenny's loving nature shows itself in intimate person-to-person contact. When she loves you, she just simply loves you. No explanation is necessary and can be easily dismissed if offered. In her maturity she has become a global lover as well. She engages in world events and cares for causes of the world's population as deeply as she cares for any given individual. She is perhaps one of the kindest and selfless people we know. There is something special about Jenny that you can only feel, not describe, a feeling that you are loved without reservation. Aside from the lovers in our personal lives we see patients who bring to us the problems that are associated with being lovers, namely the awful experience of being separated from people that they love in some way or another. Dan still loves his son who died five years ago as if he were yet alive when he speaks of him to me, and he continues to grieve this difficult loss. Sarah grieves that she can't have the connection that she so dearly wants with her husband, probably largely because he is not the lover that she is by nature. Alesha often brings into her therapy session how hurt she was that a child of a distant friend didn't respond to her birthday wish. For Alesha, loving her friend automatically means loving her friends' child. Franklyn speaks of the distress he feels in his office when his colleagues bicker because he wants all people to have an intimate connection. Mike, a seven-year old boy loves everyone in his family, his class, and his neighborhood without regard to whether they love him back. We are often touched by social media links reflecting on some kind of love-based generosity, like a child who wants only to spend their gift money for someone else in need and begins a web-wide crusade to help those in need.

This lover nature seems like a selfless approach to people, which it certainly is, but it is more than selflessness. It is an understanding that if we truly find commonality between two people, we will both be better off. Their search for connection and commonality supersedes their own wishes and desires. When they find this connection, they feel a kind of bliss that occurs when two people are symbiotic. This symbiosis can be in what they see and what they think, but mostly in what feel emotionally. That having been said, lovers can get lost in their loving. They can love so deeply, so passionately, and so graciously, that they can be naïve about the dangers of loving to a fault. They are quite inclined to slipping from *giving* to *giving in*, or from connection to enmeshment where they lose a sense of their separate existence. All of this is love to a fault just as players play to a fault, caretakers work to a fault, and analysts think to a fault.

Analysts

Analysts are quite unique in how they feel and how they engage the world with their feelings. Analysts demonstrate their love for the world and for people by looking to solve difficult problems for people. They want to understand things so they can improve things and in so doing make the world a better place for people. Their unique way of loving is not directly *for* people but *about* people. Their problem-solving orientation comes by observing what might go wrong or has gone wrong, and then figuring out how to improve things. Their mantra is something like, "If we can understand and solve problems, everyone will be better off."

How different is this kind of love for *humankind* than the love that lovers have for *individual people*. If analysts would have their way, they would be content to be in some kind of think tank looking for solutions to the world problems, or in a seminary putting together a unified theory of theology, or on a nuclear submarine looking to find ways to avoid being identified by the enemy. All of this desired activity is for the sake of the many, not necessarily for the sake of the one.

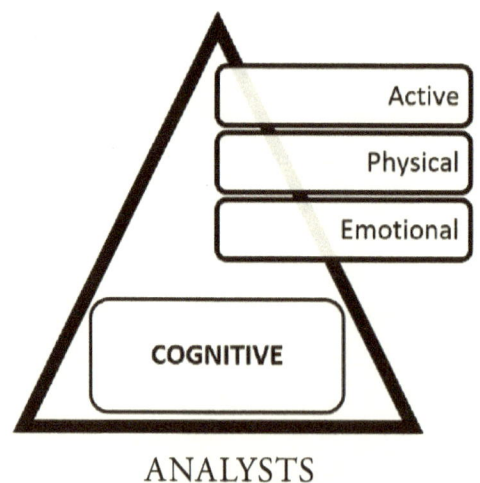

ANALYSTS

Analysts believe that the world would be a better place, different groups would get along better, individuals would be more satisfied, and relationships would be better off if only people *understood* things better. Analysts take it as their task in life to render solutions to the problems that the world, groups, individuals, and relationships have in life. Their most basic desire, their most basic love, is to understand *why* things happen. They believe that if they understand why something is not working, there will be a way to fix the problem, whatever the problem might be. It is quite important to note that analysts are not so interested in *fixing* problems as in *understanding* them. The fixing belongs more in the realm of caretakers. In fact, analysts are much more interested in improving things more than fixing or maintaining things. Understanding why something doesn't work could be a government operation, a sports team that is underperforming, a machine that is broken, a financial dilemma, a relationship, or what they think an individual is doing wrong. They want to understand how things work or don't work so they can be improved, whether property, projects, or people.

The "things" that analysts seek to understand and improve upon often are people. They are expert at seeing what is wrong with what one has said or done, or what they think people should do or say. Theirs is a stance towards people quite apart from the connection that lovers seek, a distance that gives them an opportunity to help people with the problems that they believe people bring on themselves because of their lack of understanding. While lovers are the most easily distressed by a misunderstanding or disconnection that they might have with someone, analysts find a difference of opinion as opportunity for further analysis and discovery.

There are many analysts in the world: many in the public eye, many in families, and many in movies, whether biographical or fictional. When analysts come to our office, they always come with the intent of understanding why something isn't working, often in their relationships, with the implicit hope that if the people in their lives would only understand things better, all would be well. Again, their aim is for understanding so they can lend some direction as to how things could be improved, whether the "things" be a person, place, job, or idea. Analysts believe that their analyses to problems and suggested solutions to these problems are their best way of loving people although they may not actually use the word "love" when they suggest what they think people should do. Understandably, people are often offended by analysts' suggestions and feel that the analyst has intruded upon them by telling them what to do. Analysts are often bemused by the fact that people hearing their suggestions do not always respond favorably. As a result, analysts try to "correct" the misunderstandings that people have of what they said. The analysts who seek our help are not seeking help in understanding their feelings, much less their emotions, because they deem such things as secondary to the truth that they seek to find and display to the world. We frequently find these folks in unhappy relationships partly because they have been working hard to improve their family members, friends, or work associates.

Sam cannot fathom why his wife takes offense at his suggestions that she should spend less money and become more prompt in her life. Sam believes that frugality and promptness are what normal people do, "normal" being equated with what he sees as correct in the world. He has tried in vain to "help" his wife by identifying her so-called problems and render solutions irrespective of what she might think or feel. It is beyond Sam's conception of how things work in the world to conceive that his wife would be hurt and ultimately defensive when he says such things to her. The patients like Sam that we encounter are generally people of good character and often deep thinkers, always looking for the truth, but the truth they seek often runs into causing disharmony. Just as players play to a fault, caretakers work to a fault, and lovers connect to a fault, analysts analyze to a fault.

We trust that you have noticed several things in this brief description of the four temperaments as they relate to you. Likely, you have observed that you have characteristics that predominate in one or two of these temperaments, but also noted that you have some characteristics of all four of them. You might also have found that you are not exactly like any one temperament even if you have the predominant elements of one temperament. You may also have begun to identify that your preference of experience and expression of feelings falls largely into one of the four temperaments. The experience of feelings is much easier to identify with the four temperaments because with little variance, each temperament fits into one of the four elements of feeling expression. You might, for instance, conclude that you are a player because you experience and express your feelings largely in your body. Or, you might be an analyst experiencing or expressing feelings in cognition, a caretaker experiencing and expressing feelings in action, or a lover with a predominant feeling of emotion. As you continue to read, consider how you feel based on your temperament. First, identify how you experience your feelings according to your temperament and then begin to recognize how you express these feelings. We trust that you will also find yourself understanding how other people in your life deal with these important feelings. Our intension is that this understanding of temperament as it relates to feelings will help you understand yourself better and other people better.

TEMPERAMENT AND FEELINGS

Players and feelings

Because of their penchant for experience, players' feelings tend to circumnavigate around their *physical experience* as they engage the world. Players' feelings are almost always intensely physical. They may emote, think and act in some way as they attempt to express their feelings, but their primary means of expression remains physical. In fact, if a player does not have a physical experience with something, this something will not be exciting, and very likely the player will be bored. It is from this gift of physical experience that players express their feelings, which as we have noted, is the first element of feelings that humans experience. In fact, even when players demonstrate the other elements of feelings (emotional, cognitive, and active), they continue to demonstrate the physical movement that is so typical of players.

The typical expression of feeling for a player is its physical presentation is often displayed in physical mannerisms, like arm or hand gestures, facial grimaces or smiles, or in some quick body movement, or in many cases, a simple exclamation of joyfulness that radiates from their whole body. I speak regularly to a person on the phone who reports that he is compelled to walk around his home while talking to me. I think of other player-types who seem compelled to move their legs or feet when sitting or standing around waiting for something to happen. In addition to whole body movement like walking while talking, players often move their hands and fingers in ways that approximate a kind of sign language. We know of a person with a strong player element in her nature who learned American Sign Language in a day because it was so natural for her to demonstrate what she said by using her hands. It is nearly impossible for some people to speak about something without using their hands to describe what she is talking about. We wonder if the stereotypical hand movements of native Italians might display a player nature implicit in Italian culture. That both of us have strong player components in our temperaments might explain why we are always excited to return to Italy.

Players' communication of feelings is not limited to their hands, nor for that matter to their appendages. If a player is truly trying to communicate something, you will observe her whole body in some kind of movement, perhaps even gyrating as her body is a kind of body sign language that is an attempt to express her feelings. We suspect that many professional dancers might be players especially dancers who take to the genre seamlessly. We have watched many actors who seem compelled to use their bodies in this way making me think that many players end up on stage where they can use this means of body communication. Sometime, just turn the sound down for a few minutes while you watch a favorite movie and see which actors are best at communicating physically, whether with their whole bodies or just through simple facial gestures.

Because players are so good at communicating feelings physically, they are less good at doing so verbally. While some players do well with words, like improv actors and standup comedians, most players are not professional in their playing but still attempt to communicate their feelings with words. Unfortunately, their "words" may not be in the English dictionary. They might just create a word out of various syllables that seems to communicate what they feel; they might use a good bit of blue language because swearing, as we know, comes largely from the right hemisphere of the brain, the housing for emotion; or they might simply move their body is some fashion to communicate a feeling. I have heard players open their mouths and seem to speak but no words come out at all; rather, just this facial grimace or wide grin that seems to communicate their feelings. It is as if just opening their mouths and moving their facial muscles is a language all of its own. Such physical presentations do, indeed, communicate some of what the player is feeling, but it might be challenging for someone unfamiliar with player's physical-feeling language to understand what is being communicated. When I have been in the company of players gyrating, grimacing, and generally moving about in their attempts to communicate what they feel, I feel enticed by the apparent fact that my player friend is feeling "something" while having no clear idea of what my friend is trying to communicate.

If you are in the company of a player in some kind of conversation or engagement, you would do well to watch more than listen, feel more than think, and *sense* by intuition what your player friend is trying to communicate. You will have more success understanding a player's feelings that he demonstrates physically than trying to insist on hearing words that make sense to you. You might have more difficulty in developing a sustained relationship because of your player friend's propensity to excitement all the time. It can be difficult to engage players because of their energy-based way of life as well as their tendency to engage you physically.

Caretakers and feelings

As we noted previously, there is a similarity between players and caretakers: they both involve some kind of physical experience, but the ways that they express feelings are vastly different. Players are play-oriented, excitement-oriented and physical in their expressing their feelings; caretakers are production-oriented, property-oriented, and physical in their expressing feelings. When caretakers express their feelings, it is almost always in the care of property or some activity that is productive. Recall that caretakers view property as having intrinsic or spiritual value that needs to be cared for.

We have three neighbors whom we suspect are caretakers by temperament. Luke, our nearest neighbor, manifests his caretaker temperament regularly with the hands-on work of splitting wood and the overall maintenance of his property. Many times, over the years I have watched him first unload hardwood from his pickup, chain saw them into uniform lengths, then split these lengths by hand, and then stack the wood in large piles somewhat resembling a symmetrical mound or pyramid, the most efficient manner I have ever seen. While his finished work is actually creative in vision, I have no doubt that the beauty of his wood stacks come first from a perspective of caretaking before it is about beauty. To observe him at this work is truly enjoyable because of his hands-on efficiency. My other caretaker neighbor, Lonnie, whom we mentioned above, is the best of what it means to be a true tradesman. A roofer by trade, he is ready and willing to do anything that we might need, or what anybody might need in the neighborhood. His work is speedy, efficient, and of the best quality. He approaches such projects with complete confidence and care even if he has to make last minute adjustments to his work. My third caretaker neighbor, George, lends me his wood splitter once a year. When I come to retrieve it, he is usually working on something in the garage, like a small engine that needs repair, splitting wood, or cleaning up debris on his small acreage. As long as he is busy, he is happy and satisfied. For all of these good neighbors, doing is their expression of their deepest feelings.

Whenever I am in conversation with any of these three men, the talk is never about emotions, or thoughts, or relationships. Rather, we talk about wood, engines, house repairs, teaching kids how to play basketball, or any other chore that is on their minds. For George, Luke, and Lonnie, when we are talking about wood and wheels, we are talking about feelings. When Lonnie finished his work on our chimney last night, and again this morning when he picked up the 70-foot lift he needed to repair the chimney, he was all smiles and very vibrant as he looked over the work he had completed. He was "talking about his feelings" by smiling, looking, and musing about what he did to make something work. Not all caretakers like to split wood or repair machinery, but all caretakers revolve their lives around the use and care of property. Ask one of your caretaker friends what she or he has been doing, and you might end up hearing about the games they played with their grandchildren, their planning for a party, the car they are working on, the house project they are considering or some other activity that they see as a way of expressing their feelings.

It is in this valuing property as if it has spiritual value that can become problematic for caretakers. When caretakers talk about the care of property that is so important to them, they are expressing their feelings, but many people on the receiving end of such a conversation do not understand that talk about property for caretakers is sharing their feelings. Over the years I have known my caretaker neighbors I have heard very little from them about play as we normally think about the term that is typical of players, love that is typical of lovers, or thought that is typical of analysts. If you have a friend or family member who is a caretaker by nature, you might find yourself a bit bored hearing of his or her "feelings" that always have to do with property and doing, but not much of anything else. Caretakers can give you the same report of what they have done over and over. They speak repetitively because they don't mind repeating what they've said or what they've done. They don't get bored with routine because routine and repetition are expressions of their feelings.

Conversation between life partners both of whom are caretakers usually involves care of their common property and often the care of their children or grandchildren. Most of the Christmas letters we receive are from caretakers who report a list of things they have done, people they have seen, places they have gone, or projects completed over the year. It is through the reporting of their routines and activities that they talk about feelings. Sometimes, however, caretaker couples fail to spend much time playing, loving, or thinking, which then can lead to difficulties building relationships. Caretakers working…to a fault…can be problematic in their lives and in their relationships because the caretaking is usually done alone and so doesn't register with some as a connection.

Lovers and feelings

While *feelings* are no more important to lovers than to someone with a different personality construction, lovers are much more adroit at incorporating *emotions* when they express their feelings because emotions are at the heart of what it means to be a lover. Lovers are also aware of other people's emotions just as caretakers are aware of others' productions and players are aware of other's play. Because of their passionate nature, lovers are intensely aware of the *emotion* that is associated with their feelings although they are no more aware of their actual *feelings* than people of other temperaments. This greater awareness of the emotion associated with feelings often compels lovers to express what they call their "feelings" because they equate feelings with emotions.

Because of the centrality of emotion with lovers' expression of feelings, their emotions are often intense. It is common for lovers to say something akin to, "I just feel it and I know it is true." This "just feel it" intuition-like experience is basic to all people, but lovers' intuition is invigorated by emotion. We can call this phenomenon *intuition* but with the caveat that all people have intuitive feelings, but not all people emotionalize their intuitive feelings. The primary emotions that lovers have are joy and sadness, but they can also experience and express intense fear and anger. Recall that joy and sadness are the two emotions associated with love as we noted previously while fear and anger are defense-based emotions. While lovers experience fear and anger, sometimes very intensely, they are particularly drawn to the love-based emotions of joy and sorrow. Thus, we have discovered that the best way to describe people with this love-based temperament is to call them "lovers." Because lovers emotionalize their feelings, they appear to have more feelings.

While lovers' expressions of feelings are largely emotional, they also have feelings that are expressed physically, cognitively, and in activity. Yet while lovers think, speak, or act out their feelings, their emotions tend to dominate all of their expressions with an appearance that can be quite demonstrative. They tend to make strong statements of opinion infused with emotion but not necessarily informed opinions. They may engage in some activity that will be laced with emotional expressions like opening their arms when they see you in the grocery store or slamming the door when you have offended them. When a lover says that he "just feels" something, we might call this emotion, but he could just as easily put his fist to his chest and say that his body feels something that is important. Because of their emotional and physical awareness of feelings, lovers tend to be strong in their statements, which can be very emotional. Tears can come to lovers quite easily, whether tears of joy or tears of sadness. Laughter comes just as easily, which makes lovers easy to like. You might be drawn to lovers because they seem to feel your emotions, perhaps even more than you do. They may even attempt to tell you what you are feeling emotionally, and be equally distraught if you challenge their perception.

Because of the emotional centrality to their experience and expression of feelings, lovers can get themselves in relational trouble without meaning to. Lovers are first and foremost looking for connections with people, but these connections are primarily emotional, so they look for common emotions, common thoughts, common values, and common interests with the people in their lives. When a lover has expressed her emotion-based feelings to someone, she unwittingly believes that this other person will have the same feelings. But, if as so often happens, her friend has a different opinion, or does not share the same emotion, the lover can become quite upset. Lovers have an unspoken operation something like, "If I feel it, you should feel it because we are connected." Recall that Cookie knew that "*we* like Pedro's." It does not naturally occur to lovers that the other person may, indeed, have different values, thoughts, and intuitions about the topic at hand. Many fruitless arguments have erupted because lovers, in their desire for connection, have mistakenly believed that their emotions and the underlying feelings should be shared by all.

Analysts and feelings

Analysts have just as many feelings as the other four temperaments but you would never know it. In fact, they are often accused of "having no feelings at all" or of being harsh and uncaring. Analysts feel very deeply but they tend to keep the emotions associated with feelings to themselves and tend to express themselves through thoughts. In that way they are quite different from lovers who lead with their emotions. Analysts tend to reside in matters intellectual and intuitional. While you will rarely hear an analyst use the phrase "I just feel," you may easily hear the phrase "I just know." But when an analyst does use the term *feel*, he tends to really be speaking of his thoughts and intuitions more than his emotions. Listen to scientists, many of whom are analysts, whether one in the social sciences or the physical sciences, and you will often hear the speaker's feelings in the form of data and theory. If lovers' moto would be "I feel therefore I am," analysts' motto would be "I think therefore I am." Rene Descartes, who coined this last statement, might have been an analyst himself. If you look hard and listen carefully, you will be able to detect some emotion from an analyst but you will rarely hear anything about the speaker's physical feeling unless it is something like "I know it in my head!"

The primary operation for analysts is understanding, something that often occurs in the form of problem-solving, and secondarily in problem-preventing. They actually *love* problems to solve, and so their joy in the world revolves around queries, questions, and complexities, all of which are directed towards understanding and then towards making improvement with that understanding. If a caretaker's penchant is for maintaining property and accomplishing chores, an analyst's desire is to make the world a better place by having an understanding of how property works and how it can be improved with suggestions and solutions. This generally comes in the form of ideas and suggestions more than "just doing something." They want to make the world better, but in doing so, they might not look at the specifics of people the way lovers do, property the way caretakers do, or adventure the way players do. Analysts love the world, which might include their people, property, and play, but their love for the world is more philosophical. When analysts express their *feelings*, they are looking to answer the question Why, not the What of caretakers, the Who of lovers, or the When of players.

While the primary operation for analysts is problem-solving, the operative words for analysts are *understanding and improvement*. In their desire to improve the world at large, the football team they watch on TV, or their intimate friend, they look to identify problems and offer solutions to these problems. There is deep passion in analysts' desire to understand and improve and then possibly solve problems, but this passion can be heard as critical. Jokingly, we sometimes say to analysts that their operation in life is something like, "Let me love you the way I do best, by telling you what you did wrong, and what you should have done." As you might expect, such an approach to problem-solving is not always well received.

As we proceed in our discussion of the four temperaments as they relate to emotions, consider how you operate in life in one or more of these temperament descriptions and in the primary means of your feeling expression. You might remember conversations you have had that turned out to be unfruitful or harmful, which might have had to do primarily with differences in how people experience and express their feelings. See if you can begin to recognize the temperament of people most important to you.

Expression of Feelings According to Temperament

Primary Temperament	Temperament Value	Expression of Feeling
PLAYER	Experience	Physical
LOVER	Connection	Emotional
ANALYST	Understanding	Cognitive
CARETAKER	Property	Active

TEMPERAMENT AND EMOTIONS

Recall that there are four basic emotions: joy, sadness, fear, and anger and that these four emotions occur in couplets: joy and sadness being love-based emotions while fear and anger are defense-based emotions. These four emotions, as well as combinations of these emotions, are but one way of expressing our feelings. It is with this framework of understanding emotions that we approach the study of how people of different temperaments experience and express their emotions. Just as we all experience and then express our feelings though a physical, emotional, cognitive or active elements, we all experience and express our emotions though the love-based and defense-based couplets according to our temperaments. We propose that people of different temperaments have preferences for expression of their emotions. Furthermore, each temperament has a preference for the expression of the defense-based emotions and a preference for the expression of the love-based emotion. Thus, everyone tends to be more fluent with one defense-based emotion (fear or anger), and more fluent with one love-based emotion (joy and sorrow). This means that we all tend to be conscious of some emotions and not conscious of the other emotions that we have. This does not mean that people feel more of one emotion than another emotion, but that they are better able to express some emotions more than others. In other words, the emotions that you hear from people do not constitute the entirety of their emotional experience. They are just better at expressing some emotions more than other emotions.

As we examine the four temperaments' inclinations towards expression of their emotions, our intention is first to help people of all temperaments know what they feel consciously and then understand what they might feel unconsciously. While people of different temperaments tend to be better at expressing one of the love-based emotions, their preference for joy or sorrow is interesting but not particularly problematic. When people feel safe and confident, they always feel joy first regardless of their temperament. It is more important to know that the unconsciously felt defense-based emotions of fear and anger often drive people to say something without their awareness of that driving force. Famous Gestalt therapist, Fritz Perls, said, "Awareness is curative", but we would prefer to make an adjustment to that statement suggesting that "awareness of one's emotions helps people communicate their feelings." If you have discovered your preference for feeling expression, you might now be able to see your preference for emotional expression.

Our goal in this discussion of emotions and temperament is to help people become more successful at communicating their love-based emotions. To do this our task is to help people recognize and trust what they initially feel emotionally. When you become more fluent with joy and sadness you will be more successful at communicating your love-based emotions and become less reliant on defense-based emotions and other negative presentations of yourself. Except in the very rarest of instances, our primary emotion is love-based. The rare experiences where our primary emotions are defense-based are those when we are in truly life-threatening danger. By nature, we should experience far more joy and sadness than we do fear and anger. Sadly, most of us have not matured enough emotionally to access the more important love-based emotions. Instead, we default into expressing our defense-based emotions.

Our task in the present discussion is to help you understand what you feel from your core level and how to express it through love-based emotions. We will focus on which defense-based emotion people experience, which love-based emotion that they tend to express, and the unconscious emotions that occur in all people. Our overall task is to help you be more aware of all of what you feel emotionally so that your emotions serve you and others around you but do not dominate you. The framework we use in this discussion of temperament vis-à-vis the **love-based emotions** is this:

- We all experience the feeling of love when we have something that we love.
- Our experience of loving something brings the emotion of joy, while the experience of losing something brings the emotion of sadness.
- We all *experience* the emotion of joy before we experience the emotion of sadness.
- We tend to *express* this feeling of love predominantly with either joy or sadness according to our temperament.

The framework we use in this discussion vis-à-vis the **defense-based emotions** is this:

- The emotions of fear and anger are natural in the face of real or imagined loss.
- Our experience of past loss tends to be anger, while the experience of future loss tends to be fear.
- We always *experience* the emotion of fear before we experience the feeling of anger.
- We tend to *express* the emotion associated with loss with fear or anger according to our temperament.

As we proceed with this discussion of temperament and emotion, we will highlight how some people express one of the love-based emotions more easily and one of the defense-based emotions more easily but that the other two emotions that are not expressed yet operate with everyone even if they are not aware of these emotions. This seemingly convoluted understanding of expressed and unexpressed emotions will become clearer as we discuss people of all temperaments in light of the emotions they express or fail to express. Consider what you feel emotionally and how you tend to express these emotions.

Players and emotion

The primary love-based emotion that players express is joy. Players are absolutely at their best when they are truly enjoying themselves in some way. They can become so lost in this joyful activity that they are oblivious to anything else in their environment. They are, we might say, "in a zone," namely a zone of joy. Due to their playful and experiential nature, players look for joy, find joy, and tend to express joy at any moment of any day. You might often hear from players the simplest of exclamation "I am just so excited" or "that was SO fun!" Players who have an analytic temperament might talk about how interesting something is, a book they are reading or a lecture they have attended because their playful excitement blends with interest in learning and understanding. If they combine their player nature with a lover nature, they might be excited and joyful about an intimate experience with someone, or if they combine their player nature with a caretaking nature, you might hear their joy in fixing the roof. Players do not *experience* any more joy than people gifted with the other three temperaments; they just hope for it to be there, see it when it is there, and enhance it whenever possible. Our daughter Krissie was certainly at her best when she displayed the joyful experience-base she had in life. Krissie often commented that one of the best times in life was when we took her white-water rafting in Alberta, a classic player type of adventure. At Krissie's celebration of life her aunt Karen said that the most remarkable thing about Krissie was her outrageous laugh, so indicative of players.

If players' conscious love-based emotion is joy, their unconscious love-based emotion is sadness. Simply put, they are much better at expressing joy than they are at experiencing sadness. You can think of it this way: players prefer joy so they push sadness down. Players often struggle with the fact that so much of life does not lead to experience, excitement, and joy. If given half a chance, they will work to enjoy every moment of every day and make those around them enjoy those moments as well. Because so much of life is not devoted to experience and consequent joy, players fall prey to being bored with much of life and can consequently become quite depressed when they can't find much joy in what they are doing. To mature emotionally, players need to learn to trust the sadness that always follows joy, just as losing something always follows having something. What very often happens with players when they face loss or potential loss is that they find some kind of quick fix. These quick fixes can easily turn into addictions, whether chemical (alcohol, drugs, caffeine) or behavioral (eating, buying, gambling, promiscuity). When players have fallen into some addictive behavior, they are actually trying to avoid the deep sadness that they feel when life is not exciting and joyful.

The primary defense-based emotion that players experience is fear. Thus, they are conscious of the emotion of fear much more than they are aware of feeling anger when they are in a potentially dangerous situation. Players experience fear more readily than anger because they are so inclined to try the new and different, even the dangerous. The combination of their most conscious love-based emotion of joy and their most conscious defense-based emotion of fear creates the excitement that you so often see with players. You might hear a player express this fear/excitement readily as he or she attempts to do something that could be dangerous. We have a "Swedish son" as we call him, a man now 46 who spent his senior year in high school with us as a foreign exchange student from Sweden. Andreas is now a pilot by trade who originally took up sky diving, but then gravitated into mountain diving, a particularly dangerous activity. Listening to his stories of skydiving and mountain diving recently, we could hear this mixture of fear and excitement. He has no reservation of admitting that he is scared, but also excited, when he dives out of a plane or off a mountain.

Note the players in your environment who are, for instance, always on the edge of something exciting, always wanting to explore and investigate, but then without notice, you also see in them the anger, or even rage, that seemingly comes out of nowhere when they are deprived of having the opportunity or thing that they want. These outpourings of spontaneous, sometimes uncontrolled anger, are eruptions of the unconscious defense-based emotion. While the fear that we see in players may be fairly reasonable because of their adventurous nature, the anger that you sometimes see is quite unreasonable and can seem dangerous. So, players engage the world consciously with joy and fear, but sadness and anger unconsciously operating. This means that players are mature with joy and fear but not mature with sadness and anger. As a result, players can either fall into boredom or a deep depression because they don't have a mechanism to simply be sad, or they can become irresponsibly angry when they are deprived of what they want in life. I often have player children brought to me for evaluation because of their outrageous explosions of anger, but the parents also say that they are "just so fun and friendly" at other times. Player children are more inclined to these explosions of their unconscious anger than player adults who might sublimate the emotion of anger into an addiction of some kind.

Caretakers

Caretakers are like players in one way: their love-based emotion of preference is joy. However, they express the defense-based emotion of anger when they feel some kind of danger or experience some kind of attack. The joy that caretakers feel shows mostly in their production, most often with their hands-on work but occasionally with production that occurs in other ways, like writing or creative projects. You can see caretakers, like our roofer neighbor Lonnie mentioned earlier, simply look at the roof he put on our house and quite simply feel great joy in his accomplishment. This kind of stand-back-and-admire an accomplishment is quite different from the joy players have in excitement and experience, but it is joy nevertheless. Caretakers don't necessarily need someone with them when they enjoy what they are doing. They can just go about the task in front of them and with a gusto that could be extremely pleasurable without any visible evidence that they enjoy the process. They're good at enjoying the experience of doing something just as much as players enjoy some exciting experience.

Caretakers are less good at the other love-based feeling, sadness, which remains largely unconscious. Their generally positive attitude towards what they are doing does not leave much room for simply feeling sad when things don't go well for them. While they generally have a positive attitude in their approach to life, they are not well-equipped to deal with mistakes and disapproval that would naturally lead to the feeling of sadness. A caretaker can mature in emotional expression by adding to his natural tendency of joy of accomplishment the sadness that naturally occurs when something doesn't go right. Unfortunately, caretakers tend to run away from feeling sad and end up expressing anger at disappointment. I have a patient who, sadly, suffered a serious back injury leaving him largely paralyzed. His life had been replete with doing, whether at work or at home. Now unable to swing a hammer or even to move his legs, he is quite despondent. While he was very good at enjoying his work, he was never very good at any kind of failure, criticism, or disappointment. Years before his unfortunate accident he came to me because he knew that he got angry too easily. We succeeded in that endeavor to some degree, but now we are facing the need for him to feel this profound sadness associated with this profound loss so that he can find a meaningful life ahead for him. He is not good at facing loss of any kind, much less the profound loss he has recently suffered that has seemingly robbed him of being a hands-on doer.

The defense-based conscious emotion for caretakers is anger, while their unconscious defense-based emotion is fear. Caretakers are inclined to quickly and easily blow up, usually because something didn't go as planned. The laminate flooring didn't work the way they hoped it would, the compressor jammed just when they were finishing a job, their partner didn't hold the glue gun right when they were trying to fix that old plate, the report didn't get finished in time, the presentation at work was not successful, or the car just wouldn't start when it was supposed to start. Caretakers get angry when things don't work "the way they're supposed to work. They tend to be the ones who throw the hammer at the wall, yell at their coworkers, and otherwise display an immaturity of emotional expression of anger. They know that things might break if you throw them and people will get hurt if you yell at them, but they too easily give into their emotional immaturity when they meet with some unexpected challenge with the property that they cherish.

Caretakers are good at anger, if we understand "good" to be an ability to feel and express anger as a means of defense. At the heart of caretakers' defense-based emotion, however, is a deeper sense of fear. They are less good at allowing themselves to experience fear that always precedes anger. Because they don't allow for a normal amount of fear, it tends to build up unconsciously in their systems. This unacknowledged fear often leads to a deep sense of anxiety. They talk it away, think it away, and often work it away, but anxiety doesn't "go away" with talking, thinking, and working. It goes away when you realize that you are afraid and then take a moment to let it run its course.

Lovers
We see more expression of sadness in lovers and analysts than we see in players and caretakers. Lovers and analysts do not *have* more sadness, nor do they *have* less joy. Rather, they tend to *express* the love-based emotion of sadness more often than they express the emotion of joy. Let's look at lovers first in this understanding. The proposal that lovers express sadness more easily than joy might sound a bit weird because it might sound like lovers would be better at being happy than at being sad. But such is the case, so allow us try to explain this understanding of how lovers experience and express the love-based emotions. Recall the many lover people we met while on our "grieving journey" over the days and weeks following the death of our daughter. While not all the people we met were lovers, when we shared our story of grief, lover people, to a person, *felt sad with us* and many came immediately to tears as we shared our loss with them.

To say that lovers' visible emotion is sadness is not to say that they are depressed, which most certainly they are not, but rather to note that lovers have an intrinsic feeling of connection with people who have loved and lost something. Lovers do not think of their sadness as something wrong to feel but something right to feel as it is deeply related to their love of people. They know implicitly that the more you love, the more you will lose, and when you lose something, you will feel sad. Lovers know that losing something requires the emotion of sadness. There are often challenging moments with a departure from a lover, however brief the separation might be. In these moments, say when you are about to leave someone's house, you might find the lover holding on to you tightly as if you shouldn't really leave. This can put you in a difficult place, wanting to go and being pulled to stay. In such a circumstance your lover friend is aware of her feeling of sadness at your departure. You might be aware of feeling joyful at having had a good evening together. You're both feeling love for each other, but you each display different love-based emotions: you for what you had, your friend for what she lost.

Lovers are more expressive of the fear in the defense-based emotions than of anger. While they love easily and quickly, they are intrinsically aware that they will lose what they love, particularly when they love someone. Lovers are so aware of potential separation and other forms of loss that they exhibit a kind of anxiety much of the time. This awareness of potential loss can keep lovers from truly enjoying the moment of loving something and enjoying something. It is to their credit that lovers know that all good things end, but they can be so aware of the potential loss that they work too diligently to prevent loss of any kind, particularly loss of connection with another human being.

While lovers are conscious of and expressive of fear, they are not so conscious of the potential emotion of anger that can result from a loss. Because they are not aware of anger as a natural defense against attack, they are not as mature in the expression of anger when it comes to them. Lovers can display the best of kindness and generosity easily, and even be aware of the potential of some kind of separation or loss, but when they actually experience that loss, they can become excessively angry. It is remarkable that these, the most connection-oriented of all temperaments, can become so overcome with anger that they can say the unkindest things to people that they dearly love. Why would someone who loves as deeply as lovers do, become enraged to such an extent that he or she would end up yelling or screaming at the very person that they love? They do so because while their fear is the more basic defense-based emotion, their anger is much less mature and so surfaces in defense. They can defend themselves against loss or attack by appropriate fear, but they often do not manage the emotion of anger that can come up with any kind of separation or any kind of disagreement.

Analysts
Analysts are similar to lovers in their being conscious and expressive of the love-based emotion of sadness more than the emotion of joy. We note again that this fact does not make analysts any sadder or depressed than other people, but rather that they simply know that we live in an imperfect world where things go wrong, people are hurt, and mistakes are made. Such things make them sad. Recall that analysts want to make the world a better place, and as a result are inclined to see what is wrong, hurt, or mistaken. Because they see such things, they see much more of the sadness in the world than

caretakers and players who are inclined to ignore the difficulties of life and charge ahead into playing or working. This strength of being aware of the great amount of loss and difficulty in life inclines analysts to focus on how things could be better, but in this focus, they see much more of what is wrong or mistaken than do people of other temperaments. They can speak of the difficulties of life and admit to the sorrow of life without actually feeling despondent. Their focus on truth, namely seeking truth and speaking truth, brings to the world the possibility of making things better by first seeing how things really are. Very often, things are not as they should be and analysts know it.

With their penchant to make the world a better place, their focus can be primarily or singularly on what could be improved. Because analysts are so good at seeing what is wrong, they comment more about what is wrong, or could be wrong, than they focus on what is right. This amounts to analysts being much more conscious of the necessity of feeling sadness in life than of the necessity of feeling joy. There are times where I have seen analysts be afraid to enjoy a good moment because of the possibility that the moment might not last. My brother in-law, the consummate analyst, is unable to enjoy a moment of success while we watch a football game together because he is so aware that a lead in such a game could evaporate at any time. Good a person as Dennis is, he is not good at enjoying the moment. As a result of their penchant to feeling sad, analysts can almost be unable to enjoy a moment of joy without "automatically" declaring how it won't last. Thus, joy lies mostly unconscious for analysts because they're so good at sadness. An analyst who matures emotionally allows herself to feel joy without undue fear of losing the feeling.

Analysts are conscious of the defense-based emotion of anger more than the emotion of fear. Thus, they rarely display fear of attack, but rather defense against it in the form of being angry. In their desire to "make the world a better place," they are inclined to see what is wrong and attempt to correct what is wrong without particular reference to how their words sound. Like caretakers, analysts are inclined to express irritation or anger easily. They see more of the world, see more of what is wrong with the world, and become angry that so many things are wrong. They are not any angrier than people of other temperaments, but they tend to express it more easily and more frequently. We hear from our analyst patients that they are often perceived as angry when, in fact, they are not so much angry as they say angry-sounding words or expressions in their daily walk and talk. Because of their problem-based orientation to life, i.e. preventing and solving problems, they often run into problems that cannot easily be solved or problems that other people fail to resolve. Simply put, analysts get angry rather quickly because they see that something is not working out as they hoped it would and know it could, usually because someone is not doing what should be done, or they themselves are not succeeding in doing what is right to do.

While conscious and expressive of anger easily, analysts are less conscious and rarely expressive of the other defense-based emotion, fear. The danger with defense-based emotions that are not conscious is that they operate on their own; they operate to motivate a person to defense. So, with analysts who are good at being able to be angry when something is wrong or mistaken, they are less good at feeling appropriate fear on the same occasions. Analysts can be overcome by a deep-seated fear that something will go wrong but express anger instead of the underlying fear. Analysts who mature in their emotional awareness and expression admit that they might not know what to do, where to go, or how to fix something rather than quickly moving into some form of anger at some error that has been made or misjudgment that has been made.

We have examined how people of all temperaments tend to be conscious of one of the defense-based emotions and one of the love-based emotions. No one is conscious and appropriately expressive of all four emotions although that is the goal of emotional maturity: to know how you feel, communicate how you feel, and govern how you feel so your emotions do not dominate you but serve you as your serve humankind. You serve humankind because you know and respect yourself and are then able to understand and respect others. Being aware of how you express your love-based emotions and how you express your defense-based emotions contributes to a personal maturity and eventually to a social maturity.

Let's summarize both the love-based emotions and the defense-based emotions:

Temperament and Expression of Love-based Emotions

Primary Temperament	Expressed Emotion	Unexpressed Emotion
PLAYER	Joy	Sadness
LOVER	Sadness	Joy
ANALYST	Sadness	Joy
CARETAKER	Joy	Sadness

Temperament and expression of Defense-based Emotions

Primary Temperament	Expressed Emotion	Unexpressed Emotion
PLAYER	Fear	Anger
LOVER	Fear	Anger
ANALYST	Anger	Fear
CARETAKER	Anger	Fear

As we noted earlier, we acknowledge that our temperament paradigm is but one way of understanding human differences in personality and ultimate psychological and social functioning. We mean no dishonor or disagreement with other systems of personality analysis and invite readers to explore those other systems. Our task remains primarily to help people communicate their feelings by understanding themselves first and other people second. In order to be successful at expressing and communicating feelings, including their emotions, we suggest that it is important to know not only what one feels, but also how we are all inclined to express our feelings in one of the four ways we have outlined, namely physically, emotionally, cognitively, or actively. We also need to know how we naturally tend to express our emotions, namely the four emotions of joy, sadness, fear, and anger. Finally, we also need to be aware of emotions that we feel but tend not to express so that these unexpressed or unconscious emotions do not dominate us beyond our conscious awareness. We will be discussing how we can use this understanding of feelings, emotions, and temperament in the next few chapters when we get down to the business of how we speak and how we listen, all based on how we feel.

SUMMARY:

1. Depending on their temperament people experience and express their feelings quite differently:
    - People with a "player" temperament tend to express feelings physically.
    - People with a "lover" temperament tend to express feelings emotionally.
    - People with an "analyst" temperament tend to express their feelings cognitively.
    - People with a "caretaker" temperament tend to express their feelings in action.
2. People of all temperaments can mature in their awareness and expression of their feelings by noting the elements of feelings that are not natural to them.
3. Depending on their temperament people experience and express their emotions quite differently:
    - People with a player temperament express joy as their love-based emotion. They tend to feel fear as their defense-based emotion.
    - People with a lover temperament express sadness as their love-based emotion. They tend to feel fear as their defense-based emotion.
    - People with an analyst temperament express sadness as their love-based emotion. They tend to feel anger as their defense-based emotion.

- People with a caretaker temperament express joy as their love-based emotion. They tend to feel anger as their defense-based emotion.
4. Emotional maturity begins with understanding the emotions that you feel most easily, this followed by learning about the emotions that you might not so readily feel or express.

Chapter 4

Expressing Feelings

DO YOU EVER WONDER why people so often use the word "like" so frequently when they speak, especially when they want to express something that is important to them? Some people scatter the word "like" so frequently in their descriptions that it can be the predominant word in every sentence. I have heard, as you certainly have heard, people actually using "like" several times in succession, often at the beginning of a sentence or when they are unsure as how they might proceed. I once heard, "Like, like …like, I, like, think, I like, feel that this is, like, very important." When people use "like", they are suggesting that what they are saying is an approximation of some sort or as a superlative. Someone could say, "She's, like, beautiful," which would mean that the word beautiful wasn't exactly the right word to describe the woman's appearance. Or perhaps the word beautiful wasn't quite powerful enough.

The word "like" is just one of many words or phrases that suggest approximations. Sometimes people use "I mean" several times because they can't quite find the right word. They might say, "I mean, you know, I mean, like I mean… she is beautiful." The word "just" is also a word that suggests approximation. In churches where public prayers are common, you might hear someone begin a prayer with, "Lord, I *just* pray that …." How does the word "just" add anything to the prayer? It allows the person praying to add personal emphasis to the prayer. Another very common expression often inserted in a statement is simply, "I don't know but…", again, an expression that allows the speaker room for saying something that is approximate. How in the world can someone justify using "like" or "I mean" several times in succession, or insert, "I don't know" in the midst of a statement? People use these expressions because they *are trying to express their feelings and can't seem to find adequate words for their feelings.* The very word "like" suggests that the statement one is making does not lend itself to exactness. Something is *like* something else, but it is not exactly *alike* it. People are all desperate to find a way to express what they feel. We hope that we can be of some help in this process because people, *like, I mean, really, like, need to just tell you their feelings.*

We studied the nature of feelings and emotions in Chapters 1 and 2, noting among other things that feelings are central to life and that we need to be aware of our feelings and attempt to communicate them. We've learned that emotion is a subset of feelings. We have studied a bit about the four basic *emotions* to help us understand the deeper element of communicating our *feelings*. We have also learned in Chapter 3 that people express their feelings in different ways based on their temperament. Now we will look more carefully at how we start the process of communicating our feelings, but in order to successfully do this, we must have the foundation of *knowing* what we feel, particularly knowing what we feel emotionally. We have to know that these feelings are about us, not about the other person and then work diligently on ways to express how we feel. But we were never taught how to do this when we were children and adolescents, probably because the adults in our lives didn't know how to do it either.

THEY NEVER TAUGHT US HOW

Most of us were not taught us how to express our feelings. We weren't taught by our parents even though they loved us and were intelligent people. We certainly didn't learn about feelings from our friends because they didn't know any more about feelings than we did. Deb and I learned about feelings in our own psychotherapy sitting with competent therapists who guided us through our feelings. We learned a lot more in our relationships, particularly in our own relationship. We learned the most about feelings in the process of conducting therapy where we saw the centrality of feelings in human beings in their intense desire to be known, understood, and appreciated. We have seen people's desperate desire to be known in concert with a nearly complete inability to express their feelings so that they could be known.

In an ideal relationship people treat each other with kindness, respect, and honesty. In other words, they are *mature*. The essence of maturity is knowing who you are, because if you know who you are, who you *really* are, you will understand yourself, and then you will understand other people. A subset of maturity is emotional maturity, which is knowing what you feel emotionally. Emotionally mature people can access and express their emotions and other elements of feelings fluently without defensiveness or judgment. If they know what they feel emotionally, they will be able to utilize these emotions in their initial expression of how they feel at a core level so that they can eventually communicate these deep feelings that underlie emotions. Recall that knowing how you feel emotionally is only part of what it means to know how you feel. The other elements of feelings, as we have studied, include physical, cognitive, and productive expressions of feelings. Emotionally mature people know how to use care in the emotional expression of their feelings. They know how to use words that successfully communicate their feelings. People who are mature in their emotional expression usually grew up in environments that gave them permission to feel what they felt without shame and so they gained confidence in their expression of feelings. They learned early the difference between their emotional responses and their personal deeper feelings that are represented in emotions. Emotionally mature people know that emotions are very powerful and can be easily miscommunicated and misunderstood. Sadly, we don't know many emotionally mature people, but we do know many people who are working diligently to become emotionally mature.

We have noticed that as people have matured emotionally, their social development also advanced so that they not only knew how to express their own feelings, they could just as easily hear other people's feelings. Emotionally mature people are not only aware of how they feel and are able to express how they feel; they are also *socially mature*. They are able to understand other people, particularly other people's emotions and other elements of feelings. *They became socially mature because they had first become emotionally mature.* Socially mature people can set aside how they feel for the time being, and attend to how other people feel. People who are emotionally mature and socially mature are the happiest people in the world. They express themselves, particularly their feelings, whenever it is possible to do so. They understand how difficult it is to adequately communicate feelings and they know how to listen to others when they speak their feelings. They are happy with themselves and with other people because they are self-aware and others-aware. Such people comprise a small percentage of the population.

The purpose of our work is to increase the number of people who are self-aware and others-aware. People who are emotionally and socially mature are content with themselves and with others. The people who have made the most profound positive impact on our lives have been such people. Many people muddle about trying to express feelings and understand others' feelings without much success. Most of us were not raised in families where emotions and underlying feelings were understood, expressed, and accepted. We may have been raised in intelligent families where there were political, religious, the philosophical conversations, where opinions were discussed but where there was little or no expression of emotions. Or we may have been raised in emotionally expressive families where emotions reigned, but so much so that nobody was listening to anyone else. Or we may have been raised in very under-spoken families where no one expressed any feelings, and everyone went their own way. Loving parents do not necessarily make parents who communicate feelings well. While many people were raised in unloving families, most of us were probably raised in families where we were loved. Being loved and feeling loved does not equate with understanding feelings, much less successfully communicating feelings.

While parents and other significant mentors have the most influence with us, particularly how we express emotions and feelings, there are many other influences in our lives that shape how we understand, express, and hear feelings. Thus, if we are lucky, we learn about the expression of feelings from role models who are able to put feelings into words, often with emotion but not dominated by emotion. Sometimes, these role models came in the form of historical figures or fictional figures in books that we read. For example, Shakespeare must have been a person of emotional maturity to be able to write some of the most profound statements under the guise of his characters. How else could he write "to be or not to be, that is the question." Or his utilizing Sir Walter Scott's famous line "Oh what a tangled web we weave when first we practice to deceive." Being a history buff, I attribute to Abraham Lincoln emotion maturity in his ability to manage the emotionally murky waters of slavery, army generals, and politicians to achieve what he did for America.

We have noted a number of volumes in the annotated bibliography that provide some information regarding feelings, but we have found ourselves compelled to write the present book because we have not found a person, much less a book, that really helps us know how to "tell you how I feel." Unfortunately, the North American public learns about feelings from movies, TV, or the Internet where successful feeling-based conversation is made to look easy. Both in jest and in fact we have heard people say, "Why can't communication be easy the way it is in movies?" It is never that easy. These days, there seems to be more communication of "how I feel" in the form of emoticons than there is in meaningful communication of deep feelings. While communication is difficult in general, communication of feelings is more difficult, and it is especially difficult when I communicate my feelings with emotion. In fact, it is so difficult that it is never possible to communicate my feelings perfectly to anyone at any time.

Unless we have good models from whom we learn how to express ourselves, social factors inhibit effective feeling-based communication. School, social media, sports, TV, church, and our whole culture are not particularly helpful in this endeavor:

- Middle school and high school social "drama" make it hard for teenagers to express feelings without being criticized, ignored, or gossiped about. Girls suffer more from words, as in gossip, while boys suffer more from feeling inferior as they compete with other boys athletically or academically. Furthermore, teenage years are fraught with excessive expression of emotions that rarely communicate deeper feelings.
- Social media and electronic communication, like texting and emails do not help kids learn how to communicate emotions. Most texting is about information with very little emotional content. Adding emojis

to emails may be cute but these faces don't do much to express how people really feel on a core level. Some research suggests that emojis may even have unintended negative consequences to those who receive them.
- The American culture itself does not enhance emotional expression. Ours is a very production-driven society, not one that engenders relationships based on emotion, the expression of emotion, and the resolution of conflicting emotions.
- People do not spend enough time expressing their feelings to get good at it. They would rather watch TV, drink wine, eat, shop, gamble or a host of other diversions. If people spent as much time working to effectively express their feelings as they watch TV or surf the net, they would be a lot happier.

We enter romantic or other intimate relationships wholly unprepared for engaging in emotional communication, much less the larger element of feeling-based communication. But enter into relationships we do, however unprepared to engage in feeling-based conversation. The issue here is that most of us were not raised with a good understanding of what we feel and how to speak of these feelings and hence, most of us are not very good at understanding what other people feel when they say something with an emotional element. This whole array of difficulties in expressing feelings has led most of us into a good deal of *shame* associated with expressing our feelings. We might even feel shame for just having feelings at all. It's not for our lack of trying to communicate that we fail to do so. We all try to communicate our feelings. Our intent in the present work is to lend some direction to the communication process by noting the complications and barriers that we all run up against and suggest specific ways to practice communicating feelings. As we initially noted in Chapter 1, feelings can be expressed physically, emotionally, cognitively, or in activity. That having been said, the largest barrier we face is not with the physical, cognitive or active. Rather, it is the words we use to express our feelings, words that are laden with emotion and dominated by emotion. So, how can I talk about my feelings, particularly when I am emotional, and be successful at that endeavor?

TALKING ABOUT FEELINGS

We all want to have positive and productive conversations built on good communication. Such conversations begin with knowing how I *feel*, and then doing the difficult part of translating these feelings into *words*. Much of the content of this book is about how people can speak their feelings and hear other people's feelings, but importantly, *it is not always necessary, valuable, or possible to talk about feelings*. It is important to know that *feelings are not words*, and that *emotions are most certainly not words*. So, when we attempt to speak our feelings, the words we use are always approximations of feelings, never perfect, and often quite imprecise. In the 1980's movie, "E.T. the Extra-Terrestrial," the alien character ET communicated by sending out a kind of beam from his chest to the other person's chest and communicated his feelings. Oh, that we were all ET's, but we can't beam our feelings to someone else the way ET did in the movie. People actually think that if they feel something, and maybe say a few words about their feelings, that they have successfully "beamed" their feelings. We can't expect others to "just know" our feelings. The painful reality is that *I can never perfectly communicate my feelings in words*…but I must continue to work at it. If I give up on saying how I feel, I will end up with a soul filled with feelings but no soulmate with whom to communicate how I feel.

Since we don't have the ET-like beaming ability to communicate feelings, we have to use other means, namely words. But words are not always the best way to communicate feelings. We have noted that about a quarter of the population expresses feelings primarily cognitively, almost exclusively with words, but the other three quarters of people communicate their feelings predominately in ways other than words, namely physically, emotionally, or productively. Artists and artisans communicate feelings in their physical art forms, perhaps most notably painters and sculptors. Photographers do the same, and even more so now with computer enhanced photography. We have always known that "a picture is worth a thousand words." Only carefully chosen poetic words can compare with the communication that a painting or photograph can provide of a wondrous sunrise or sunset. I have a friend, Bud, who posts photographs of sunrises nearly every day. For Bud, a photographic artist, every sunrise photo speaks a different story. When we attempt to express our feelings in words, this feeling that we have is unique to us, so unique in fact, that we can never really communicate this feeling in words. When I see a sunrise photo that Bud has posted on Facebook, I can know more about his feelings than I would if he would just write about them.

Most of us are not artists, photographers, or sculptors. I (Ron) have no artistic ability whatsoever and so I am heavily reliant on words to communicate feelings. I do pretty well communicating with words, but the people who do the best at putting feelings into words are poets and musicians. I love the story of one poet who struggled heartily to find a phrase that would somewhat adequately describe the end of the day. After searching for hours for the right words, he came up with "waning dusk." Can you see the picture that the phrase "waning dusk" paints? The best I can do when I see a beautiful sunset is to reference that poet and "feel" the beauty of a waning dusk. Poets can do quite well with wordsmithing partly because we give them *poetic license*, which means that we allow poets freedom to use language that is imprecise to communicate *feeling*. Artists have *artistic license*, such as demonstrably seen in much modern art. Musicians have *musical license*. We should give each other *feeling license*.

LICENSE IN SPEAKING FEELINGS

Not only do we have poetic license, musical license, and artistic license, we also give novelists *literary license* in order for writers to communicate adequately, often in the realm of feelings. We allow grammatical errors in poetry and music as well as variations on rhyme and meter in poetry and seeming discord in music. We can even give such license to speakers and authors because sometime it is more powerful to say something that is grammatically wrong in order to make a point. The best example is the use of the word "ain't". I don't like the word ain't because I grew up in a family where proper English grammar was essential when speaking. Ain't was a four-letter word in my household. However, I know how the use of that "wrong word" can make some expressions all the better. The former slave, Sojourner Truth, made the famous expression, "... and ain't I a woman?" This expression became a hallmark for equality not just between blacks and whites but between genders. The use of the word ain't for Sojourner may well have been part of her natural conversation, but her use of ain't magnified the significance of the *feeling* she had about equality of all people. Sojourner communicated with her words despite the fact that they could be considered grammatically inaccurate and imprecise.

Our point here is that in order to learn how to communicate our feelings we will need *license* in that effort. Giving license to people who want to express their feelings is giving them the opportunity to express a passion with imprecise words. One of the most dramatic and frequent use of such license is in swearing. We know that swearing and cursing originates in the right hemisphere of the brain, which is the housing for most emotions among other operations, while most other words and language skills come from the rational left side of the brain (Damasio, 2003, Goldberg, 2001, LeDoux, 1996, Ornstein, 1997). We know this because if someone has a left-brain stroke with damage to the word-based part of the brain, that person will not be able to speak, but he will be able to swear. Clearly, swearing is not so much "verbal" or cognitive, but rather emotional.

We recently heard a standup comic use a good deal of cursing in his performance. It was amazing how emotionally powerful his humor was when laced with blue language. People curse because they are trying to put emotion into their statements. Different cultures and languages use different words for swearing, but these words always originate from the right side of the brain and are emotionally-laden. The difference between, "She is beautiful" and "She is fucking beautiful" has nothing to do with sex, nor with an attempt to offend, but rather an attempt by the speaker to put emotion into his statement. Over the years we have worked with many folks who are of a more conservative faith. These folks, for the most part, find the fact that cursing is a right brain phenomenon relieving because they "feel" the need to use strong words but have been taught that all swearing is sinful. Jesus used Aramaic cursing when he called the Pharisees "painted gravestones" or "brood of snakes" Such expressions would have much less impact in today's English but they were powerful emotional statements 2000 years ago in Palestine. I understand that a Japanese term that translates as "stupid" in English is equivalent to English foul language. The time of life where there tends to be the most cursing is adolescence, a time when young people are experimenting with their emotions and trying desperately to communicate their feelings.

People need freedom to speak their feelings as well as they are able, and they need a lot of freedom. We label the freedom to express their feelings *emotional license*. In other words, we need a wide berth when we speak our "feelings" because feelings are not words, they are inexact, and they are often emotional. While the words may be wrong and even offensive, *the emotion they are trying to express is never wrong,* nor is the feeling underlying the emotional expression ever wrong. Emotional license does not mean that it is good to shoot your mouth off and say whatever comes to your mind. It means that we all have a hard time expressing our feelings and we need to stumble around until we find words that *approximately* express what we are feeling. When you attempt to speak your feelings with words, you are saying that the words you use are *like* your feelings, but the words are not *exactly* your feelings. And this stumbling around has much to do with the fact that we have deep feelings, that these deep feelings are often tied to primary emotions, and that these feelings and emotions do not lend themselves to clear and rational expression. Any expression of emotion can be offensive, especially to people who find such expressions unacceptable. What they mean by "unacceptable" is that the emotional words offend them.

EMOTIONAL EXPRESSIONS CAN OFFEND

The fact that cursing and swearing frequently offends is an important aspect of this discussion because many emotional expressions often offend the people who are listening to these expressions. I am sure that the Pharisees were quite offended by Jesus' using "swear words". Some readers were offended by my statement utilizing the F-word in the previous paragraph. But interestingly, other readers might have been entertained, and might have identified with their own such expressions.

The odd thing about emotional expressions is that they are often intended to be friendly statements, but still offend. I have said, "I hate you" in jest when a competitor on the basketball court stole the ball from me. This statement means the exact opposite of what the words suggest. I do not "hate" my competitor. Rather, I acknowledge his superior athletic ability and make that acknowledgement with my friendly statement. "I hate you" a friendly statement? Yes, it can be, but of course it can mean just the opposite. How such a statement is said, how it is received, and what it really meant depend on the context of the statement. Such a statement often is made as an expression of anger at the other person (or group) but it can be a kind of friendly teasing of one person to another. In a brief perusal of books at our local book store I noted no less than 15 books with "fu*k" in the title, clearly an attempt to put emotion into these titles. The uplifted middle finger that I often get from a certain competitor in my regular pickup basketball game is usually such a friendly teasing. University of Wisconsin students at football games always have such an assault from one student section to another, which leads to an even more potentially offensive statement from the other student section, kind of like antiphonal swearing. In all this swearing the thousands of students are laughing at one another and at themselves. But at the same time many people in the stands cover their ears so as to avoiding hearing the swearing. A jovial and exhilarating expletive could be the emotional equivalent of "Awesome, shucks, no kidding!" but it might not be understood as such.

It's not just curse words that offend. All emotionally laden statements have the power to offend. I can express a political opinion with some emotional power to my statement and bring offense with the combination of fact and feeling. I can raise my voice when speaking and scare people. I can speak of something that is so dear to my heart that I "become emotional," and offend in the process of tearing up. I can be expressing my fear at my spouse's driving procedure and offend her by stating my emotion without ever intending to offend. *Emotional statements, especially the most important ones, almost always offend.* It is important to keep in mind that whenever we speak with powerful emotions, we cause emotions in our audience, something that we will discuss specifically in the next chapter.

The most strongly stated feeling-based statements are generally highly emotional with anger being the most predominate emotion expressed. We are living in days of tremendous political furor where people freely say derogatory statements about our political leaders. During the last presidential election, we heard more people "hate" one candidate or the other than we have ever heard in presidential debates that started in the 1950's. As I recall the opposing politicians of the 1950's was that they may have teased, cajoled, or challenged each other, but never attack the character of their opponents as we experience in today's political arena. During a recent election it was impossible to make any kind of positive statement about either candidate without hearing a powerful negative reaction from my listener. This phenomenon of intense emotionality around politics has less to do with politics than with the fact that many Americans have not matured in their emotional expressions, much less in their emotional state in general.

We have to communicate our feelings, and we have to use words to do so. This is the central theme of this book. But we have to know that when people speak their feelings, whether physically, emotionally, intellectually, or in activity, it is very likely that we will offend. We have to be ready for offense if we are speaking our feelings, and we have to be ready to be offended if someone is speaking their feelings to us. Our proposition is that we need to give ourselves and our friends' *emotional license* when speaking feelings especially when the emotion is very strong. We need to give each other the wide berth in emotional expression that we have talked about. Then, when we have expressed ourselves emotionally, or heard someone else express himself or herself emotionally, we can massage the words to better communicate. But remember, the first task is not wordsmithing. The first task is to know what you feel and then, with acceptable license, express your feelings the best that you can. Let's consider a feeling-based conversation replete with imprecise words and emotional expression. Note first how emotional expressions might offend, and then how the speaker might be more successful in communicating her emotion without losing touch with her feelings:

> ***Joan***: Don't you just hate Senator Bob. He's such an idiot. I can't believe what he said the other day.
>
> ***Andrea***: What's your problem with Bob? He just speaks his mind.
>
> ***Joan***: Yes, and his mind is not working right.

Andrea: His mind is working just fine. He just doesn't cater to all the left-wing ideas of giving money away to people who won't work.

Joan: Well, some people can't work and need government help.

Andrea: Too much government. Too many handouts. Too many lazy people.

Note how in this conversation Joan may have an opinion about Senator Bob, but the way she stated this opinion was primarily emotional. Nothing wrong with an opinion and nothing wrong with emotion, but when strong opinions and strong emotions are put together in the same package, we have the danger of inciting emotions in the listener, which is what happened with Andrea. You can have an information-based discussion, even a debate, or you can have an expression of emotion, but you can't have both. Opinion in combination with emotion is a recipe for an argument. In this scenario both Joan and Andrea have opinions and both have emotions, but neither is really listening to one another. Joan can speak her mind or her heart, but she can't speak them both at the same time, and certainly not with the incendiary language she used at the beginning. So, Joan might speak her feelings (but not her opinions of government help or Senator Bob) in this way:

Joan: I really feel bad about people who are out of work. I've been out of work and penniless and it's no fun. I remember days when I didn't know how I was going to afford my next meal. I wish that Senator Bob would do more to find ways of helping people who really need help.

Andrea: I didn't know that you ever were in the situation of being penniless, Joan. That must have been a terrible time. I've had some difficult days financially but I've never really been penniless. What were the circumstances of your financially difficult time?

> *Joan*: It was a long time ago when I was in college and worried about being able to pay tuition for the next semester. It made studying very hard. I was living on peanuts trying to finish college, which was very important for me because I was the first person in my whole extended family ever to go to college.
>
> *Andrea*: I never would have guessed that you had these troubles looking at you now being a successful real estate agent.

Note how Andrea heard Joan's feelings and emotions and she was able to connect with her friend emotionally and know her friend better. If, on the other hand, Joan wanted to have a discussion or debate about government help for those in poverty, she might have started with her opinion based on some identifiable fact, like:

> *Joan*: I've been thinking about this whole matter of poverty in the country, and there seems to be no good answer. Different politicians seem to have widely different approaches to deal with the problem. I think there is at least some place for government intervention although I am not sure how that could occur.
>
> *Andrea*: I agree with you on the poverty issue. Too many people shoot their mouths off about what should be done, and all of these answers seem too simplistic. What do you think could be a place to start?
>
> *Joan*: Well, I'm no expert, but I think there could be some kind of productive support from the government. I know you're a small-government gal, Andrea, but tell me what you think might be the danger of government help for people in real need.
>
> *Andrea*: I think the operative words you just spoke are important, at least to me: "real need." It's hard for me to see

people on the "dole" who could seemingly work, especially now that the economy is doing so well and employers are desperate for employees.

Joan: I agree with you on much of this. I don't think we should just throw money at people who can and should work. But I'm also aware that some people don't have the education that they might need to get a good job.

Andrea: Then our task might be to help people get that education.

Joan: Yes, indeed. I knew that I needed to have a good education to find a good job and I worked my butt off to get one. I think that there are a lot of people who don't have the knowledge of how they could do college on pennies the way I did.

We admit, that people don't talk singularly with the facts of this third conversation or the passion of the second one, but we think that it is important to learn to do so. Throwing out random facts with feelings never works, because *feelings* are not facts, and throwing emotion with facts is even worse. However important emotion is, emotion itself is not verbal; it is spiritual. The spirit of feelings is never wrong; the emotion in any expression is never wrong; but the words used to express feelings and emotion are often wrong, or at the very least, offensive.

HOW EXPRESION OF FEELINGS CAN SEEM NEGATIVE

We noted earlier that "I need to tell you my feelings" often suggests to the listeners that we are about to say something bad about them. We might say that we don't like the way the person behaved, or how the person spoke, or how the person ignored us at some time. This "expressing your feelings" in not really expressing your feelings. It is essentially critical and negative. If you start talking about your feelings by criticizing the other person, you are essentially being defensive. You are giving an explanation for *why* you feel what you feel rather than saying *what* you feel. You are not really saying anything about your real feelings at all, so there is no way your listener can possibly understand you, much less what he or she might have done, much less what you yourself really feel. If you really want to learn to communicate your feelings, you have to realize that a statement beginning with "I feel that you…" is not a statement of your feelings at all. You need to take the implied negative element out of expressing your feelings entirely, but that is no easy task because "no one taught you how to express your feelings."

Feelings are never really "negative," but the words we use to express our feelings sound negative, especially when you are learning to express feelings, and even more when your emotions are the dominant factor in your expression of your feelings. Ultimately, you need to feel positive about your feelings as you express them remembering that "feelings are never wrong" and that they represent a very basic and a very important part of who you are. Being "positive" about your feelings doesn't mean that you are all smiles and happy. It means that you work to have the other person understand your inner self, as hard as that may be. But when you start talking about feelings, especially if you've never done it before, it is a real challenge. You likely will sound critical to your audience, whether the "audience" is friend, foe, or loved one. There is no way around this because you have probably bottled up angry resentful feelings for a long time, and you have to get them off your chest. This, of course, asks a lot of your audience, but your listeners will need to *hear feelings* just as you learn to hear their feelings, a task that is a delicate matter that we will discuss in the next chapter.

Feelings are never wrong, and emotions are never wrong. Feelings and emotions are always about what is right because they are always about something that you value or love. The words you use to express your feelings may be wrong and they may be hurtful, but your feelings, which are the essence of you, are never wrong. This is a hard concept to adequately communicate because so often the statement, "I just have to express my feelings," means that you better get ready to hear something they don't like about you. The dislike, disappointment, and anger that people express when they "have to tell you their feelings" is really about *hurt*, not anger. When people speak of "negative emotions," they usually mean the emotions of anger in some form, like "disappointment" or "frustration." Fear and anger are two defense-based emotions that we discussed in Chapter 2, but anger and fear are not truly "negative." Fear and anger erupt when you are hurt because you feel attacked in some way.

Given all the hurdles to expression of feelings that we have noted, it is no surprise that when people say that they want to express their feelings, they usually mean they want to talk about something that they think is *wrong*. Unfortunately, people express the defense-based feelings of fear and anger more readily than the love-based-feelings of joy and sadness. Most people who feel compelled to tell you how they feel are probably not happy about something. They don't want to tell you the whole of their emotions of joy, sorrow, fear, and anger. They may simply not know how to express their feelings. So instead of saying how they real feel, they tell you what they think your "problem" is. They may not like something about you, or they may be angry about something you said or did, but instead of admitting to those feelings and emotions, they launch into an attack of you. It would be good to have people first learn to express the love feelings of sadness and joy, but this isn't where most people start. They have to start with their anger and fear feelings because these feelings are the ones that trouble them the most.

It is very unfortunate that "I want to tell you my feelings" usually means that the person is going to tell you something that they don't like about what you said or did. This happens very frequently in relationships, especially when the two people are quite different in personality type or temperament, or possibly have significantly different cultural backgrounds. I am working with a couple who are quite different in personality. The woman's psychological nature is truth oriented, namely the "analyst" type that we have discussed. She has had a strong tendency to render her opinions rather frequently and openly for many years. In so doing, she has offended many people, particularly her husband even though in her mind she was just "speaking the truth" and "trying to be of help." Her truth-speaking tendency has hurt many people, who have hurt her in turn. Over the years she has incurred more and more dislike by her husband and by many other people. This is tragic because Sharon is simply trying to make the world a better place and help people do better in life. As a result of Sharon's lifelong tendency to speak the *truth* (as she sees it), she has not only offended and hurt many people, she has incurred their reaction, which is to hurt her back.

"Hurt people hurt people," goes the old adage. Sharon believes she is simply expressing her "feelings" but these "feelings" are singularly what she *thinks* is wrong with the people around her, including her husband and several other family members. In her honest attempt to "help" people, she has taken privilege of telling people what she thinks they should and what they shouldn't do, not realizing that her uninvited analysis of their behavior hurts them. She doesn't really want to talk about the breadth of her feelings because she doesn't know how to do that. She would much rather talk about what she thinks would make life better. Note that Sharon, and analysts like her, is expressing her feelings through her cognitive function. While she hurts people *unintentionally* when she speaks her truth, her audience hurts her *intentionally* seeking revenge. Sound familiar? All of this hurt with Sharon and her family and friends is based on love and loss. Eventually, I hope I can help Sharon see that she has started the hurt-people-hurt-people process, and only she can unwind it to find love that is always at the bottom of this painful, never-ending process. We will discuss the important concept of emotional hurt more extensively in Chapter 7.

When people begin to know how they feel and express how they feel, they usually express the emotions of fear and anger, namely the "defensive emotions" that keep us alive when we are young or in true danger. This is a very difficult time for people when they are in the early stages of learning about their feelings and beginning to express these feelings with some form of emotion. Going courageously into the whole business of expressing feelings feels fraught with danger, usually because most people have never had the privilege of expressing any kind of feeling. Expressing the emotions of anger and fear is the beginning of the line in expressing feelings, and usually where people have to start.

Learning to successfully emotionally communicate is like walking into a dark tunnel. As you enter the tunnel, you have to pass through the initial fear of darkness that you might stub your toe on some unknown rock, or the anger you feel at the rock or at yourself for stumbling. This is a very crucial time in your development of a true expression of feelings, and one that most people fail to navigate successfully. The tunnel of finding and expressing feelings usually begins darkly with the emotions of fear and anger. There most certainly will be times when you think that there is no end to your anger and fear, but these emotions are only the beginning of a time when you start to express your feelings, albeit a difficult beginning. If you start with fear and anger, and allow yourself the freedom to say these emotions, you will ultimately find that the more advanced and more important emotions of joy and sadness that can follow fear and anger. In other words, you have to face the anger associated with the things you have lost in the past that caused you to feel anger, and face the fear of losing something else in the future that causes you to be afraid. When you finish feeling anger and fear, you will then feel a great preponderance of the love-based emotions of joy and sadness. Rarely can people start with joy and sadness when they "just have to tell you their feelings."

Let's consider some examples of people trying to express their feelings where "negative" feelings usually start the ball rolling.

1. *The car seat heater*

A couple whom I just recently began seeing gave me a perfect example of what usually happens when people express their feelings. More accurately, when they *think* they have expressed their feelings. During one of my first sessions with this couple I worked initially with the man for a few minutes trying to help him learn to express his feelings, particularly helping him understand and value the nature of his personality and learn to communicate his feelings a bit better. The work with the husband, Bob, was slow and methodical, and he didn't want to do the work of finding his real feelings, much less communicate them. Like many men, Bob had never told anyone how he really felt despite the fact that he had a history of emotional explosions. After a pause in the work, Bob's wife, Rhonda, volunteered that she thought she was quite good at expressing feelings and offered to give a recent example.

I was all up for it. Rhonda related a recent time when she was pulling the car out of the garage, and her husband getting in the car on the passenger's side. Then he proceeded to turn on the seat warmer for himself, but not for her. Rhonda was proud to tell me that she expressed her feelings plainly enough saying, "Thanks a lot, partner, for thinking of me instead of just yourself" as she aggressively pushed her seat heater. Then she told him that he was an idiot.

(Actually, she said to him that he was a certain body orifice.) She thought this was a good example of expressing her feelings. Rhonda truly believed that she had expressed her *feelings* in telling Bob that he was an idiot. She was quite proud of the fact that she had "expressed her feelings" to Bob. I was bemused for a moment and had to think of how I could proceed with this matter of her expressing her feelings.

I first told Rhonda that she had, indeed, felt angry, which was understandable. Then I felt obliged to say to her that she had expressed *emotion* (anger), but she hadn't expressed her *feelings* in a way that her husband could possibly understand. I wasn't very successful with helping this woman see that she did not, in fact, express *her feelings*, but rather expressed the *emotion* of anger at her husband. I had to start with what she felt: angry. She was angry at her husband for being "insensitive", but this is not where her feelings really began, and her anger, however understandable, was not the most important emotion that she had. She didn't understand what I was saying about her failure to express her more important feelings of hurt and sadness. Most people don't understand this important concept. It takes a lot of time to help people know that *anger is a secondary emotion, i.e., a defensive emotion, always stirred by hurt*, which is caused by some kind of loss of something that is loved.

Certainly, Rhonda was *angry*, but anger wasn't the first experience she had. More importantly, she felt *hurt*. More important than hurt, she felt *sad*. More important than sad, she felt a loss of something that she *loved*. Yes, she was offended, but this offense came because she has what we call a "love problem." She had lost something that she loved. In fact, in those few seconds that her husband failed to turn on her driver's side car seat heater, she lost a great deal. Think of it this way: she loves her husband, she loves their relationship, she loves herself, and she loves the comfort of a warm car seat. As a result of these things she loves, she would have loved for her husband to love her by turning on her seat heater. Carefully, I asked her, "How could your husband know all these love feelings when he just heard the 'You're a jerk statement'?" I suggested that her anger was a secondary feeling that occurred because she loved some things, lost these things, felt hurt, and felt sad. To turn this situation around so that she can express her important feelings in a way that her husband could really understand her, is very hard. I won't be able to help this couple until I can teach them to know what they really feel, and then how to express how they really feel. In situations like Rhonda's it is always hurt. The most important times of hurt are those that occur in a relationship, be it with a partner, friend, family, or work associate. The deeper the relationship, the deeper and faster hurt can occur. We would be mildly hurt if a restaurant server gave us the wrong order, but we might easily be more seriously hurt if our spouse failed to fix dinner when it was his turn to do so. We will delay a more deliberate explanation of this important concept of hurt until Chapter 7. Let's look at another experience of loss that causes hurt, that then jumps to sadness and then to anger.

1. Shoes in the house

Let's say that you like people to take their shoes off when they come into your house. We used to live in Newfoundland, Canada, where everyone always took their shoes off at the entry door. We had a party once with about 30 people, all of whom put their shows in a pile at the door as they came in. It amazed us that when people left, they left wearing their own shoes! I remember hearing from a Newfoundlander living in Florida that the only thing she didn't like about Americans is that they didn't take their shoes off when they came into her house. Imagine that this is your preference, whether you learned it at home, in your Newfoundland culture, Japanese culture, or that you just came to it yourself. Your spouse, however, doesn't have that value, so he just walks right in the house without leaving his shoes at the door. You might have said something like,

- "Look at the mess you created on the floor, I just mopped!" Or…
- "I've told you a thousand times that I don't like you to wear your street shoes in the house." Or…
- "I can't get the kids to take their shoes off at the door if you don't set an example." Or…
- "Take your fricking shoes off when you come in from outside!"

Or you might have asked a rhetorical question. Rhetorical questions are those that have an implied statement. Rhetorical questions, with or without intent are always shaming. Which of these rhetorical questions might you be inclined to ask?

- "What is wrong with you that you can't take your shows off when you come inside?"
- "Do you think we live in a barn?"
- "Why is it so hard to remember to take your shoes off when you come in?"
- "Why can't you simply take your shoes off when you come in the house?"
- "Do you expect me to clean up after you make this mess?"

If you were to have said one of these statements or asked one of these rhetorical questions, you would have communicated that:

- You are angry at your spouse.
- Your spouse is stupid, irresponsible, and disrespectful.
- You don't like living with your spouse.
- You know when and where to wear shoes better than your spouse does.

These statements and rhetorical questions are what most people say when they want to "say how they feel." They are not, in fact, communicating their feelings, at least not the really important feelings of love and loss. People speaking these judgmental statements and making these rhetorical questions have communicated anger but they have not communicated the more important feeling that underlies anger: *hurt*. Hurt is a *feeling* that leads to the *emotion* of sadness for having lost something that is important. This hypothetical conversation about shoes in the house is a conversation about what is *loved*, what is *lost*, and *hurt*. Let's explain. Consider that I am the offended spouse and my wife has come into the house without stepping out of her street shoes. What have I felt? I have felt hurt. Why have I felt hurt? I have felt hurt because of what I value, what I love. In such a case, possibly because I have a caretaker temperament, I value a clean kitchen floor. I could also say that I *love* a clean floor although love for a clean floor might not be as strong as my love for a friend or a family member. I have been hurt because someone has violated my value system. The really important *feeling* I have is hurt, and the real *emotion* that I have is sadness. Unfortunately, most of us race right by the love part (e.g. loving a clean floor), and then we race right by the hurt *feeling*, and we channel this love-based hurt into the *emotion* of anger. The most important feeling is that I have been hurt because of something I *love*: a clean floor; I love my spouse, and I love my spouse respecting my value of a clean floor. We call situations like shoes on the floor a *love problem*, not really an *anger* problem. So, how might I express the positive, love-based feeling of love? I might say something like,

- "Deb, I would like to tell you something that is very important to me. I would like to communicate something that has been a part of me all my life." (Hopefully, Deb is all ears because she knows that I want to tell her about me, about my feelings.) Then I might say...
- "I just love having a clean floor. You know how I always am picking up scraps of paper and sweeping up the crumbs on the floor. I do this because it gives me great joy to see a spotless floor." It is just the way I am as a caretaker. I love taking care of the floor. Then I might say...
- "And when I see crumbs, or paper, or mud on the floor, it seems that something has been taken away from me that I truly love." Then I need to add...
- "I know this sounds silly, but believe me, a clean floor is an important thing in my life. Somehow, I can leave the dishes in the sink all day or leave the car dirty for weeks, but a dirty floor offends me. It actually feels wrong to me." Then I transition my feelings from what I love to what I need to communicate by saying...
- "So, I will ty to communicate to you better about the clean floor value that I have." And I will end my statement by saying...
- "And by the way, I am sorry for griping at you about your wearing your street shoes in the house. I just didn't know how to tell you what was really important to me."

Nobody speaks like this. But they should. If I would communicate my value system to Deb, which in this hypothetical situation, is a clean floor, I would be communicating what I *value*. I would be communicating what I *love*. I would be communicating *who I am*. If I indulge myself in expressing anger at Deb, I will not be communicating my value system, what I love, or me. I will be assaulting *her*. Most importantly, she won't understand me any better. She will just think I am angry or bitter about something as silly as street shoes in the kitchen. It is up to me to communicate what I love. It is not up to her to somehow know what I love by reading between my angry words. I need to state something, namely my feelings. I don't need to ask questions.

QUESTIONS VS STATEMENTS

It must be obvious that someone on the receiving part of this scenario would have all sorts of thoughts and feelings. We will discuss the hearing, processing, and valuing people's feelings in the next chapter, but let's stay with the expressing and communicating feelings before we launch into how we hear other people's feelings. Consider how you might start to express your feelings under the following circumstances.

- Your partner buys a wide screen TV that costs $1500
- Your friend is always late for things.
- You and your partner have a sexless marriage.
- Your friend speaks ill of your favorite politician.
- Your spouse disciplines the children too harshly.
- Your spouse fails to discipline your children enough.

In any of these situations you could start with nasty rhetorical questions, judgments, or threats. It is actually hardest to deal with the rhetorical questions because such "questions" force the listener to try to answer these so-called questions. Importantly, all such questions are essentially negative and angry, but the underlying emotion is fear, i.e. fear of losing something. Note that all of these "questions" are really angry and critical statements posed as questions:

- *New TV*: "Peter, how do you justify spending our hard-earned money on another stupid TV? You paid an exorbitant price for the last one and now you spend another $1500. What's wrong with you?"
- *Tardiness*: "Pam, you really piss me off. Why do you always have to be late? You are just so disrespectful! Can I count on you to be on time for once?"
- *Sexless*: "Do you have a lover? Are you gay, Rob? Are you using pornography? Do you prefer masturbation to sex with me? Do you think that I'm too fat?"
- *Politics*: "Geesh, Sarah, how in the world can you support such an idiot for senator? Don't you know that he is a philanderer and a liar?"
- *Child discipline I*: "Ben, what are you, some kind of child abuser? I wonder sometimes if I should call the cops. They're kids for God's sake. Are you trying to get them to hate you?"
- *Child discipline II:* "Are you ever going to say "no" to our kids, Alice? Do you even care that they grow up to be responsible? You always give in to them. Why do I have to be the bad cop and you the good cop?"

All of these questions are not, in fact, questions. They are examples of the worst kind of criticism because a rhetorical question asks the recipient to answer why he or she is stupid, wrong, or bad. Such questions put the listener in a very difficult position because he or she has to try to answer a question that is not a question. More importantly, these rhetorical questions fail to tell the listener what you are really feeling. Such questions give nothing positive and ask for something negative. Furthermore, shaming rhetorical questions are often followed by some kind of shaming statement. Yesterday, I heard about a guy who was upset at the fact that his wife hadn't plugged the cell phone into the charger. After "asking" her, "What's wrong with you?" he followed by saying that plugging in the charger was "the least thing you could do." He shamed her twice with these shame-based rhetorical questions but had no idea that he had shamed her. His wife, on the other hand felt shamed and it triggered her history of having been repeatedly shamed by her parents. She recalled an incident in her childhood when her father used the same words,

"What is wrong with you?" when she forgot to turn the ignition off after listening to the car radio.

Instead of asking these negative questions or making critical comments, you might consider saying something positive, namely something positive about you, namely your feelings, namely your love. So, you could deal with the hurt and offense you have in these circumstances and the more important aspect of the *love* that is under your hurt:

- *New TV*: "You know, Peter, what I really love about how we do life: we provide a secure home for the kids and us. Security, particularly financial security is really important to me. You know, of course, that I lived in a family where we had to scratch for every penny. Poverty caused me to have an undue fear of the potential of being penniless. We are a long way from penniless, but sometimes I get afraid of being penniless, however silly that sounds. When I look at our finances, like what we earn and what we spend, I am always thinking, "security first; avoid poverty at all costs." When I saw that you bought the new TV, I was scared and a bit hurt. I don't like tech things much, like TVs, speakers, and computers, so I didn't understand why you bought the TV. But my hurt and scared wasn't about the TV; it was about being insecure and being afraid of becoming penniless."
- *Tardy*: "Pam, I got to tell you, I like things that are planned and orderly. I have a list for everything I will do today, another list for the things I'll do this week, and believe it, a list for things that I want to do this year. I've even thought about a list for things I want to do the rest of my life. Plans and the future are a lot of who I am. This brings me to time. I just love to be on time. In fact, for me "on time is early," which is something that I was evidently taught by my parents. My brother Jim hated it but I loved it. Jim was always late and I was always early. He actually came late to his own wedding, remember? That would drive me crazy. This "on time is early" thing seems a bit different from your "on time is late" thing. Nothing wrong with "on time is late," of course, but it is difficult for me when you're

late. Not because you should be an on-time person, just because that is how I operate."
- *Sexless*: "Rob, I have a "love problem," however silly that sounds. I love you. And loving you allows me to love lots of other things. I love doing things with you, even repairing the roof that we did last year, or going to church, or raising the kids. And I love having sex with you. It has been a special part of our relationship. I really love sex… just with you however. And I miss it. I really miss it. I miss it because I love sex and I love you. I really needed to tell you."
- *Politics*: "I gotta tell you, Sarah, that you are really a person of passion and purpose. I just love this part of you. It's like, you have a lot of passion and a lot of love. For example, the way you really love Senator Gary. It's a bit difficult for me, as you know, because he's not my favorite guy, but when you were talking about him last night at dinner, I actually wanted to like him for the way you were representing him and I realized how we are both very passionate people even if our passions are not always for the same things. We both love passionately, whether it is people, our house, or the TV shows that we like. So, when you talk so favorably about Senator Gary, I'm going to try to work harder at understanding how I feel about political figures, and try hard to listen better to your political feelings."
- *Kids I*: "Ben, you are a wonderful father to our kids. You love them beyond life. You work hard to provide them with all that we have. You would give your left arm for them, I know. I know all this love you have, and it makes me sad when you are hard on the kids. Sometimes the way you speak to our kids, especially Josh, it sounds like you don't love him. I know you would die for him, of course, but it's the words that are hard to hear. I know you love them just as much as I do, and I know we show our love in different ways. I feel hurt when I hear you speak so harshly. I just needed to tell you. I don't want to interfere with your parenting; I just want to tell you I feel sad. Only because I love you and I love Josh."
- *Kids II*: "Alice, I think you're the best mother in the county. Everyone knows it. They see you being kind and gentle to the kids, sacrificing

for the kids, and loving them so fully. You certainly know that I love them just as much, but my kind of love is a bit different from yours. You tend to give; I tend to limit. I think both of these ways are good for kids, but for me the limiting is something that kids need to learn when they're kids. Sometimes, when I see you picking up after Josh, allowing him to talk to you the way he does, and helping him with his homework that he is capable of doing on his own…well, this seems like indulgence. My kind of love for Josh is for him to face the world where he has to make his own way, make his own mistakes, and become a good man."

We are aware that most people don't speak this way. Note how much longer it takes to speak of your feelings rather than speaking against the other person. Can you even imagine a parent talking to her spouse about the discipline of the kids in this way? Not likely. But consider the other option: anger, argument and all that goes with it: threating, demanding, demeaning, disrespecting, maybe divorcing. In order for someone to talk this way, which is expressing one's feelings, it takes knowing how you feel, knowing that it is hard to express your feelings, understanding your emotion without letting your emotion get control of you, and focusing on the origin of all hurt: love. If you keep in mind that your feelings are always about love, you will then be able to work at finding words that begin to communicate your feelings.

BEING VULNERABLE

There is a cost to expressing your feelings: you will make mistakes, you will hurt people, and they will hurt you back. We cannot emphasize enough this process of your *unintentionally* hurting someone when you are trying *intentionally* to express your feelings. Hopefully, you continue to migrate around your emotions to find words that express your feelings. But when you express your feelings, no matter how hard you try to be careful and kind, you will almost certainly run into someone's soft spot leading them to defend themselves. And this "defense" will most frequently turn into an offense. Their hurt will unavoidably result in their criticizing you. You will be hurt. There is no way around this hurt. So, you have to be willing to *express* your feelings anyway and find ways to wade in these difficult waters until you *communicate* your feelings. The cost of communicating your feelings is that you will be hurt.

You can avoid being criticized by keeping your feelings to yourself, but at a great cost, the cost of no one knowing your feelings, and no one knowing you. In order to have people understand you, you will need to hang your butt out there and say something. You have to be vulnerable. When you express your feelings, you are vulnerable to being wrong in your own eyes or being wrong in someone else's eyes. You might even be right in the other person's eyes but at the cost of hurting them emotionally. Whether you are right or wrong in what you say about your feelings, you will probably offend. When you offend, you will be criticized. Your vulnerability, both to your own mistakes and to the judgments of others, is essential for you to become successful at getting beyond *expressing* your feelings to the point of actually *communicating* your feelings. But the road to successful communication is a long road fraught with danger, with mistakes, with misunderstandings, with hurt, and with rabbit trails that often lead nowhere.

The vulnerability that you feel when you are trying to express your feelings is the result of years of being alone in your feelings, unable to know them, unable to express them, and unable to successfully communicate them. You feel this vulnerability because you are afraid that your listener might not like what you are trying to say. Or you are afraid that you might get a response that implies that your feelings are unimportant, and then feel dismissed. This is tantamount to feeling *shame,* which is the feeling that someone might think that something is wrong with you. Know that when you are doing the hard work of finding your feelings and then finding words for your feelings, you will naturally want to avoid the whole process and give up because you don't want to be humiliated. You will want to run away and hide because you can't seem to get it right. You will find yourself thinking, "Why can't they get it? I feel it; they should feel it." You will feel very defensive because you will undoubtedly be attacked in some way, perhaps directly with words, perhaps indirectly with silence. You will get angry because your audience doesn't understand what you are saying or doesn't like what you are saying. You will certainly be afraid. This defensiveness will incline you to be negative in what you say about your feelings. When you start this learning process of communicating feelings, you will probably start where everyone does: finding something wrong, very often finding something wrong with someone else. The unfortunate but unavoidable truth is that you will sound negative. It is a defensive maneuver we hope to help you get past.

The whole business of being vulnerable is love-based, just like all our emotions are love-based in some way. Being vulnerable is an act of love, love for yourself and your feelings, love for the potential of being understood, love for your friend or partner, and love for a meaningful honest loving relationship.

PRACTICE MAKES IMPERFECT

Practicing the expression of feelings doesn't ever make you perfect at communicating. You will never be *perfect* at expressing yourself, especially when expressing your feelings. The very essence of feelings makes it impossible to be perfect at expressing them. Feelings are simply too complex, too beautiful, too artistic, too emotional, and too spiritual to ever be put into a verbal package that is perfect. Feelings are like so many other important things in life that never become perfect; they just get better with practice. Is a 9.5 second 100-meter dash perfect? No, just phenomenal. Did anything Mozart compose ever reach perfection? Never, just phenomenal. Was MLK's "dream" speech perfect? No, just phenomenal. People who do these phenomenal things have taken hours and years to ply their trades, and they have made many mistakes along the way. It takes time to learn to communicate feelings effectively, just like it does to learn anything of value in life. We don't learn to swim the first time we get in the water, and we don't get better at swimming just because we want to be able to swim well. We need a lot of practice to get good at anything: swimming, writing, reading, baking bread, or communicating our feelings. The expert chef has had many flops before she becomes familiar with quantities of flour and spices, the texture of the dough as she kneads, and minutes in the oven. The same is true of learning how to communicate feelings. If right now, you commit yourself fully to learn how to communicate your feelings, it will take you at least a year to become fluent at it. It has taken us many years to communicate our own feelings effectively, and much longer than that to understand other people's feelings. We are still working on it. We still make mistakes. Rome wasn't built in a day, and we didn't learn how to express feelings effectively in a day. Hopefully, it will take much less time for you to learn to communicate your feelings than it did us. But when you begin to master this difficult business of communication, it will be a thing of beauty.

Knowing that your initial attempts at communicating your feelings will be imperfect at best is challenging, but it is essential to remember. It is also humbling to realize that even your best efforts at communicating your feelings might fail dreadfully. Don't expect to communicate your feelings well to start with. Keep in mind that you are learning to express your feelings, knowing that expression comes before communication. You will need multiple attempts. These attempts are necessary to help you get to the core of what you feel and who you are. Always remember that however imprecise or inadequate your expression of feelings may be, *your feelings are never wrong*. Your feelings are, in a way, *perfect* even if the words you use to express your feelings are imperfect in some way. The mistakes you might make expressing feelings could include the following:

- You will say things that you don't really mean…because you are using *imperfect* words when you express your *perfect* feelings.
- You will begin by making judgements of the person you are talking to…because you haven't yet found your real feeling of hurt.
- You will say something one day, and then the next day you will realize that what you said wasn't quite right…because you are just beginning to understand your feelings.
- You will contradict yourself and have to start over…because feelings are not facts even though when we express feelings, we always refer to facts.
- You will ask your audience to agree with you before you are finished talking…because you are still afraid of disapproval.
- You will feel defensive when you are challenged …because you are yet feeling some shame at being imperfect in expressing feelings.
- You won't even know what to say because you don't know how to identify what you feel…but you will just know you feel something.

You won't be good at expressing feelings when you start, and you will feel awkward in the process. It takes a lot of "my bad; that wasn't what I really wanted to say", and "I am sorry, I really miscommunicated. Please let me try again" or similar *mea culpa* expressions. Wouldn't it be wonderful if we could just tell you how to express feelings and then you just do it? No such luck. You have to try. Try again, fail, and then try all the more. You have to admit to your failure. And you have to try again. Just like swimming and baking. You will get good at it…eventually. In the meantime, be prepared for mistake after mis-communicated mistake. You will eventually make fewer mistakes and have more successes. But to start with, *most* of what you say when expressing your feelings will be less than good, but it will be a start. You will need to be patient with yourself while you are practicing the expression of feelings. Poets and musicians, who are certainly the best at communicating feelings in words, spend hours and days working at wordsmithing. You would do well to spend minutes finding words for your feelings. It's worth the time.

IT TAKES WORK

In order to successfully communicate your feelings, you have to *know what your feelings are*, which is a very difficult task. In brief review, first, you have to identify what your feel *emotionally* without letting your emotions dominate you. Then you have to *think about what you might say* about your feelings. And then, you have to *carefully phrase what you say* knowing that anything you say will be imprecise at the best and hurtful at the worst. It would be wonderful if you could *feel* something, find the perfect *words* to express this feeling, and then *communicate* your feelings. Can't you just "say what you're feeling" and be understood? No such luck. It takes a huge amount of work: work to know what you feel, work to find approximate words that express your feeling, and work to re-state, re-phrase, and revise the words that you use in communicating your feelings.

This communicating feeling business is really about having sensations, thoughts, emotions, and actions that might somehow help you find the words that still might not hit the spot of successful communication. The whole process is challenging: you say things that you don't really mean; you change your mind in the middle of saying something; you fumble around with words that are imprecise at best, and dead wrong at worst; and in the end you hurt people whom you don't mean to hurt. You hurt people because words do not do justice to our deeply personal and spiritual feelings. Yet with all these challenges of communicating feelings, it is a task worth the effort because the result is life-changing and life-enhancing: people understand you. *If people truly understand you, they will like you, and in most cases, come to love you.*

Expressing feelings, and eventually communicating feelings is difficult but it is important in life and even more important in relationships. If you can improve your ability to communicate your feelings, much by identifying and governing your emotions, you will be understood, you will be loved, and you will be increasingly successful in your relationships. Communicating feelings is difficult, challenging, and fraught with danger, but if we meet these challenges with honest work, we will most certainly be happier and bring more happiness to the people around us. Successfully communicating your feelings is the first task. Then comes the real hard task: hearing someone else's feelings.

SUMMARY:

1. Feelings are perfect. Emotions are also perfect.
2. Feelings include emotions but they are much more than emotions.
3. Any expression of feelings is imprecise.
4. Any meaningful expression of feelings involves emotion.
5. We need to govern the emotional element of our expression of feelings.
6. Expressing feelings is not the same as communicating them.
7. We need to practice the expression of feelings to be successful at it.
8. Initial expressions of feelings tend to sound negative, largely because of the predominance of anger in most expressions of emotion.
9. If you express your true feelings, you will feel vulnerable.
10. When you succeed in communicating your feelings, you will feel wonderful.

Chapter 5

Hearing Feelings

COMMUNICATING FEELINGS IS EXTREMELY difficult as we have just learned. If finding the right words for feelings wasn't problematic enough, we usually hear about other people's feelings before we're half-finished speaking our own. This whole process of expressing feelings is exhausting and frustrating because it seems that we can never communicate our feelings perfectly. But if you stay with the process of feeling and attempting to communicate your feelings, you get better and better at it. Eventually, you can get good at finding words to adequately communicate your feelings even if this communication is imperfect. The better you get at communicating yourself the better you will get at hearing someone else's feelings when they are fumbling about trying to tell you what is most important to them.

Complex and difficult as it is to find, feel, and communicate one's feelings, it is twice as hard to understand other people who are trying to communicate their feelings. The good news is that it is possible to hear and understand other people when they express their feelings. It is *possible*, but it takes a lot of work and even more wisdom and patience to succeed in understanding other people's feelings when they are spoken. And it certainly takes making many mistakes. As we discuss the ways and means of hearing feelings, keep in mind the complexity and challenge it takes to express feelings because the *expression* and the *reception* of feelings are intricately connected.

Granting that both expressing and hearing feelings is immensely difficult, when it does happen—when someone actually successfully communicates their feelings and you have heard them—it is truly wonderful. It is wonderful to be heard. It is just as wonderful to hear. If you have begun to digest the importance and the profound difficulty of communicating your feelings, you might be ready to learn how to hear feelings. So, if you're up to the task of learning how to hear feelings, read on, because you can do it. Keep in mind, however, when people express their feelings they often talk in circles.

THE CIRCLES OF FEELINGS

When we are helping folks in our office with their communication difficulties, we often draw one small circle on the white board followed by three concentric circles. The inner most circle we call one's "core self." The three outer circles represent what we call *natural abilities, enhancement of these abilities, and engagement in the world* with these abilities.

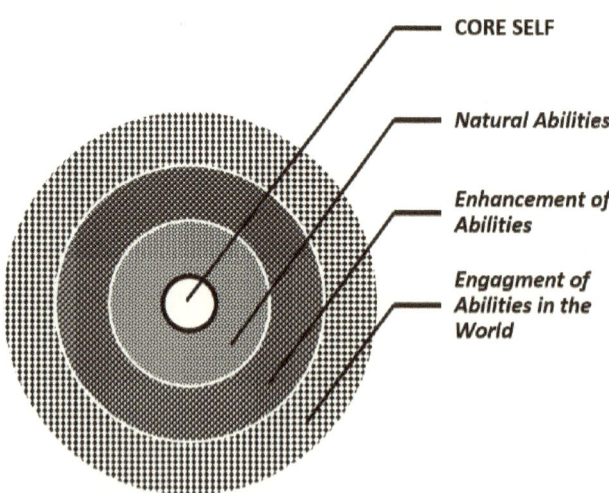

We understand these circles as abstract representations of what we might call the *levels of personhood*. The innermost circle that we call core self could be called spirit, soul, or personal essence. We could even use the Greek term

Psyche or "inner self" as Claus (1980) suggested. For some clients, we can identify this central part of themselves as God inside them, or perhaps "godlike." We believe that *feelings* originate in this nugget and then proceed outward through each of the circles until they are expressed. We sometimes use the expression "spiritual genetics" to suggest that our inner core is a unique spiritual inheritance and that our expressions of feelings generate from our core self, or spiritual core. We believe this core self is perfect, or perhaps the better word is *pure*. People admit that they feel some kind of essence inside of them regardless of whether we call it personhood, core self, spirit, soul, or God. People appear to have a natural sense of having "inherited" a kind of goodness or purity, whether from God, from physical evolution, or from the universe at large. An important purpose of any therapy should be to help people find this sense of goodness and purity because it is from this pure core self that all else erupts, particularly *feelings*.

The first concentric circle beyond the godlike nugget or core self represents the *gifts and abilities* that the person has. This first circle represents the many elements that make an individual distinctive, such as natural personality factors, like the ones we discussed in Chapter 3, but this circle also includes intelligence, gender, and physical factors. Much of the difficulty people have in expressing and hearing feelings results from people failing to understand their gifts and abilities. If you can't see your natural abilities and value your natural abilities, you will not be able to proceed to enhancement of these abilities, much less an effective engagement in the world.

The second concentric circle represents how these natural gifts and abilities have been *enhanced*: shaped by family, language, and culture and whether these gifts have been personally developed. Gifts and abilities are enhanced equally by one's social environment and by one's own efforts. This second concentric circle represents personal achievements of some form, perhaps artistic, physical, scientific, or literary. It is also important to note that cultural enhancement and personal development of one's talents becomes the basis for self-esteem. Self-esteem does not come from natural ability, nor does it come from family, friends, and culture. It comes from personal success and failure, which naturally leads to self-enhancement of one's natural abilities, and is rooted in one's core self.

The third concentric circle is some kind of *engagement* with the world, which includes expression of feelings. This means some kind of demonstration of these abilities, which could be speaking by someone gifted with speech, artistic expression by someone with artistic talent, athletic expression by someone with natural kinesthetic ability, or the expression of any of the personality characteristics we discussed in Chapter 3. This third concentric circle is where feelings are expressed. But remember that these feelings originate from the godlike core self and have progressed through one's gifts and abilities into some kind of expression of feelings. It would be great if a person could just reach into their core self and somehow magically communicate their feelings to someone else whenever they wanted to do so. But core self does not lend itself to words because it is spiritual in nature. Core self is something we feel and know, but can't ever adequately communicate because it is way too deep within us and there are no words that can describe one's core self adequately. This is why the outer circle, our attempts to express our feelings, is so often emotionally laden: we are striving to communicate our internal self with externally expressed words. While we can't find perfect words to describe our core selves, we can find words that describe our feelings, which are always based on our gifts and abilities, which in turn are a representation of our core selves.

It is in this third circle where we engage the physical world with what we do, and the social world with what we say. This arena of life is also where we experience the result of our expressions, which can be success, failure, approval, or disapproval. Self-esteem is primarily developed through success and failure. The more success *and* failure, the better one's self-esteem becomes because the person becomes familiar with the process of improvement, which primarily comes from failure and an examination of the causes of failure. Becoming familiar with the joy of success and the sadness of failure, namely the two primary feelings having to do with love, leads to self-esteem. Self-esteem always precedes esteem that comes from other people. It is absolutely necessary in life to have people like you, and it is equally necessary to have people *not* like you. If you have established good self-esteem based on your own observation of your successes and failures, you can then profit from other people's assessments, both positive and negative. Self-esteem based on other people's judgments is not real self-esteem; it is the esteem of others. Unfortunately, many people seek to build their self-esteem around other's judgments of them, which can lead to undue dependency on approval and fear of disapproval.

This third, most outer concentric circle of personhood, is where communication, or the lack thereof, occurs. We cannot "beam" our feelings ET-like to people however much we would like to. We have to say something or do something to communicate these feelings. If children are given the opportunity to frequently express themselves in some way, they become more and more familiar with the joys and sorrows of such expressions. If children engage in these expressions sufficiently, they do not demand perfection of themselves in communication, nor are they unduly afraid of failure or disapproval. Expression of feelings, whether in physical, emotional, cognitive, or productive forms, ultimately leads to both healthy self-esteem and healthy social esteem. Ideally, a person comes to know and trust that they have a godlike core self, then realizes that they have talents and abilities, then engages the world with these abilities, and finally expresses feelings that erupt from this process. Unfortunately, many people have not had enough self-expression, together with the consequences of expression, to be confident in expressing feelings. Instead of talking out of these *concentric circles*, they talk in *confusing circles*, which makes it very hard to understand their feelings.

LISTENING TO CONFUSING CIRCLES

The expression of feelings begins with one's core self, then proceeds through awareness of one's gifts and then enhancement of those abilities until you express these feelings in words. When you are in the process of listening to someone speak their feelings, it can be helpful to think of this process in reverse: you are hearing words, words that are expressed through one's abilities, abilities that come from one's central core, a core that is one's godlike spirit. It asks a lot of listeners to keep in mind that their friends are speaking words that are two generations away from the feelings they so dearly want to communicate. This means that you, as listener, need to hear words that are spoken but be thinking of the feelings that the words represent and the core self from which these feelings emanate.

We conceive of all people having these concentric circles: their spiritual/ core self, personal gifts and abilities, and engagement with the world, which includes the expression of feelings. So, while it is not possible to communicate my core self and feelings directly to someone, I can, with practice, succeed at communicating my feelings, albeit imprecisely. If I make an honest attempt to communicate my feelings, I will naturally roam back and forth between my core self, my gifts and abilities using words that do more and more justice to expression of these feelings. It is no surprise that people seem to be "talking in circles" and "go around and around" when they try to communicate their most important feelings. When truly listening to someone, you will be hearing primarily from the third concentric circle, namely words. If you listen very carefully to someone trying heartily to express feelings, you will have a sense of the person's core self, which is a reflection of their spiritual essence. If you can get to that point, which is tantamount to feeling your friend's core self, you may very well be the first person in your friend's life who has ever done so.

If you are really going to work at understanding your friends and partners while they go through these various cycles and circling, you need to keep in mind that words in the outer circles are representations of core self. So...

- You have to wait through those rounds that your friend wades through as he or she works to communicate their core self.
- You can't get stuck with the words that are used.
- Much of what you hear will not make sense to you. Some of what you hear will seem silly or irrelevant to you.
- You might hear self-dismissive statements like, "I don't know what I am talking about" or "I don't know why I feel this way." You will hear lots of "like…" or "I mean…" or "I don't know how to say this" statements.
- Some of what you hear will seem to be flat out wrong.
- Some of what you hear will be offensive to you.

Your task in all of this is to learn to *hear their real feelings*, which is tantamount to *listening to another person's core* being expressed.

HEARING AND FEELING

There is an important difference between physically hearing words and comprehending what the words mean. We have discussed the immense difficulty of finding words that approximate what you feel. We discussed how we *feel* something before we choose to speak about this feeling, and how we have to muddle around with imprecise words to express an approximation of this feeling. If you can keep in mind that it is hard for you to adequately express your feelings, you will be better able to comprehend what your friend is saying when she is expressing her feelings. If one word can have very different meanings to two people, consider how many meanings a phrase, a sentence, or a series of sentences might have to different people. Listening to feeling-based words is a challenge indeed, but it is a challenge worth taking. Sometimes, you have to focus on the sound of the words more than the words themselves.

Some sounds bring an immediate awareness as well as some rudimentary understanding of the meaning of the sound. If we hear a siren while driving on a highway, we immediately look behind us and then to the side of us to see the emergency vehicle so we can decide what to do next. We immediately know the siren means to "take notice" because we are obliged to get out of the way. In other words, a siren means, "Figure out what is going on and then take action: do something and do it quickly, but think first so you do the right thing." The siren means "take notice and then take action."

When feelings are spoken, they are like a siren that tells you that something is coming but you might not yet know exactly what is coming. When you hear a friend speaking her feelings, especially if she is rambling through emotions trying to find the way to her feelings, you usually don't understand what she is saying and you are often uncertain what to do. Maybe you should say something, but you don't quite know what you should say. If you respond, should you tell her what you think, or how you feel? Should you correct her if she says something that isn't factually accurate? Should you agree with everything she says even though it seems illogical or unjustified? We ask ourselves all these questions in a heartbeat. Then, we usually do the wrong thing: we *speak*. The right thing would be to *listen*.

Listening to feelings is fraught with danger because of the emotion involved in the matter of expressing feelings: the emotion of the speaker and the emotion of the listener. Recall that emotion is always a part of feelings, but that the essence of feelings is much more than emotion. Anytime someone is expressing their feelings, the words that they speak will always evoke emotion in us. If we are to succeed in understanding someone's expression of feelings, we are obliged to do double duty: we need to hear *their* emotion-laden words as well as recognize and feel *our own* emotional response. We have to be aware of that our friend is trying her best to express her feelings but that undoubtedly, she will be emotional in this process. Furthermore, her expressed emotion will ignite emotions in you. This is perhaps the biggest reason that hearing feelings is more difficult than speaking feelings. To listen to someone expressing feelings that are often expressed with emotion, to work hard to understand what this friend's feelings are, and to simultaneously know what you are feeling emotionally puts a great strain on your brain. You can manage the brain strain if you learn to contain your emotion. We will shortly discuss the whole matter of *emotional containment*.

The terms hearing and listening are often interchanged, but the elements of these two neurological functions are quite different. Hearing occurs in the *parietal* part of the brain, roughly in the area of your ears, which is the auditory part of your brain. That auditory information, whether it is verbal or otherwise, then goes through an immediate process of getting to what we might call the thinking part of the brain, the *frontal lobe*. But before sound actually gets to the frontal lobe, it passes through another part of the brain that we might call a transfer point, the *hippocampus*. It is the hippocampus that facilitates the processing of most of our sensory input such as sounds. Even more importantly for our discussion, the hippocampus also processes emotion. So, when you hear that siren, or any startling noise, you have an immediate emotional response, fear. It is fast, less than a second, but you *feel* potential danger before you even look to see if it is a cop behind you or an ambulance rushing nearby. Our brains do this for us in order to protect us from the possible danger that loud noises often signal.

A similar neurological process occurs when we hear someone speaking their feelings. We hear the words spoken and we notice the emotion with which the words are spoken. Very often, however, the emotion associated with the words spoken, or the meaning that the words have for us causes our own hippocampus to kick into gear. We have an immediate emotional reaction, which could be fear, anger, joy, or sadness. Of these four emotional reactions by far the most important one is fear. Our brain is always taking care of us and protecting us from perceived danger, so if I hear a loud noise like a siren or something else that causes me alarm, my fear reaction will be almost immediate. The hippocampus that ignites an alarm system with sounds that suggest danger, like a siren, also ignites an alarm system when we hear words that suggest danger. The simple expression, "I need to tell you how I feel" or "you hurt me" might easily suggest danger, the danger that your friend is about to criticize you. So, if you hear some "feeling" from your friend that you perceive as an attack on you, your brain will immediately go into protective mode making you "defensive." Recall that the emotions of defense are fear and anger. You cannot stop your brain from "protecting" you when you feel assaulted. You can't avoid feeling defensive. *You can, however, govern what you say when you feel these things*. And you can listen.

LISTENING

Listening, as we are using the term, is primarily a cognitive activity even though it has to do with emotional material that we feel when we hear certain things. To listen we have to first know what we feel *emotionally* and then use our *cognitive* capacity to manage our emotions. In other words, we have to know what we feel emotionally before we think rationally, and certainly before we speak. If you try to think about what your friend has said without first noting how you feel, you will not be listening. Instead, your emotions will dominate your thinking and lead you to some kind of emotional reaction. Worse yet, you will speak out of your emotion. To be able to really listen to someone, we have to recognize what emotion the person's words have stirred in us and then, just as fast, we have to find a place to store them, to put them aside while we continue to listen to the other person. It would be good if we could just muse about what we've heard from someone who is speaking their feelings, and let it go at that, but it is just not possible to do so. It is hard to listen to emotionally expressed feelings because we always feel something emotionally before we even have a chance to think. If we aren't aware that we have an emotional reaction, our emotion will take control of us and lead to emotion-based thinking, or worse yet, emotion-based speaking. We will become defensive and probably insist on expressing the emotion that has erupted in us. We have to allow ourselves to register what we feel emotionally so that our feelings won't impede the listening process. We discussed the process of emotions in Chapter 2, namely that *we always feel before we think*. The process is: 1) hear, 2) feel (emotionally), and 3) think. The only way you can get to thinking is to allow yourself to feel emotionally.

We are not suggesting you avoid feeling your emotion because that is impossible. We are suggesting that you be aware of your emotion and hold on to it while the other person is speaking. We call this process "giving room" for your own emotion while you are allowing another person to speak their feelings. Giving "room" to your emotions means taking a moment to be aware of what you feel and then consciously placing these emotions on hold for a while. When Ron offends me with his emotional expression, I actually think to myself, "ouch, that hurt," which is an internal acknowledgment that what Ron said to me hurt me. When I engage this listening/feeling process effectively, I take a breath in order to give myself a moment to allow for my emotional response. In order to contain the emotion I have, I find it valuable to create an image of a small box into which I can store my feeling of hurt. Then, silly as it might sound, I tell the hurt "you are safe in this box for now, I will come back to you." In this way I can continue to listen to Ron's feelings and allow myself to have an emotional reaction without giving vent to my emotion, which would essentially be getting defensive. You may find a different picture process by which you can recognize your emotion without giving vent to it. This cognitive process is not thinking away your emotions but rather it is feeling your emotions so you can think about them later, and talk about them later.

Consider this sequence:

- *Hear* someone's words as their attempt to express deep feelings, feelings that are laden with emotions.
- *Note* your own emotional reaction to these words.
- *Contain* your emotional reaction. Perhaps make mental note of your feeling reaction and plan to speak your feelings at a later time.
- *Think* about what the person is saying.

Almost no one does this whole process. When people hear other people's expression of emotionally-laden feeling, they tend to over think, over emotionalize, or over speak. You can't avoid thinking and you certainly can't avoid being emotional, but you can avoid speaking. Our primary suggestion is that you recognize the power of your emotion and keep it to yourself. When your friend is telling you how she feels, you will most certainly hear more than you are prepared to hear. In that moment you will be predominately emotional, so you will not be able to effectively think about what she is saying. We want you to know what you feel emotionally without expressing your emotion. Because you will always have an emotional reaction to someone else's words, you will have an even stronger emotional reaction if your friend is making a feeling statement. You must keep in mind that *true listening hears, feels, and thinks, in that order.* If you can be aware of your emotional reaction, without reacting, you will be able to *manage* your thoughts and your feelings. This requires patience. This also requires practice.

Understanding the essence of words can be helped by understanding the origin of words. The etymology of the word patience is from both Latin and Greek, and the essence of the word is "long-suffering." Simply stated, if you are patient, you are suffering through something. The Greek word for patience is *makrothumia*, a rather odd sounding word but if you separate this word into *makro* and *thumia*, you will learn something important about patience as the Greeks understood it. Simply translated, *makrothumia* means "long passion." It is interesting that patience as conceived of by Greek and Latin philosophers was not so much peace of mind or calm, but quite the opposite: much feeling, much emotion, and perhaps much suffering experienced within a period of waiting for something. We propose that if you're going to truly listen to someone's words and manage your own emotional reaction to those words, you might be very passionate and very emotional. In fact, you might very well have to *suffer* through hearing words that have a powerful emotional impact on you. This is no easy task. Truly, "patience is a virtue."

The true listening experience that we are suggesting is not passive. It is not just a courteous silent presence while someone else is talking. Listening to another person's feelings goes beyond hearing the words and it certainly goes beyond the courtesy of keeping your mouth shut. Indeed, you have to be silent and contain your emotions, but you also have to think. You will not be able to think clearly if you are unduly emotional or just waiting your turn to speak. Patient, quiet listening is very emotional, but it can lead to great insight. It is hard to listen to what is being said by your friend while trying to understand the feeling under his words while experiencing the emotion that accompanies his words. Your thinking during this listening process includes reminding yourself that the other person is working hard to find, feel, and communicate feelings, knowing that this is always an imprecise process at best. You will only be able to listen to someone else's feelings if you have worked hard to express your own feelings and can appreciate the arduous process. Giving your friend a wide berth in his expressing his feelings requires you knowing what you feel and keeping your feelings to yourself. We call this process of knowing what you feel without expressing it *containment*.

CONTAINMENT OF EMOTION

When you have some emotion while hearing someone else's feeling and emotion, you need to engage in *containment* of your emotion. Containment is *knowing* what you feel, *valuing* what you feel, and *keeping your emotions to yourself*. Containment is distinct from *repression* of emotions that leads to stomachaches and headaches, and distinct also from *expression of feelings*, which includes emotional outbursts. When you contain your emotion, you know that the insertion of your emotion (and opinions) will interrupt the other person's process of trying to communicate with you. If you insert your own thoughts, your words will undoubtedly be emotion-laden, and your friend will then have to try to attend to your feelings instead of his own. Furthermore, if you express your feelings while the other person is expressing his, you are not really listening, and you are certainly not hearing and understanding. Your job is to try your best to understand what your friend is feeling. Know this: *if you have some strong emotions while your friend is speaking his feelings, you are very close to understanding him.*

During this time of containment, you will have to do both a cognitive process and an emotional process in tandem. You will have to hear what your friend is saying (cognitive), know what you feel in reaction to what she feels (cognitive), value what you feel (emotional), contain what you feel (emotional), and remember to attend to your friend (cognitive). If you have children, you have learned how to do this kind of listening because you know that children express their feelings emotionally all the time, and much of what is expressed simply needs to be heard, not corrected and not challenged. The true listening process is the same with your friend. You have to let your friend be temporarily inadequate in feeling expression while she works to say what she really wants to say. True listening to adults, which leads to understanding, comes when you can pay your adult friend the same privilege you pay children: hear, feel, listen, and eventually understand.

Containment is perhaps the most important task in really hearing another person's feelings. But even though we can train our brains to contain, containment is much more than just being quiet. Containment is much richer and personal than just listening to words. Containment is *love-based* because it is knowing and valuing your feelings, knowing and valuing another person important to you, knowing and valuing that she is struggling to express her feelings, and believing that this struggle will eventually lead to your understanding and loving her better. Knowing your emotions and valuing your emotions while temporarily having a deeper respect for your friend's feeling is an act of selfless love. Practicing this kind of containment creates and augments character in you but it is certainly not without emotion. You can do this kind of containment only if you have good self-esteem. If you feel compelled to interrupt your friend while she is speaking her feelings, you are displaying a lack of self-esteem and ultimately a lack of social-esteem for your friend.

If you can contain your feelings without expressing or repressing them, you will be doing what only one in 1000 people do. I am reminded of Kipling's *The Thousandth Man*, who is a person who "will stand by your friend…and will sink or swim with you in any water." This is the person who seeks to know how her friend feels, but in so doing is able to keep the focus on her friend's feeling and not on her own emotion. Most of us are not particularly selfless when it comes to our feelings. We selfishly think we should have the right to say whatever we want, especially in a highly emotional conversation. We have the right to *feel* whatever we feel, but we don't have the right to *say* whatever we feel at any time. This kind of listening requires the hearing-feeling-thinking process over and over again graciously giving your friend emotional license to find his way into his feelings. As you get better at governing your emotional response to what you hear, you will simultaneously get better at understanding people. You will also be improving your own self-esteem while simultaneously improving your social esteem.

Unfortunately, many people believe in a kind of magic when it comes to expressing and hearing feelings. As avid Star Trek fans, it was always interesting to see the "empath" Deanna Troi be able to "feel what other people were thinking." Some people may have some kind of special ESP-like empathic ability, but most of us are not so gifted. Instead of assuming or guessing what the other person is feeling, true listening is allowing your friend to go through round after round of rational, irrational, emotional, esoteric, and pragmatic statements until you actually get a real grasp of what he really feels. True listening is waiting while the person goes deeper and closer to their core self. The essence of truly listening to people when they are expressing their feelings goes beyond the hearing part, the emotional part, and the thinking part. *Real listening is working to understand the essence of the person that has just been expressed in emotionally laden terms.*

We can never perfectly understand what people really feel when they express their feelings, but we can understand them better, which is the crown jewel of communication. When you begin to really understand someone's feelings, you are beginning to understand them. You might think of this moment of understanding as an "aha" moment. We call this the *fourth element* of listening, which is *spiritual,* or maybe *intuitional,* whichever term seems best to you. This fourth element is being alongside the individual as they approach their own core self. Whatever we call it, this important ingredient of understanding means this: arriving safely at a place in your emotion and thinking that you are *more interested in your friend than you are in yourself.* So, this process of listening to people's striving to express their feelings is not only good for them, it is good for you. When you improve at listening and hearing, you become a better person.

When you reach the goal of understanding your friend's feelings, you have arrived at having a sense of your friend's spiritual core. When you reach this goal, you experience a sense of safety in relationships, a safety that allows you to love people regardless of your emotions, regardless of your thoughts, regardless as to whether you agree with them, and even regardless of whether you like them. This level of safety in a relationship puts you in a place of loving the person unconditionally. It is from this point that you and the other person can connect on a deeper level and both be more enriched in the relationship. To get to this level you often have to listen to a lot of complaints.

FEELINGS VIA COMPLAINTS

One of the most difficult things in the process of hearing people's feelings is hearing their complaints. As we noted in the previous chapter, many of us didn't learn to express a breath of feelings when we were growing up and so we are generally not good at it. It might have been OK for us to share our positive feelings, like happiness, joy, and excitement, but most of us did not get the opportunity to express hurts, disappointments, fears, and anger when we were kids. Because these normal feelings did not get expressed in childhood, they did not mature. Had we had the opportunity to simply express disappointment, sadness, and hurt, we would have learned that these emotions are quite normal and quite necessary as we face the world when we lose things. As children, without the opportunities to express such emotions as simple disappointment, we felt helpless in the face of such disappointments. When we feel helpless, we will tend to express this feeling of helplessness by complaining about how external factors in the world do not allow us to be ourselves, which amounts to feeling that the world is not giving us what we want. It is this fault-finding that is the basis for most of the complaining we hear when someone is trying to express their feelings. Fault-finding always leads to complaining. Underneath complaining is always a feeling of helplessness, which is really what we are hearing when people are doing their emotions in route to their feelings.

It would be good if people could avoid complaining, which is tantamount to saying what they don't like about something. Most people will take every opportunity to complain about something when they are expressing their feelings, but this is where most people have to start. Complaining is simply a funnel for the felt sense of helplessness in life. Eventually people need to learn to express the breadth of their feelings, which is always about what they love and value. If you are beginning the hearing and listening process, be prepared for hearing complaints at the start. If you are to get better at hearing feelings, you will have to listen to these complaints without speaking a word. This will be hard. You will want to defend yourself from a perceived attack on you, correct the seeming errors of what you are hearing, ask questions that are probably rhetorical and critical, or have a discussion about the "facts" that your friend has expressed. If you are really listening, you will always keep in mind that you are not so much hearing facts as you are hearing feelings.

The listening process that we are suggesting requires several things of the listener, not the least of which is self-esteem, which itself is built upon knowing what you feel. In order to do this kind of listening, you need to understand yourself, like yourself, know your strengths, know your weaknesses, feel confident, and feel humble. In other words, you will need good self-esteem in order to contain your feelings and master patience. This is a tall order for most of us, but it is the only way we can truly listen and truly understand people. You will not be able to truly listen if you are plagued with a desperate need to express your feelings in the midst of listening to someone else's honest imprecise attempt to express feelings. You cannot be successful at this very difficult task of true listening if you don't how hard it is to express feelings. True listening requires a great deal of restraint in favor of a generous giving of time and emotional license to people when they are doing the nearly impossible task of communicating their feelings.

Listening to someone in the way we have suggested is an act of love, but it is not to be confused with being someone's doormat or a dumping ground for someone's emotional abuse. Sadly, most of us have not been taught how to express our feelings with appropriate emotion and appropriate governance. Yelling, screaming, vicious attacks, and undue swearing is never valuable. We can give children the freedom of violent expression because children are not vicious and poisonous in their words. They just yell and scream. Giving an adult emotional license is not the same as allowing that person unlimited freedom to attack you. Rather, we are suggesting that talking about *feelings* is very difficult, both for the speaker and for the listener because feelings do not lend themselves to words very well. If your friend is really trying to communicate, she wants you to know how she feels, but she certainly will have difficulty with that endeavor. You might need to give your friend a wide berth of emotional expression and complaints, even complaints about you, before she can find her own feelings, much less express them. Giving a wide berth requires love and humility; being a doormat is neither.

HELPING PEOPLE EXPRESS THEIR FEELINGS

One of the real dangers of people maturing in the process of good psychotherapy is the problem that their maturity has on their relationships. Maturity is essentially the development of a sense of *self*, namely who you are. Our principal way of helping patients understand who they are is through helping them understand their feelings, their emotions, and their temperaments. When someone has really begun to understand herself, like herself, and express herself, she may find that her personal maturity does not translate to relationship maturity. Personal maturity is wonderful because it means that you are less angry and less afraid of others' disapproval. But the other people in your life may not share your insight into such things as feelings, self, and communication. If that is the case, you are in the very challenging situation of knowing something very important about feelings, emotions, and communication that others don't know. The challenge is to use your personal maturity to carefully assist other people find their personal maturity. Knowing yourself, liking yourself, and communicating yourself does not mean that your partner can do the same. When you have found this wonderful feeling of self-value together with an ability to communicate your feelings, there is a great danger of thinking that everyone has the same ability. So, your challenge is to be aware of your own feelings, work diligently at understanding others' feelings, and then carefully find delicate ways of assisting people to express their feelings. There are two dangers in this procedure: (1) trying too hard and too fast to get the other person to communicate the whole business of feelings that took you months to develop, and (2) being your friend's bootleg therapist.

We encounter the difficulty of knowing quite a bit about feelings, and quite a bit more about psychology in our daily lives. Over the last few days we have encountered various people in our families, friendships, professional lives, and more casual contacts all of which were replete with feelings. Usually, the people we were talking to were not aware of their feelings, and in many cases, they had no interest in understanding anything about feelings. So, we needed to have a varied approach to these important people in our lives depending on what was possible to say, what was not possible to say, and what was possible to do. There are times when you just listen, and there are times when you might be able to lend a bit of assistance to your friends in understanding that they are expressing feelings. (We have altered some of the nonessential data in these stories to protect people's identities.)

Times when you just listen and govern your emotion

- A family member spoke quite abruptly about his political preference just as I had just spoken mine. I acknowledged his opinion as "certainly valid" and said that, indeed, his preferred candidate was quite bright and had many good ideas. I judged this as a time when it was unwise to express any more of my political preference, much less anything about my feelings since he expressed his so vociferously and clearly had no interest in my opinion, much less my feelings. I deemed it the greater part of wisdom to not only keep my feelings to myself, but to give some credence to his feelings even though he was quite unaware that his "opinion" about his preferred candidate was certainly a feeling-based opinion. This is not to say that his opinion was wrong, but rather that it was feeling-based and that my relative did not know that it was feeling-based, much less what his deep feelings were that had led to his political opinion. So, when I eventually left my relative's company for the evening, I felt a bit sad that it was neither possible for me to help my relative express his feeling, but certainly impossible for him to hear my feelings.
- We were recently in the company of an old friend whom we had not seen for several years. We were looking forward to this reunion for some time thinking that it would be a time where we could catch up on what each of us had felt, thought, and done over the intervening years. The evening began quite simply by our friend telling us about a project she had just been involved in over the past six

months or so. Her expression was initially ripe with passion and deep feelings. We listened intently to the story. And then we listened a bit less intently to the continuing story that took perhaps a half hour. And then, we listened to another story and another story, all good stories, but in the telling of the stories, our friend seemingly lost the passion and was just relating facts. We had a pleasant departure that evening and left with the standard hugs and handshakes, but this departure, like that of our family member, was difficult for us because we were left with many feelings, mostly sadness because it wasn't a reunion so much as it was a monologue. The speaking and the listening was a one-way street and we were disappointed. We concluded that Rebecca was not a person who could share feelings as feelings, nor could she be genuinely interested in our feelings and thoughts. Our own feelings of disappointment passed after a day or so. We now can focus on the good history we have had with Rebecca while being a bit more reticent to place ourselves in the purely listening situation again.

- We receive a local newspaper only on Sundays, a paper that usually arrives well before 6 AM and in time for us to pull an espresso, sit back in bed, and read the news for the day and the week. It is the only time we do such things and it is a time that we enjoy together, sharing stories we each read, caching up on the news, and taking a cursory look at the Sunday ads. This morning there was no Sunday paper at 6, nor at 7, nor at 7:30. Finally, I drove down to the local Kwik Trip and bought a paper so we could go through our Sunday routine. Then we had some important yard work to complete before the day ended, so we began that work in the front yard with shovels and rakes. About 9 o'clock, a car drove past and threw our Sunday paper on the sidewalk. Then we heard an extensive explanation as to why the paper was late: two carriers had quit-one was her son; they can't find replacements; distribution was dropped at the wrong site and a host of other factors. We expressed our appreciation for her explanation of the delay of the paper delivery, and she soon drove off. We were both a bit chagrinned at this situation because it was, again as many such situations are, ripe with feelings: our feelings and our delivery person's feelings. But these feelings were not expressed as feelings, rather as explanations. Our delivery person was distraught, certainly for good reasons, but just relayed the facts of the paper delivery delay, not her feelings as such. We did our best to hear her feelings-via-facts without expressing ours. It was obvious to us that this was certainly not a time when this kind harried woman was capable, much less interested, in hearing our feelings. Situations like that are not terribly important in the long run, but they are examples of times when people want to express their feelings while at the same time not knowing that they are expressing feelings.

- If you happen to live in an old house like we do, you know that old houses have their problems, and you need to keep on top of things that deteriorate with age and use. The foundation wall was one of those things that we dared not ignore anymore as it was bowing into the basement and crying for repair. We contracted out the project estimated to be as much as six weeks. Five months later the project was finished with the various tradesmen blaming the other for failing to get the project completed in a timely manner. The best they could all do was to blame the other tradesman, and they all tended to blame God for sending rain with inopportune timing. Never did we hear anything like an apology, or a personal statement of disappointment for not being able to honor their agreement on time. We worked diligently to contain our feelings, which were immense and aimed to avoid expressing anger or any kind of legal threat because we were aware of the pressure that they must have been under to finish this project along with all the other projects that were behind schedule. Only once did I indulge myself saying to the cement guy that it was "difficult" to not have the project done, only to hear in return 20 reasons why things weren't done. The whole project was replete with emotion, and certainly important feelings under the emotion, but little of either was ever expressed. This is an example of many in life where everyone's emotions are running full speed but the best thing to do is to keep them under wraps. It's an effort to do so.

Times when you assist the person to express their feelings
We spend many hours a week helping people in our office learn what they feel, accept their feelings, express their feelings, and eventually communicate their feelings. Helping people in our office learn about their feelings in the professional setting is satisfying work. Things are not so easy if we are having dinner with friends who are not seeking our counsel but are expressing deep feelings. It is one thing to listen to an old friend tell stories that are only marginally interesting to us, but it is quite another when someone expresses a deep feeling without knowing that he is expressing a deep feeling. We have to speak graciously and kindly but avoid the tendency of going into therapist mode. We advise you to do the same: gracious assistance to a friend without falling into doing therapy over the chicken dinner. We have found it valuable to start with the genuine listening that we have discussed as so central in hearing people's feelings, and then adding a statement that amounts to "I understand how you're feeling" or "That must be very difficult," or another statement that suggests that the thing that our friend has just said amounts to a deep feeling even if she doesn't know it is a feeling. I have sometimes found it helpful to go a step further with a statement like, "That sounds like it is very important to you." Such statements affirm the feeling even if the word feeling isn't used. Sometimes, such statements are dismissed quickly, while other times we find that we are privileged to hear someone's deeper feeling without the probing or careful analysis that we might execute if the person were in our office. It is impossible to leave our therapist hat at the office, but we have found ways to put it on briefly and then remove it just as quickly so we can go on with dinner.

Whether dealing with an emotionally unsophisticated tradesman, good friends at dinner, a challenging family member, or a cashier who expresses something that is truly a feeling, keep in mind that *almost everything people say spontaneously is a feeling statement.* You don't have to tell your friend that he has made a feeling statement, but you need to know that you have heard a feeling statement. You need to listen as much as you can honestly listen, but not listen beyond your ability to genuinely listen. Avoid rendering your opinions, much less expressing your feelings to give your friend the privilege of expressing his. Avoid answering your friend's questions because his "questions" are a desire to elicit your agreement with his statements. Keep in mind his fact-sounding statements are feelings not facts. This is a tall task. Sometimes, the best thing you can say is something like, "That sounds like a really important feeling you have about…." To help your friend learn to express his feelings without going too fast or being too much of a therapist, consider how Mike might graciously help his lifelong friend Sam express his feelings.

> **Sam:** "I'm really bummed out at work lately. My boss is so sloppy in his directions. He doesn't seem to value doing something right. He just wants to get it done and go on to another project".
>
> **Mike:** "What's he done that is sloppy, Sam? I know a little about your work but I don't know what all the particulars are."
>
> **Sam:** "OK. I got to the office this morning and there was a pile of stuff on my desk, some of it hand-written so sloppily that I couldn't even read it. Then he barges into my office and complains about a couple of other things that he thinks should have been done yesterday."
>
> **Mike:** "You know, Sam, I know you are a person who likes to have order in your life and you are really good at following through. It's one of the things that I really admire about you. It must be very hard to work with someone who is different from you in this regard. You know, of course, that I'm a bit sloppy myself. I think it is part of my player temperament. I would guess your boss is a lot like me in some ways."
>
> **Sam:** "Thanks for that reminder. Maybe the boss is a player guy like you. I never thought of that. And yes, you are right, it is really important to me to have an order to my day." "I just don't like the difference."

Mike: "Yup that is the most important thing, being who you are. I am glad that we can be such good friends even though we are different."

Sam: "I know you never set out to intentionally irritate me, Mike. I will try to think of my boss in the same way."

Understandably, this would be a much longer conversation than what we have proposed, but we intend to suggest that even in the simplest of conversations, we can be of help with our friends by identifying that what they have said is a personal value, and perhaps a core feeling. If you can do that, you will help people understand themselves and like themselves without ever admitting that you are really talking about the central element in psychology: feeling. All this discussion about knowing how you feel, knowing how other people are feeling, and keeping your feelings to yourself is a challenge. Sometimes, you are just not up to the challenge.

WHEN YOU DON'T WANT TO HEAR SOMEONE'S FEELING

As important as feelings are in life, and as central as they are in any relationship, we know that life is not all about feelings, and we know that it is not necessary to have a feeling-based conversation every time you feel something. You have to honor this feeling that you "just don't want to hear someone's feelings," as odd or unkind as that sounds. If you try to push yourself ahead to listen, you will most certainly not be truly listening, and your friend will know that you are just putting in your time. These times call for a simple, honest, and loving statement like, "You know, as important as your feelings are to you…and to me…I just don't have the energy right now." Then you might add, "Give me a minute, or an hour, or a day, and I will get back to you when I can really be the listener you deserve."

Recall that we noted in Chapter 4 that you don't always need to express your feelings. Sometimes, you just need to feel them. You feel content just to feel something and might even realize that this feeling needs to be kept private, at least for a while. Likewise, there are times when you just don't want to hear someone talk about their feelings. Maybe you're tired, maybe you have something really important that you need to do, maybe you have heard enough complaints from people all day that you don't have it to listen to any more feelings from anyone. Maybe you have so many feelings yourself that you would like to share that you don't have the listening ear necessary for true listening. You need to honor these times and respect yourself before you try too hard to honor and respect someone else.

SUMMARY:

1. *The feelings that you hear are never wrong.* The words you hear may be wrong, critical, or inadequate at the best, but not wrong.
2. *Being quiet is a cognitive process.* You need to be prepared to listen to multiple attempts before you hear the real deal.
3. *Being quiet while people are expressing their feelings is difficult.* Keep in mind that true listening is an act of love, but not an easy act.
4. *Listening is making sense* of what your friend is saying, or trying to make sense of it. Wade through the words and try to connect with the feelings.
5. *Emotional containment is the key to successful communication.* Containment is governing your emotion. Communication often fails when listeners cannot contain their emotions.
6. *Communication can be gloriously successful.* When you are able to contain your feelings, you can really begin to understand the other person's feelings. You are near the ultimate goal of true communication.
7. *You get to the place where you feel what the other person feels.* When this happens, you have the wonderful experience of connection.
8. If you can keep your head about you and *think*, and keep your heart about you and *feel*, you will be able to keep quiet and listen.
9. When you are able to *feel deeply* and *think clearly*, you will be able to love better, if never perfectly.

Chapter 6

Rules of Engagement

THE BEST WORD TO describe this expressing and hearing feelings might be *careful*. We need to be careful in how we express our feelings and even more careful in how we hear other people's feelings. Given that we need a great amount of care in these two processes as well as the patience with ourselves and everyone else, there are some rules of engagement that we would like to suggest that makes communication possible.

RULE # 1: REMEMBER THE POSITIVE

The major focus of this book is to help people understand their feelings and communicate them more effectively. While feelings are never wrong and never "negative", there is a tendency to think of feelings as having to do with something that is wrong or negative. As we have suggested, "I need to tell you how I feel" tends to be a precursor to telling the person that there is something you don't like about the person. We have attempted to reframe talking about feelings from something *wrong* to something *right*. It is essential that people know how they feel, value how they feel, and then work diligently at communicating how they feel, but there remains a strong tendency to look at what is wrong with something when we talk about our feelings.

We previously noted the initial "negative" nature of feelings when they are expressed caused by years of suppression of feelings as a whole and a lack of adequate understanding of feelings in order to find words that express them. While there are no negative *feelings*, the emotions of sadness, fear, and anger tend to be stored up more than the feelings of joy. It would be wonderful if we could first help people express these joyful emotions as they learned to express their feelings, but that tends not to be the case. Most people are too wounded and wearied from keeping sadness, fear, and anger inside to be able to express much of anything joyful. Hence, we are confronted with the phenomenon of starting where people are, which sadly, is with these more difficult emotions.

So, what is the positive to keep in mind as you work towards communicating with those you care about? The positive is that you are learning to identify your core self and working towards sharing your basic goodness with others. You are worth the work. As you look deeply into yourself, you will find more and more to be joyful about. Likewise, as you learn to express your feelings, you will find more and more joy in your expressing yourself. There is a genuine human beauty of wading through speaking and hearing feelings. Having communicated yourself or hearing people communicate themselves settles the soul and engenders a true sense of connection.

RULE # 2: THERE IS A TIME & PLACE TO TALK ABOUT FEELINGS

"There is a time for all things. There is a time to be silent and a time to speak." (Ecclesiastes 3.1). These words reportedly spoken by Solomon 3000 years ago remain true today. There is a time and a place where people can express their feelings. Even more importantly, they need a person who is willing to hear what they have to say. Ideally, the time, place, and person provide a setting that is safe for them to wander into the dangerous waters of expressing their feelings. We therapists have the privilege, and the responsibility, of providing these things to the people who choose to see us. Therapists are very often the first people that someone has talked to about their feelings without feeling judged, feeling wrong, or feeling stupid. Most of life, however doesn't afford us those three luxuries of time, place, and person when we want to express our feelings. So, while a therapy office should be a good place to express feelings, a grocery store is not such a place, nor is a time after you come home from a party of drinking or when the kids are around. Even if you have the right time and place, you cannot adequately communicate your feelings if the person listening to you isn't interested in you and your feelings. If you're going to really talk about yourself and your feelings, there needs to be a time and a place for it with a person who is willing to make the investment in listening to you speaking feelings.

The problem with feelings is that they occur instantaneously. You "just have a feeling" and then you go through the physical, emotional, cognitive, and activity based processes in order to perhaps say something about this feeling. It would be great if you could just feel, just speak, and just be heard. No such luck. You can only do this when you are in the confines of a therapist's office or perhaps sitting calmly on an ocean beach watching the waves roll in. Most of the time feelings come at times and places that are not conducive to you wandering about with this vague "I feel something." Furthermore, when you "just feel something," it is very likely that you are overly emotional and not in control of what you might say about your feeling. Talking about feelings should not be a time when you simply spew out some kind of feeling laden with emotion. Your listener will not be prepared to listen to your feelings and will be broadsided with what you have to say, and you will likely begin your feelings by expressing what is wrong with your listener. Remember, if you are going to talk about your feelings, you need a *wide berth* in which you wonder through the murky waters of "feelings" working honestly to find words that do some justice to these feelings. This wide berth requires sufficient time and a safe place. So, think clearly about the time and place where you can have this wide berth.

When you *think* about a time and place, you should not be focusing on what you feel emotionally. You should be thinking of where it is safe for you to just feel, a place where you can talk about your feelings. This thinking is not planning out all that you want to say, and it is certainly not a time when you prepare for an all-out assault on your partner for what he or she said or did. It is not thinking about *what* you might say or *how* you might say it. It is thinking of *when and where* you can give yourself the freedom to wonder about in these murky waters of feelings. Talking about your feelings should be an intentional exercise, not a reactional event. Delaying a conversation until you find a good time and a good place gives you an opportunity to cool down a bit and restore your equilibrium so you are not wholly emotional but yet still feel the passion of what you want to say. If some important feeling comes to you when you are in the grocery story, you could say something like, "Mary, something important just came to mind. I want to remember this thought (or feeling) and tell you about it later." And you might add, "… that will give me some time to formulate my thoughts (and words)." Ron and I do this frequently at the end of our clinical days. I might say to Ron driving home from our Madison office "I had a very painful session with Judy today. I can't talk about it yet, but I do want to tell you about it later." This gives me the privilege to recognize my passion for the work I do and gives Ron the knowledge that I will need to debrief a difficult session.

This may be a challenge when you begin to note how you feel and begin to value how you feel because it is likely that you will be excited about the prospect of telling someone how you feel. You can make a statement about your feeling that gives your friend or partner an opportunity to be excited about hearing your feelings without actually making a plan to do so.

RULE # 3: REMEMBER THE FUTURE IS IMPERFECT

Bear with me while I indulge myself a bit. I happened to be one of those kids in school who loved grammar. I loved diagramming sentences, easily distinguished between adverbs and adjectives, and could differentiate a gerund from a participle or a phrase from a clause. While most people think that such things as gerunds and participles are unnecessary understandings for common speech, I find such understanding of language friendly. I know better than to correct someone's grammar, much less to suggest that he or she should understand gerunds, clauses, and placement of pronouns, but for me it always *feels* wrong when I hear something like, "Me and Grandma…." When I jokingly talk about the pluperfect with Deb, she rolls her eyes and says something like, "to where did the perfect fly? or "certain shades of blue are perfect". More to the point, what do grammatical terms have to do with the business of feelings?

It is not the pluperfect that I think of when I talk about expressing feelings. It is the *future imperfect*. Without a discourse on the technicalities of the future imperfect in English grammar, let me just use this term to describe how your feeling-based expressions in the *future* will be *imperfect*. You really need to have this firmly planted in your mind, not the grammatical structure, mind you, but the fact that your future expressions of feelings will, indeed, be imperfect. You need to know that your words will be imperfect because you will almost certainly *not* be understood when you start expressing your feelings.

Imperfection of any kind is understandable. Lots of proverbs are about the importance of imperfection in the world: such as M. Gandhi once said "My imperfections and failures are as much a blessing as my successes." or Anatole France said: "I cling to my imperfection as the very essence of my being."

We agree with the essence of such quotations with an important caveat: *imperfection is hard to accept*, and it is particularly hard to accept when we have done our best. And it is harder yet to accept when we want to tell you about our feelings. The Apostle Paul of the New Testament said, "If I speak with the tongues of angels and have not love, I am nothing." I might rearrange this statement for my own purposes like, "If I speak with love but have not the right words, I will fail to communicate." I might even say, "Even if I have the best of intentions, and even if I have great love at the source of what I say, I might fail to truly communicate that love, much less the feeling that underlies all love." Love is not enough when it comes to feelings. Love is great, and love is the "greatest of gifts," another thing Apostle Paul said, but it is not enough to have love, passion, and feeling when communicating. You have to use words, all the while remembering, these words will be imperfect.

We discussed the importance of adding, correcting, and re-stating our feelings in Chapter 4. Re-stating and improving our communication of feelings needs regular use of "My bad here" or "I haven't communicated very well" and "Let me try to express myself better," or "I'm not yet very good at this business of talking about my feelings." Such statements are not an admission of personal insecurity or something wrong with you, but simply a humble statement that you are doing your best, knowing that *your best is imperfect*. When you say such things, you admit that your words are inadequate to fully communicate your feelings but that you are going to give it your best try, and that you are going to continue to try to get better at the feelings-into-words task. Please note that for you to be quickly able to state these *mea culpa* statements, you will have to feel confident in yourself knowing that your core self is pure and your feelings are a reflection of that purity even if the words you use are imperfect. Most angry words originate from one's personal insecurity and fear that something is wrong with them instead of knowing and feeling this perfect inner self expressed with very imperfect words.

RULE 4: ONE AT A TIME

Eventually, you and your friends will have reciprocal feelings. You will speak to each other and listen to each other giving everyone a wide berth in your expression of feelings. Communication ultimately has to be a two-way endeavor for the relationship to be healthily evolving. But that won't happen for a while. Having said that, you need to understand that the act of *expressing* feelings is a one-way process. At any given point in the process of expressing feelings, only one person can speak at a time. It is not a two-way process and it is certainly not taking turns. Contrary to what most people think about a feeling-based discussion, it is not back-and-forth talk about feelings. When we teach people about feelings and their expression, we start with this rule, which we believe is not only the ground rule of engagement but also the rule that is hardest to follow. Recall that feelings expressed generate feelings felt, that when I express my feelings, my very expression will create emotions in my listener. Giving the person who is speaking feelings a wide berth is extremely hard to do and requires an amount of emotional maturity that many people don't have.

One-way conversation is not easy to explain, especially to someone who has had a lifetime of two-way bantering and the arguments that often ensue. Learning how to move from two-way arguments to one-way communication of feelings is difficult to do without falling into the pattern of "my feelings statement lead to your feeling statement." Let's consider Max and Judy already had a conversation where Judy tried to communicate her feelings only to hear Max' reaction and feelings as soon as she spoke hers. Consider how Judy now attempts to communicate to Max how she needs to speak her feelings without hearing his.

Judy: "Max, what you just said is really important to me. You said that you, too, have feelings. I have offended you, and you understandably would like to tell me about how I have hurt you. I think it is very important that I hear your feelings, and I really want to. If it is possible for you to do so, I would like to postpone your feelings for the moment and come back to them later. I'm afraid that if I don't continue trying to tell you how I feel, that I will lose the feeling or get in the way of you expressing yours. Your feelings are just as important as my feelings."

Max: "Why can't we just take turns: you say something, and then I say something? You tell me about your feelings and I tell you about my feelings."

Judy: "That sounds reasonable. And that is what I have always thought, and that is what we have always done. But what I am reading and trying to do is quite different. The idea is that communication of feelings, and perhaps communication of any sort, starts with one person expressing their feelings. Think of the arguments we have got into when I had a feeling that caused another feeling in you, and we ended up fighting. Then we never get back to what started the fight, which is the fact that one of us made a statement of feelings but didn't get a chance to finish talking. I am trying to avoid the tendency of one person's feelings getting in the way of the other person's feelings."

Max: "It only seems logical that we take turns. You speak your thoughts and I speak my thoughts and we find some compromise."

Judy: "It is very reasonable to take turns expressing our thoughts, and we do that all the time, especially when it relates to things common in our day, like where to go, or what to do. But I am learning that this business of "feelings" is much more difficult to communicate than thoughts. Thoughts can be quite rational and practical. But feelings are not always rational, and they can be very emotional. The idea is this: if you are speaking your feelings, I have to keep my emotions out of the way, even if I have strong emotions. My task when you are speaking about yourself is to understand you. If I interject my feelings into the discussion, especially if I am emotional, I will not really be trying to understand you." I will end up only defending myself and then we end up in some kind of argument instead of really understanding each other better.

Max: "This sounds a bit weird, but maybe I can try it. I still want to know when it is my turn to speak."

Judy: "If I do this right, I will finish what I have to say and hopefully communicate my feelings to you. If I do that, I will be ready to hear your feelings. It's kind of taking turns, but the turns are not back and forth."

Max: "Still seems weird, but I'll try it."

Granted, in an emotionally mature relationship, the expression may become more efficient leading to a more swift exchange between partners, but it always starts with one person speaking their feelings. As good as the two of us are at this rule, we violate it frequently, much to our great chagrin. Governing one's emotional reaction to a statement of feeling takes more than we have at certain times. So, if we can't do it all the time after decades of practice, we expect it will be difficult for you to do especially when you are first beginning to express feelings and hear feelings. A note: when we do go awry in this rule of engagement, we each are more prone to recognize it and can then go back to the "my bad" even in the midst of a conversation, and that often makes all the difference. We work daily on being aware of the complexity of speaking and listening to feelings.

A corollary to speaking "one at a time" is this: whoever starts to express feelings gets to finish. The purpose for this rule is to provide the speaker with enough time to get through the feelings that need to be expressed. Ideally, the speaker needs an unlimited amount of time, which could be minutes (usually) or hours (not recommended). If the speaker has to worry about finishing in a few seconds or minutes, she will be less likely to get to the words she needs to find to express her feelings. The listener can't have the idea that it is "his turn" and just wait finger-tapping until his friend is finished. He has to give her the time she needs. Arguments can be entirely avoided if people follow the "whoever starts gets to finish" rule. That having been said, it is awfully hard to listen, wait, and focus on understanding the person who initially started the feeling-based conversation, especially when you hear something that you *feel* is wrong.

RULE # 5: IT IS NOT ABOUT AGREEMENT

If you are going to do the hard work of expressing your feelings, you can't be worrying about what your partner is feeling about your feelings, let alone how that person might interrupt you. Your focus needs to be on your own feeling and finding your way through the murky waters that are the very nature of feelings. An effective therapist should be able to assist you in exploring your feelings and ultimately finding words for them but when you are daring to speak yourself to your partner or friends, unless you have an emotionally mature listener, you really are on your own and it requires courage. You need to become familiar with speaking your feelings and in so doing gain confidence regardless of the response you might get. Ultimately you need to be listened to, then to be heard, and eventually to be understood. To get to that place requires you to step out and begin even though it may be difficult. You have to be the brave one for this to come about.

You don't need to ask questions when you speak your feelings. The only reason you would ask questions when you're trying to speak feelings is that you either want assurance from your listeners that they agree with you or you are trying to get out of a deeply emotional and deeply personal statement. Asking questions, which are usually in the form of, "Don't you agree with me on this?" or "Do you understand what I mean?" only invites your listener to either take the invitation to begin their dialogue or gives them an easy out of just agreeing to avoid hearing more. If you ask a question, you are changing the rules of this endeavor from you speaking your feelings to an interchange of ideas. If that happens, you might have a good conversation about theory, fact, or history, but you won't be any further getting your listener to understand you. Talking about feelings is not based on question-and-answer because it is not about agreement. It is about feelings, this undefined, central ingredient of your soul.

Keep in mind that *you* are speaking about *your* feelings that represent *your* core self. You don't need someone's correction, addition, or approval to do this. You need courage. If your listener does her job, she will let you wander all over the universe with words that are inaccurate, and even inflammatory and not interrupt you. If she really understands you, she will no longer be concerned with the moments of "disagreement" or "dislike" that he had when you were speaking. This is the person you want your listener to be: someone who listens to you and comes to understand you when you speak about your feelings, or at least works hard to understand you. This feeling-communication program asks a lot of the speaker and the listener. If your partner gives you the wide berth that you really need when you are talking about your feelings, she will learn that the liking and disliking disappears, and in its place, she will have a deeper understanding of you. When the demand to have agreement is given up, there is the real possibility that your love for each other will increase. Eventually, there will be some reciprocation, some back-and-forth talk about you, but that can come only after you have finished talking and feel that you have been successful in communicating your feelings.

RULE # 6: IT TAKE TWO TO TANGO

When you begin to understand the importance of your feelings and begin to communicate them, it can become disappointing that the important people in your life are not equally able to express their feelings, much less hear your feelings. They simply haven't learned what you have learned and so they don't know how to speak feelings and how to listen to feelings. In fact, they may not even be interested in your feelings because they have never successfully communicated their own feelings. They might be more interested in their work, reading, or watching a football game. We have frequently heard people say or ask, "How do I get them to do what I am learning to do with feelings?

Tough question. Tougher answer. Learning about feelings can be dangerous to relationships because once people realize how important and how central feelings are, the more they will be inclined to talk about their feelings. For that reason alone, it is dangerous for one person in an intimate relationship to do self-examining therapy if the other person isn't doing the same thing. In fact, depth therapy of any kind is dangerous for relationships because one person in a relationship might outgrow the other person in personal development and subsequent personal expression. This new world view can have deleterious effects on the relationship if the other person is not onboard with such learning. Good therapy increases one's self-awareness and self-esteem and often increases the person's desire to engage at a deeper level with friends, family, and life partners. Hopefully when someone is doing good therapy, it begins to "rub off" on the significant other in their life and so the other chooses to come on board and begin to examine for themselves their own deeper feelings. This then begins to set up the opportunity for a joint learning experience. The old adage "it takes two to tango" speaks of a real relational dance. It takes two to tango, and it takes two to do feelings, which means expressing feelings and hearing feelings.

If you are going to try to express your feelings to, say, your partner, s/he has to at least be patient with you if not equally interested in the process of feeling expression. This is not an easy situation to handle because your partner may not understand what you are trying to do. Even if you find the best time and place, and use the best of feeling language, you might immediately run into your partner feeling offended and turning to defense. If you are diligently trying to deepen your relationship with expressions of feelings, but this expression creates defensiveness in your partner, you will need to carefully manage the conversation. Recall how Judy managed the situation with her partner Max when Max jumped right into the conversation with his feelings in reaction to her expression of feelings. This kind of management is not easy to do because it could easily be interpreted as "controlling." If you approach this talking about your feelings with an understanding that it takes time to learn to tango, you can be patient with those whom you love the most.

These are some of the things to keep in mind when you begin to speak your feelings and simultaneously work on helping your listener to listen:

- Speak your feelings the best that you can, however imprecise your words might be.
- Noting your partner's defensiveness, apologize for having brought offense. Remember that apologizing for offending is not saying something is wrong with what you feel or what you have said. Rather, an apology is an acknowledgement that you have unintentionally offended someone.
- Keep in mind that you care for the person you are talking to, and you want to deepen the love you have for each other. If you didn't care about the person, you wouldn't bother trying to express your feelings.
- Admit immediately that you are trying something new in the realm of talking about feelings and that you are not good at it yet.
- Then say something like, "I'm sorry for offending. I'm not good at this. Let me think a bit more about what I'm trying to say and get back to you." Then do your best to simply hold off on the feeling expression until things have settled down. Then after a while you might try again but with the preface, "I have been thinking about how important you are to me and I would like to try again to tell you some of what I have been feeling. I am not very good at this, but I really want to tell you about myself."
- Learning the relational tango is about a good deal of strategy, patience, and practice.

If you find yourself in the situation when your friend is unable, or perhaps just uninterested in hearing your feelings, allow us first to suggest what you should *not* to do:

- Please don't tell her that something is wrong with her and she needs to go to therapy.
- Please don't get mad at her because she is just doing what everyone does: reacting with emotion to your expression of feelings.
- Please, don't just throw your hands up and walk out the door or threaten a divorce. At all costs, avoid an argument, especially a tit-for-tat hurt-for-hurt screaming match.

This phenomenon where one person is working diligently to express feelings while the other person in the relationship is not yet onboard is the most difficult part of the expressing feelings program we are laying out for you. Facing someone who dearly loves you but who does not understand what you are trying to do requires a good deal of patience, kindness and forbearance. First, remember that you both are doing your best to communicate and you are trying a new strategy to be understood, but your partner is also doing his or her best to communicate in the way they always have done it. If you stay patient and kind while you attempt to communicate your feelings, your partner may eventually see the value of communicating feelings-into-words. In the meantime, you might end up with a conversation something like,

> *You:* Dan, I'd like to tell you an important feeling that I've been having.
>
> *Dan:* So, does this mean that I have done something wrong?
>
> *You:* Not in the least. This "feeling" is not about you whatsoever. It is about me.
>
> *Dan:* So, why don't you just tell me your feeling, whatever that is.
>
> *You:* I'd like to do that but I have been learning that communicating feelings is always a challenge.
>
> *Dan:* Why is that? You just say what you think and that's it, right?
>
> *You:* Yes, thinking is part of it. And emotion is part of it. And doing something is part of it. It's a bit complex.
>
> *Dan:* I don't understand. Can't we just say our feelings and be done with it?

You: Perhaps eventually, we can, but I must admit that I don't think I have been very good at sharing my feelings. I think I need to work better at this process.

Dan: I don't get it. What is the "process"?

You: I don't exactly know myself. I'm still learning. I just wanted to let you know that I'm going to try really hard to express my feelings that have to do with me, not you.

Dan: That would be a relief because when I hear, "I need to tell you my feelings," I get ready to be criticized in some way."

You: That is my bad for sure. I have not been good at expressing my feelings. But I'm committed to getting better at it so that you know me better. Perhaps, I can get even better at hearing your feelings.

Dan: That may take some time.

You: I think it is worth it. How about a little walk?

RULE # 7: FINISHING YOUR FEELINGS
You will discover that there is a natural end to your feelings. This natural end is actually a beautiful thing, and you need to recognize it. The natural end is that you have a sense of completion and that you have succeeded in saying what you needed to say to the best of your capacity. You will know this because you will no longer feel compelled to "have to tell you my feelings." If you arrive at this natural stopping point, make it a full stop, albeit with some care and some appreciation for the opportunity to have expressed your feelings. If you have had success with finding, feeling, and expressing your feelings, you will feel both comforted and exhausted. So, express your appreciation, kindly excuse yourself, and go for a walk. You will need some time alone to feel through what you have said, what you should have said,

and what you might say the next time. It is likely that you will have stirred feelings in your listener, which might actually be the next feeling-based conversation.

There are times, however, when you feel finished not because you are done with your feelings, but because you have expended all of your energy and have run out of steam. This is an important distinction to make because it happens often, especially when you are first learning how to express yourself. Running out of steam happens when the work is too hard and you just need a break, or because you found more feelings than you knew you had. These additional or deeper feelings should be contained until you are more prepared to speak them and when you have found a refreshed place and time to talk. This is the time to express appreciation and excuse yourself.

If you don't get tired out with the business of expressing your feelings, and you aren't overwhelmed by the sheer volume of feelings that come pouring out, you might simply feel peaceful. A natural end is a feeling of peacefulness, and it is a time when you, quite literally, have nothing more to say. You are done. You are finished. And you are surprised that you feel so good. You have worked hard and you have a right to stop at a good stopping point, a natural stopping point. This might come as a surprise to your listener, and s/he might not be ready to stop, likely because s/he has a lot of feelings that they would like to say. But this talking about feelings has been about *your* feelings, not your friend's feelings, and it best to stop the feeling conversation with the simple statement, "I am finished."

RULE # 8: CAREFUL USE OF "YOU" WHEN SPEAKING FEELINGS

The primary difficulty of expressing feelings, especially to an intimate partner, is that you will most certainly say something about the other person: what he or she said, what they didn't say that you thought they should have said, what they did, or what you thought they should have done. It is almost impossible to engage in communicating your feelings without some reference point. Most reference points are things that have been said or done. And when it comes to what you think was wrong, it is likely that you will speak of someone else doing it. For instance, you might start with, "Roger, when you left me the other day, I felt hurt." We know, and hopefully now you understand, that you are talking about yourself when you say, "You hurt me." "You hurt me" is equivalent to "I am hurt" but most people say the former rather than the latter. It is not easy to see that *you are talking about yourself even though you mention the other person* in the process. Your statement is and should be about *your hurt, not so much about what Roger said*, and certainly not about what is wrong with him for having said something that hurt you. If you do this feeling expression effectively, you will start with the point of reference like "Roger, you..." but never use his name or the pronoun "you" again, nor reference again what he said or did. Then you can talk about how you were hurt singularly because you value something or love something. When Roger is onboard with this understanding of communication, he will eventually know that you are talking about you, not him, when you talk about your hurt. Even if he knows that your feelings are about you, he will still have emotion in response to your feelings. Ideally, he will know his emotions and keep them to himself.

SUMMARY:

1. *Remember the positive:* Your feelings reflect your core and...the more you speak about your feelings, the less they will be negative, but this may take a while.
2. *There is a time and place for talking about feelings.* Find the right time and place.
3. *You will be imperfect and imprecise in speaking feelings.* "Practice makes imperfect"
4. *One at a time.* Work diligently to speak the entirety of your feelings without diversions and without "help" from your listener.
5. *It's not about agreement.* Feelings are not facts although all feeling-based words include facts. You can disagree with the facts but feelings themselves are never wrong.
6. *It takes two to tango.* Ideally, both speaker and listener are working the program.

7. *Whoever starts gets to finish.* Feeling conversation is not give-and-take and it's not taking turns. It is courageous speaking and patient listening.
8. *Note a natural end to a time of feeling-based expression.* Enjoy this time, enjoy being quiet, enjoy the fact that you expressed your feelings to someone whom you love.
9. Use *careful use of "you" when speaking your feelings.* You might start with "you did this or that…" but your feelings are about you, not your listener.

Chapter 7

It's All About Hurt

IN CHAPTERS 4 AND 5 we discussed the importance of speaking feelings and hearing feelings. We have discussed *hurt* in these chapters and noted how it frequently interrupts the process of both speaking and hearing feelings. Hurt isn't any more important than other feelings or emotions, but it is what often screams the loudest when it comes. We must remind you that hurt, as a feeling, is another of those important phenomena in life that are *real but undefined*, like time, life, and feelings. Recall also that we have to be very careful using such undefined-but-important words so as not to make something out of nothing. Phenomena like hurt can be understood by observation and consequences, not by definition. In other words, we *feel* hurt and see the results of being hurt even if we can't exactly define hurt. We are compelled to use this word *hurt*, unpack it, and find ways of using the word hurt as a *tool* of conversation about feelings without using it as a weapon.

Hurt is a central ingredient in a person's experience and expression of feelings, and it is even more important in relationships, whether intimate or casual. We need to be intensely aware of hurt, particularly our own hurt, the difficulty in adequately communicating hurt, and then become aware of other people's hurt. Hurt is a good word that implies something very important about a person because hurt is always generated by love and is always a precursor to the emotion of sadness. The more you become familiar with hurt, the better you will be at being understood and the better you will be at managing your own hurt and understanding how other people get hurt. As a result, you will be better at loving yourself and at loving other people.

While hurt is a key word in the business of feeling and expression of feelings, it is loaded with potential danger. If you properly and effectively understand your experience of hurt, you will be able to communicate the most important thing about you: what you love. More specifically, you will see that you love a lot of things, a lot of people, and a lot of ideas. You will see that *every time you are hurt, you will have lost something that you love*. Furthermore, if you listen and understand other people's hurt, you will be able to understand what they love. Unfortunately, the word hurt is not always used as a tool for self-understanding and communication. Rather, it is used as a weapon. We would like to take hurt out of the purview of attack and criticism and return it to its rightful place, a place of love. If we can speak of our hurt without attack and if we can listen to others' hurt without defense, we will find a truly remarkable way to communicate our feelings to one another.

HURT IS A LOVE PROBLEM

What in the world does "Hurt is a love problem" mean? It means that hurt is intrinsically and basically related to loving something. Here is how hurt generates from love:

- I love something.
- The thing that I love is attacked in some way.
- I lose this something that I love.
- I feel hurt.

Feeling hurt is not the end of the line. If I allow myself to feel hurt, lots of important things happen, all of them having to do with love. The first thing that happens when I allow myself to feel hurt is that I feel sad. Recall that sadness and joy are the two emotions associated with love: I feel joy when I love something, be it person, place, thing, or idea. I feel sadness when I lose something. So, if I would simply allow myself to lose something that

I love with grace, I would first be hurt and then I would be sad. The more we are practiced in this, the quicker we get to feeling sad…and eventually finish being sad. Sadness always ends if I allow it to run its course. Then, after feeling sad, I would go on to loving more and loving better. *Sadly*, this is not where the process usually goes. Instead of allowing myself to simply feel sad when I am hurt, I will generally run right past the feeling of sadness. I will run into fear and anger so as to protect myself from further hurt. This running past the love-based emotion of sadness into the defense-based emotions of fear and anger keeps us in a state of hurt but does not heal the hurt. In the pages that follow we attempt to help you learn how to feel hurt and finish hurt so you can love again and love better. When sadness, and the hurt that precipitated sadness are finished, you are in the desirable place of being able to love again, love better, and love wisely because you know that *everything you love will eventually be lost*. All the more reason to love more and know that whatever I love, I will lose; and when I lose something that I love, I feel sad.

We see that the phenomenon of hurt, the feeling of hurt, is a very central ingredient in life and particularly important for emotional maturity and ultimately for social maturity. Our belief is that everyone experiences hurt regularly, and the key to emotional and social maturity is to be aware of the hurt and the subsequent emotion of sadness that naturally occurs. It appears that there are some people who may not actually experience hurt and sadness, or perhaps they move so fast away from hurt that they fail to recognize it. Such people might not actually truly love anything or anyone, and as a result they may not actually be hurt. People who seem not to love anything are called psychopaths, an ugly term that should rarely be used. Psychopaths may like a lot of things, such as money, sex, property and power, but they may not truly love anything. As a result, they may not actually be hurt or feel hurt when they lose something because of this lack of love. They do however, tend to get quite angry when they do not get what they want. Importantly, there are very few true psychopaths around, but there are lots of people who run from hurt into anger.

You don't have to be a psychopath to get angry. All people get angry from time to time. However, anger is always an escape from hurt. Review the process that occurs when anger sidetracks the normal process of love-loss-hurt-sadness. The process begins the same but then takes a dramatic turn.

- I love something.
- This thing that I love is attacked in some way.
- I lose this something that I love.
- I feel hurt.
- I feel sad, but just for a moment then quickly...
- I become afraid that I will be hurt more, so...
- I override both the sadness and the fear that I feel and...
- I get angry in order to forestall the feeling of helplessness (helplessness is always a part of sadness).
- I express my anger.

Note how anger was not the first emotion that occurred. When I am hurt, my first real emotion is sadness, that followed by fear, and finally by anger. Unfortunately, this movement from sadness to fear to anger takes less than a second, so most people don't actually realize that they have been hurt, sad, or afraid. They just know that they're angry. This is why we have such expressions as "he just erupted into anger" or "she just gets so volatile." We experience the anger as if it came from nowhere, but anger never comes from "nowhere". Anger always comes when we feel we have to protect ourselves. A good part of our work with people is to help them understand that hurt and accompanying sadness always precedes anger, and then help them know that their hurt has come from the loss of something they love. Hence, hurt is a "love problem."

We need to make brief note to the possible overuse of the term "hurt." In such cases the term hurt is used as a subtle attack on the other person rather than a statement of one's feeling and what has been lost. A statement that begins with "I am just so hurt..." usually leads into an attack of some kind because it is generally followed by "because you..." did this or that. We want to bring the expression, "I am hurt" out of the negative arena that the expression normally has and into the realm of feelings, particularly the feeling of love, specifically the loss of what is loved.

When people say that they "have to tell you their feelings" and then immediately tell you how you have hurt them, they usually say things in anger. When we hear someone say that they are hurt, this statement almost always comes in the form of, "You hurt me *when*..." and then go on to tell you what you have done wrong. "You hurt me" should be an expression of *me*, not about *you*. "You hurt me" suggests that I have loved something and that I have lost something. If I can stay with the "me" part of this statement, I will then have the opportunity to talk about what I love. "You hurt me *when*..." is always going to implicate the other person. "You hurt me because..." can be an enlightening statement about what you love. Speaking about hurt as a personal experience that often occurs in an interpersonal situation is delicate, and it takes the emotional maturity we talked about in Chapter 4, Expressing Feelings. The expression of hurt is complicated because not all people are hurt by the same things.

DIFFERENT LOVES, DIFFERENT LOSSES, THE SAME HURT

We all know that our differences are what makes life interesting. And, while it is a wonderful thing when we discover that someone else likes what we like, there is that important distinction that stems from our core self that we are still different people. We are different people because of our passions and loves.

We don't love the same things. We love different things and we express our love in different ways. Because we all love differently, we feel differently when we have lost something that we love. We all get hurt when we lose something, but we don't all get hurt by the same losses. This means that you could be really hurt by some loss that wouldn't hurt someone else simply because the other person didn't love what you love. The love that you have, which lies underneath the hurt you feel, might not be understood by anyone but you because people do not love the same things. Because our core selves are all different, we love different things. Over just the past week we have heard of people's hurt and the things that they have loved and lost. These losses include:

- Favorite sports team loses a game
- Opportunity to play soccer lost

- A vacation opportunity lost
- Missed airline flight
- Hand burned
- Death of a pet
- A foreclosure of a house
- The filing for divorce
- Loss of an old friend
- Loss of money at a casino
- Unfaithfulness by a spouse
- Disappointing time with a granddaughter
- A political candidate lost an election
- An idea that might have saved the company $100,000
- And many experiences of being hurt by someone's words

All of these losses were due to someone's love for something. Look at these various losses and consider which ones seem important to you and which ones seem unimportant. For instance, the first on the list is "the loss of a sports team." The individual who reported this feeling of hurt was truly devastated when his favorite team lost to a previously low rated team. Very few people would understand why Jack would be so upset because they might think this is "only a game and not really important in the grand scheme of things." For Jack, in the exciting moments of the game, his favorite team is the thing he loves more than anything else in life. Some of the other losses noted above might seem understandable while others might seem trivial to you, but they are not trivial to the persons who were hurt by these losses. What was it like, do you think, when Jack told his wife about how terrible he felt when his team lost? Did she get it? Did she understand that he was hurt? Did she understand that he had a *love problem*? Those of you who are true sports fans understand feeling hurt by a sports team losing a game that most people care nothing about. In some places of the world wins and losses of sports teams is almost a life and death phenomenon, as is sometimes seen with the riots that occur after some soccer matches in England, the hockey games in Canada, and cricket matches in India. These riots are expressions of anger but the first feeling is one of sadness.

The second item on the list above has to do with a teenage girl that I recently saw after a period of several years. I originally saw her just after the death of her mother. This time, her father brought her in for a very different reason: she had been caught stealing something from a friends' home. As a result of this violation of the law she was not allowed to play soccer in her tenth-grade year in school and may not be allowed to play the sport for the rest of high school. With a little encouragement to admit to her *feelings*, she said the loss of soccer was far worse than the loss of her mother. Can you believe that? Soccer more important than the death of a parent? Yes, true. I am the only person she has dared tell this to, and I am glad to be able to understand her feelings, her hurt, and her his sadness of this great loss. We could make similar judgments, for or against, the hurt and sadness that the other people have over the various losses they suffer, but the hurt is the same, and the sadness is the same: they both come from having lost something they love.

The things we love may be different but the experience of love is the same: Love is based on having something that is important to us, being attached to something, revering something, and valuing something. We can share loves and values on some things but no two people love the same things with the same vigor. It may be quite difficult to understand how someone can deeply love soccer or a football team more than people, but if we want to have a relationship with someone, we will eventually need to understand what they love. Understanding someone's love for pets, people, or property doesn't mean that we share the same love for such things. It means something much more important: there is a piece of the person's soul that is connected to the thing that is loved. When you see what and how someone loves, you see something quite precious: you see a part of their core self. The people we described as "analysts" in Chapter 3 often love ideas, dreams and possibilities more than people and things practical. How difficult is it for someone with, say, a lover temperament to understand his analyst friend's love for ideas, or, a caretaker's love for property, or a player's love for excitement and adventure?

It is in the realm of speaking about hurt that much difficulty originates in relationships. Much of the loss and hurt that people suffer has less to do with things as it has to do with words. Sometimes words that are spoken, sometimes words that are unspoken. Because hurt does not lend itself to exact words, it is even harder to explain how someone's words can hurt us. We know this, however: words hurt.

HOW WORDS HURT

A popular reaction to verbal teasing that we grew up with in the 1950's was, "Sticks and stones can break my bones, but words can never hurt me." While this old adage was undoubtedly presented to help formulate strong character, it is woefully untrue. Words can be immensely painful. We can, for instance, offend people with our words when we speak our opinions. While opinions are seemingly attached to facts, the heart of opinions is in one's *feelings*, sometimes very close to one's core self. Opinions are the third form of the feeling expression, namely the cognition that comes after the physical and emotional elements and before the action. Every opinion has been conceived first with some kind of inner feeling from one's core that has passed through the physical and emotional elements and become a thought. So, when I express an opinion, I am expressing a feeling. People sometimes easily express their feeling-based opinions not always knowing that this opinion can hurt someone else who has a different "opinion." This does not mean that we should never say anything or be so worried about hurting someone that I never speak our feelings. It is just important to know that when you speak your *mind* about something, you are also speaking your *heart*. When you are speaking from your heart, you are speaking about your feelings, perhaps positive feelings that bring joy, perhaps hurt that brings sadness. However well spoken, well thought out, well felt out, words can be wonderfully fulfilling or horribly devastating.

Words hurt because they *represent* things that we love; they are symbols of things that we love. This means that words represent something, but in so doing, what they represent can be very far reaching. For instance, if someone says that you are an idiot or calls you stupid, the words "idiot" and "stupid" may not be important or accurate, but the implication is that your whole person is flawed. It is much easier to digest someone telling you that you are not a good artist, or even that you slur your words, than it is to hear the all-encompassing words like idiot or stupid. When I get mad at a friend and call him an idiot or something worse, I hurt his *feelings* because he has placed a hope in me that I will find him acceptable and of value.

Not only do words spoken hurt us; words that are *not* spoken can hurt us. Household partners, colleagues, and friends can be hurt when they are not appreciated for their individual contributions to their household, work, or their overall demeanor in caring for each other. We live in such a word-dependent society that words, or the lack of words, can have a powerful effect, both positively and negatively. Whether hurt is from words that someone has said or not said, hurt always results in sadness.

If I am working at something that I really love, there is a natural thought that accompanies this love-work: I want to share it. I want to tell the world, or at least I want to tell an important person about what I love. I want to tell someone how what I have done, what I have accomplished in my work, represents what is important to me. It is important for people to talk about what they love. This wanting to share a love experience is natural and good. It is the same love that you share with a friend when you are looking at a beautiful sunset or starlit sky. Sharing what we love is natural to us. It is important to learn to speak about the things that you love without the expectation that the other person will automatically share the feeling, or even understand your feeling. It is particularly hard to talk about something that is important to you when you know that your friend or partner doesn't love what you love. The task in this matter of talking about what is important to you first involves you're knowing what you love, learning to communicate what you love in terms that other people can understand, and ultimately understanding what other people love. If you can do these three things, you will not be able to avoid all hurt, but you will be able to reduce the frequency of hurt and the intensity of hurt that so often comes when we love different things.

Deb, wannabe master gardener, tells me about various plants, flowers, and soil just about every day, often several times a day in the summer. Not being a naturalist the way she is, I do not share the passion for nature that she does. So, it behooves Deb to tell me about what she loves, and it behooves me to listen to all this garden stuff if I am to understand her. But understanding her passion for things green is more than understanding such things; it is hearing her feelings and sensing her core values, one of which is an appreciation and respect for nature. I regret that in the earlier years of our relationship I would dismiss such nature talk as irrelevant because I don't love nature the way she does. Now, I am compelled to listen when she talks garden because when I do, I know her better, understand her better, and love her better, even if I don't love nature the way she does. However hard I work at listening and understanding, I often fail in that endeavor, and when that happens, Deb might easily feel hurt because I lost interest in things green. The work I do to hear, listen, and understand Deb's nature passion is not unlike the work she does to hear, listen, and understand my passion for playing basketball. We have both hurt each other in our earlier years together because we did not really understand that our core values were different. It is in this realm of failing to understand different loves, values, and passions where much hurt occurs. And when hurt stores up, it always turns to resentment.

WHEN HURT TURNS TO RESENTMENT

It's hard enough to be hurt and express hurt in situations that are seemingly benign like gardening or basketball, where you are doing something that you like to do. It is much harder to admit to hurt when you are doing something that you don't particularly want to do. Resentment is essentially silent anger that occurs while doing something you don't want to do or having done something you don't want to do. For as much as Deb likes working her gardens, she hates paperwork. Many years ago, before we first found Becky, then Cheri, both jewels as office managers, Deb did the health insurance claims required by our profession. This was a task that she truly detested, but it seemed to her a necessity. I needed to walk gingerly when she was fighting with some insurance company about what she deemed was our reasonable claim for our services for one of their insured. Before Becky and Cheri took this insurance load, Deb was frequently hurt by the challenge of justifying what we were doing with our clients. Think of it this way: we work diligently to serve someone, often helping them get through very difficult times or elements of their lives. This is a difficult task but very rewarding, especially when a client finds a way to really enjoy life after a long period of life dissatisfaction. Then, after hours of valuable person-to-person work, Deb had to do a completely different kind of work, something that she truly did not like and was certainly not good at. She had to justify in tangible terms why an insurance claim should be paid. This was "stupid" in Deb's eyes, because the value was in healing not proving the worth of the healing. Doing something "stupid," like filling out an insurance claim, after having done something quite profound, like saving someone's life, brought resentment to Deb. Why did she resent the insurance work? Because she loved using her time effectively to do something good for someone, then had to spend equal time doing unfulfilling work.

During those difficult times for Deb, now years in the past, I did not regularly express my appreciation for her doing this "stupid" work. You may not feel appreciated for the work you do or the sacrifices and losses you experience, especially for the things that you do that you don't want to do. Consider the case of a young couple with young children both working hard on the necessary tasks, one at home with the children with all that implies, the other early in a career, often working 60 hours a week. If they enjoy their work, they can be completely beat and yet feel this pleasant exhaustion while watching some inane TV program at night. A hard day's work, even if it's exhausting, can lead to a sense of accomplishment and pride. But having worked hard at something, even if you really like it, leads to a certain need for appreciation. When a person is working hard at a job that they like, there is a natural tendency to want recognition and appreciation for their hard work.

When that same person is doing something that they don't like doing, there is an even greater need for recognition and appreciation for the work. Consider how this might work with Patty and James. If she has worked hard, Patty might say something like,

- *Patty*: "James, I gotta tell you that as much as I enjoy working at the office, sometimes the workload is overwhelming," and then go on with something like, "Like, today, I had 50 emails to answer, some of them trivial, some of them important, so I had to go through each one to see which one needed my immediate attention. About that time Rita insisted that I assist her in dealing with some frustrated supplier."
- *James*: (Ideally says nothing, maybe shuffling his feet saying he is sorry for the difficult day she had.) James' silence might lead to Patty adding a statement like:

- *Patty*: "The whole day was overwhelming. To tell you the truth, I could just scream. I'm glad I like my job most days because when days like this come, I would prefer to be flipping burgers."
- *James*: says nothing, or perhaps, "Sounds like an awful day."
- *Patty*: "Yes, awful."

How different this conversation would have been if Patty had come home complaining about work and failed to talk about the fact that she loved her work. In the scenario we have painted, Patty admits that she both enjoys her work and feels overwhelmed by it. This two-part feeling expression gives James and opportunity to simply hear her feelings. Note that in this scenario both parties are abiding by the Rules of Engagement that we talked about in the previous chapter: Patty is saying how she *feels*, and James is listening to how she *feels*. This conversation might be short or it might get extended, but it has started out on the right path: speaking feelings and listening to feelings, albeit replete with a lot of emotion. This conversation is not so much about work, or even the exhaustion or frustration about work; it is about Patty's feelings, namely the love she has for her work and the challenges that comes with loving her work.

Instead of speaking of the breadth of her feelings, Patty might have said something like, "I can't stand my job. They just ask too much of me. I don't know why I continue to do this job." Had Patty just expressed her frustration, the conversation could easily have gone very differently. James probably would have felt assaulted and hurt, and could easily have said something crude to her like, "You can't quit; we depend on your insurance benefits, don't even think about that!" Negative statements are not good feeling statements because they are entirely defense-based emotions, entirely negative, and entirely about someone else or something else and they draw negativity in return. Had Patty just railed about work, James would have had no chance to really listen to her feelings, much less understand her feelings. He would have felt assaulted by Patty's complaints instead of being intrigued by her feelings. Instead of engendering understanding and compassion from James, Patty probably would have been met with quite the opposite. James would have been "defensive." Why would James feel defensive in this situation? Because he would have felt "attacked" with what is wrong with the world, not what is right about Patty. It is impossible to hear complaints without feeling a need to defend oneself. Complaining about something on the outside of me, like people and places, always leads to feelings of helplessness and resentment on the part of the person listening to the complaints. This situation could easily have escalated into Patty remaining focused on what she didn't like compared to the balance of both what she likes and doesn't like.

If you consider times when you have felt resentment, you will discover that most of these times have had to do with three things: 1) you weren't understood about what you said, 2) you weren't appreciated for what you did, or 3) you were assaulted by someone's complaints. Resentment can be prevented or healed by learning to express your hurt feelings and hear hurt feelings from others more effectively. A complicating problem, however, is that old hurts always complicate current hurts.

OLD HURTS

The largest psychological impact we have in life comes from our families of origin. Likewise, the most profound hurts in our lives have come from childhood and adolescence, usually because we didn't have the wherewithal to feel hurt, express hurt, and finish hurt. When most people speak of being hurt, they speak of things that are in the present not realizing that hurt in the present is always aggravated by hurt that has occurred earlier in their lives. Our attempt in this chapter is to help people recognize the hurt they have in the present and finish that hurt so that they do not drift into anger, anxiety, and depression. Feeling, expressing, and finishing hurt in the present is often difficult because current hurt is so infused with old hurt. It is almost impossible to be hurt by a small current assault without old unfinished hurts tagging on. This is why people get so out of sorts when they get hurt by someone's words. Those words are precariously stacked on top of a mound of old hurts, ready to topple with one more hurtful experience. A good deal of our work is to help our clients understand that the small hurts that might occur in a day can only be faced and finished if they are not infused with the larger older hurts of their earlier lives.

All hurts have to do with love in some way, and childhood hurts are no different. While abuse, neglect, and other traumas cause profound hurt, there are other experiences in childhood where we have been hurt by having lost something that we love. It is not so much the hurt that has occurred in childhood that affects us negatively, but the lack of appropriate expression of hurt that causes us difficulty with being hurt. Deb was raised in an environment where emotional expression was not permitted, while I was raised in family that was too permissive of emotional expression. So, while Deb needed to learn how to express her emotion, I needed to learn to govern my expression of emotion. Neither of us was raised in a family where there was an appropriate amount of freedom to express emotions and consequently develop emotional maturity. In these very different childhood environments, both of us were hurt, but in quite different ways. There are many other forms of hurt that occur in childhood, sometimes with undue limitations and rigidity, sometimes with no limits at all. In all of these experiences, we have lost something that we have needed and loved: appropriate emotional expression, appropriate love, appropriate limitation, appropriate freedom, and appropriate encouragement and challenge.

No one has a perfectly appropriate childhood. As a result, we all come into our adult lives with some "unfinished business" related to loss and accompanying hurt. Todd, was raised in a family where there were no limits placed on him whatsoever. He had the run of the south Chicago streets where he found his way into gangs, drugs, and early life promiscuity. Todd knew at the time that there was something wrong with the way his parents raised him. In truth, they didn't really raise him at all; they just let him find his own way. He raised himself the best he could, which amounted to doing anything he wanted to do, getting away with most of it, legal or illegal, and paying no consequences for his behavior. Todd came to find and to love his wife in his early 20's but was clearly unable to develop an intimate relationship with anyone. Intimacy for Todd was sex, drugs, and rock and roll. Understandably, he was not prepared for what it means to talk about his feelings, much less hear his wife's feelings. He did what he had always done: be prepared for danger at any moment and got angry when he was challenged in any way. I noticed when he came into my office, he immediately looked for the best exit in case of danger. Danger in my office? Yes, in Todd's perspective, any new place, any new person, any new situation is potentially dangerous. Todd was hurt with the freedom he had as a child, which we might also suggest was a lack of appropriate love in the form of limitation. Todd came to me thinking that he had an "anger problem," but Todd doesn't have an anger problem. He has a love problem. He wasn't loved right as a child and was deeply hurt by this lack of love together with the lack of limitation.

Many families exert too much limitation, usually combined with anger. People who have been raised in unduly strict environments are often more aware of the hurt that they received. Rigid families have what we call "passive abuse" by not allowing any freedom or opportunity for children. People growing up in such circumstances feel a hurt that is deep inside and hard for them to articulate. The hurt such people have is due to the fact that they haven't had the opportunity to learn by trial-and-error, which is the only way a person develops self-confidence. John was raised in one of those families where there was no room for liberty or choice. For example, even though John was a potentially great athlete, his father wouldn't allow him to play sports, always retorting back to John's request, "because I said so, and that is all there is to it".

The path John took with his life was substantially different from Todd. John has led a life based on avoiding conflict and responding to other people overly carefully. He became so good at being responsive that everybody liked him. He was always someone's something: son, father, husband, worker, brother, and work colleague. By the time I started seeing him at age 64, he had never had a sense of himself apart from his roles of worker and someone's relative. When his wife found someone else after 30 years of "pleasant marriage", he was devastated. He had done in his marriage what he had done with every other aspect of his life: he did what people wanted him to do with nary a blink. I think his wife never knew him as a whole person. Despite the kind and honest person he was, she did not know him. It never occurred to him to say much about himself in the form of expressing his feelings. When he came to my office, he was overwhelmed by the hurt of his wife's leaving him but the real hurt of his life began in his family where he wasn't allowed to have an opinion, much less a feeling like disappointment, hurt, or sadness. He was quite the opposite from Todd who had unlimited freedom, but Todd and John share the experience of old hurt that shows itself in current hurt.

Old hurts come in many forms but they are always "love problems": too much, too little, too inconsistent, or too much lost. The task we all have is to see what we loved, what we lost, and whether we have adequately finished these lost loves. Whether the loss comes from too much indulgence, too much limitation, or terrible abuse, childhood hurts remain in our souls until we find ways to finish these old hurts. Unfortunately, we tend to bring these old hurts into our adult relationships and mistakenly think that we are able to face, feel, and finish new hurts when we don't have the emotional mechanism to do that.

NEW HURTS

We normally think of hurt existing in intimate relationships but hurt can occur in any aspect of life. We are often hurt inadvertently by peripheral events and peripheral people in our lives. It is important to recognize the hurt that you experience in your work, in your play, and in your marginal relationships as well as the hurts you experience by the people you love. Because we tend to most easily recognize when our loved ones hurt us, we often fail to consider how we get hurt by those who are briefly or tangentially in our environment. Lots of relationship harshness and consequent hurt that occurs with our intimate others comes because we haven't found ways to feel hurt at work and play by people who are far less important to us. Work or social environments are where we spend most of our time with people, and it is the place where most hurt actually occurs. Because work is not the place to express feelings, especially feelings of hurt, we store up more hurt there than anywhere else. And it is a primary reason we are hardest on our intimate partners when we come home from work.

Work is not the only place where hurt occurs outside of the home. It also occurs in recreational and informal settings. Given my propensity for playing basketball I have the rather frequent experience of feeling hurt on the court. There is a court-based expression that has come into common usage, namely, "My bad." "My bad" is an interesting expression that used to be singularly heard on the athletic playing field. It is interesting in that it occurs regularly and often in my experience, so much so that there is a rare game when I fail to hear the "my bad". I have mused of the frequency of this self-effacing statement in comparison to the fact that people rarely admit to errors in most other spaces of life. I find the necessity of using the expression rather frequently given my limited basketball skills, and most players are all too generous with my limits. I do recall one time when I said, "My bad" after some failure on my part, a young buck retorted with, "Well, it's not your good!" Now, several years later, I recall the hurt I felt with this young man's comment. Here I was admitting my mistake, whatever that might have been, and he took privilege to hurt me. While trivial in its content, I did feel hurt. Clearly, the basketball court was no place for me to make any note of my hurt, much less admit to it to my attacker. These playful scenes where one would think everyone would be having a good time in cooperation with teammates and competition with competitors are frequent places where hurt occurs.

There are many such situations outside the realm of recreation where you get hurt but the situation does not allow you to feel hurt, much less express it. Someone pushes in front of you in the ticket line: you are assaulted, you have lost your place in line, and you are hurt, but it is unlikely that your attacker has any interest in hearing your hurt. You are finishing up buying groceries at the checkout and encounter that rare grouchy clerk who is obviously doing this job for the paycheck, not for the intrinsic value of scanning your groceries. Not long ago we had our grandkids at our cabin for an Independence Day celebration replete with fireworks over the lake. My grandson was disappointed because I didn't dare let him light one of the skyrockets. He was hurt. Nothing wrong with his wanting to light the fireworks, but he was hurt when I declined his request. Hurt comes in all sizes, shapes, and situations. The key in all this is to know how to deal with it.

While work, play, and brief encounters can cause hurt, by far the most hurt that people have experienced has come from family members, very often siblings. If we are hardest on our most intimate partners, we are next hard on other family members. Some of the most damaging times of childhood occur between siblings. You can get away from your friends in school by avoiding them or finding new friends. You can get away from people at work also by avoiding them or quitting your job. You can eventually get away from you parents by moving out. You can finish school and get away from teachers that you don't like. You can quit a sports team if you don't like the other players or the coach. You can even divorce your spouse, but you can't divorce your siblings. Siblings can be harder on each other than any friend, parent, coach, or teacher. Some of the worst "hurt" stories we hear while listening to a client's history are "sibling stories". Not always, but often the hurt inflicted by siblings is generally worse than any other social hurt because siblings naturally love one another even if they don't like each other. I was hurt by my siblings; my children were hurt by their siblings; my grandchildren are hurt by their siblings; my parents were hurt by their siblings and I can only guess that you readers have experienced the same thing.

RESOLUTION OF HURT PART I: FEELING THE EMOTION OF HURT

What do we do with all this hurt: hurt at home, hurt with my intimate, hurt with my relatives, hurt with friends, hurt at work, hurt at the grocery store, and hurt in play situations? You do the following in order:

- Recognize hurt when it happens.
- Remember that hurt always comes from love.
- Prevent hurt from migrating into anger.
- Determine whether you have the place, the time, and the person with whom you can share hurt, and if not,
- Consider coming back to this hurt at another time.
- Note that the feeling of hurt may have evaporated on its own.

We trust that you are becoming familiar with this process of feeling and finishing hurt.

Recognizing hurt usually begins by knowing that you are angry. If you recognize that you are angry (or less likely, recognize that you are afraid), you can look deeper into yourself and find the hurt that preceded and precipitated the fear and anger. This is a difficult process and you will not want to do it because admitting to hurt implies you're are helpless. In fact, *in the moment of hurt you are helpless*. You are helpless because you can't unhurt yourself and you can't turn back the clock and avoid the hurt altogether. The only valuable thing you can do that is good for you is to recognize it and prevent it from migrating into anger. As you get used to this feeling hurt, you will become friendlier with it, you will come to realize that the feeling of helplessness is short lived, and you will actually prevent getting angry. But this is not something that is easy to do, and it will take you a while to catch hurt before it migrates into anger.

Remembering that hurt always come from love helps you see that you have lost some of what you have loved. We discussed this matter of love underlying hurt throughout much of this book but it behooves us to review it here. If you have been hurt, you have lost something that you valued (or loved). People get hurt for different *reasons*, all of them *reasonable*, at least reasonable to the person who is hurt. Caretakers get hurt when property is wasted; analysts get hurt when their ideas are rejected; lovers get hurt with they have lost some connection, and players get hurt when they are not able to physically demonstrate their feelings. We get hurt for different reasons from "external hurts" and from "internal hurts."

External hurts are those that come from someone or something outside of yourself. We are focusing in this chapter on the people who have hurt us with what they have said, but we can certainly be hurt by what people did, or for that matter, what the environment did to us. In the case of what has been said to you, you have been *assaulted* by someone (usually unintentionally), but you might also have been assaulted by the weather, by a religious intolerance, or a political movement. External assaults are easier to see because you can see the effect of the hurt because of your emotional reaction. If someone says your hair looks stupid, you know you are hurt, or at least you know that you are sad or angry. Likewise, you know that you are upset when it starts to rain on the day you forgot to take your raincoat.

Internal hurts are much harder to recognize as assaults because they come from you. Many people have said to us that they do not love themselves, but this is rarely true. Often, they don't *like* themselves, or more accurately, they don't like something about the way they look or sound. Sometimes they don't like the shape of bodies, their limited ability to read, the way they walk, or even their limited ability to play chess. They may also not like what they have said or done, which upon hindsight seems "stupid." No one likes to make mistakes, but when made, they are always disappointing. Mistakes always hurt you, but more accurately, you have hurt yourself. Internal hurts are also "love problems," namely that you have lost something that you love: yourself. We previously noted that it is natural to love oneself, so when I criticize myself, feel ashamed of myself, or chastise myself, I have lost some of this natural self-love. Unfortunately, the concept of self-love has been misconstrued and misunderstood by many people, including many well-meaning writers and religious leaders who propose it as vanity, pride, or hubris. Self-love is a recognition of the goodness inside of you, not to be confused with what other people think of you. Desiderata says it well: "If you compare yourself to others, you will be vain or bitter, for always there are greater and lesser than you." You cannot love yourself too much because seeing your inner goodness is essential in life. When you truly see your own inner goodness, you will then be able to see and value both your successes and failures in life without self-condemnation. When I hurt myself with undue self-criticism and by comparing myself to others, I am hurt indeed.

Prevent hurt from migrating into anger. Anger is the normal human reaction to feeling helpless because anger is part of our nature to be used in truly dangerous situations. You need to be angry, or at least raise your voice and act angry, if someone physically accosts you on the street. Anger, or the appearance of anger, is left over from our more primitive state when we needed to look angry to protect ourselves from predators. When you see a lion attacking a prey, two elk vying for supremacy, or the many other natural animal competitions, you see that the animal looks angry. The same is true for you as a human. You need this angry *look* or angry *voice* when you are really attacked, but chances are, you won't be really physically attacked any time soon. Years ago, Deb was hiking alone in the Redwood Forests. Prior to her hike she stopped in at the ranger station and commented that she had seen signs to be aware of mountain lions. Deb asked the best course of action should she encounter one. The ranger, assuming she was with others asked "how many in your party"? "Just me" said Deb. The ranger was a bit taken back and then said, "Well, first, make a lot of noise as you go along; second, if you see a cat, try to look big and sound mean; third, if he comes at you, well, run like hell."

Most of the time, you aren't going to encounter wild cats or be accosted in the street. You do however, often get angry as a knee-jerk reaction to something that has happened that has hurt you. When you get angry, you have skipped over being hurt, and you need to retreat to this more basic feeling that has to do with love, not with protection from some predator. The "predator" generally is that young insecure guy on the court, the cashier who has an unhappy marriage, the brother-in-law who copes with his unhappiness with off-color jokes in front of the kids, your four-year old acting like a four-year old, the 14-year old who knows nothing but says everything, or your spouse who said something that hurt you.

If you can recognize that you have been hurt, avoid allowing hurt to migrate into anger, and know that you have a "love problem," *you can decide what to do about your hurt*. This process naturally brings you to a place of considering what you should do about the hurt you have suffered. Specifically, you need to consider whether you should say anything about your hurt, and if you do, when and where you should say something about it. *You can think clearly about your hurt only when you're no longer in a defensive emotional state.*

RESOLUTION OF HURT PART II: THINK BEFORE YOU SPEAK

In order to be able to speak clearly about your hurt, you have to be able to think clearly about your hurt. The only way for you to think clearly is for you to be aware of all the emotions associated with hurt. Every thought we have has some emotional foundation, a foundation that cannot be ignored or repressed. Recall from Chapter 1 that our feelings are first physical and emotional before we come to thinking, much less saying something. We cannot meaningfully express our feelings without knowing that thoughts do not come to us without first passing through an emotional grid. Speaking our thoughts without going through the emotional process always leads to miscommunication and often into arguments and rage. We have to think clearly before we speak, but the only way we can do that is to have felt through all emotions that have occurred in the process of expressing our feelings. If we speak without first recognizing the emotional-physical foundation of feelings, our speech will be infused with unfinished and ungoverned emotions. The task of speaking feelings is to recognize and respect the emotional content of feelings without allowing the emotion to dominate and without disregarding the emotion.

In order to speak about our feelings of hurt, we have to apply the basic principal of how to speak any feeling:

- Know what we feel.
- Recognize the emotional component of our feelings, such as helplessness or sadness
- Allow this emotion to run its course
- Think clearly, and then
- Speak

This five-part process of speaking feelings, especially when hurt is involved, is a difficult assignment. Most people do not go through this process effectively because they get stuck in being unable to know that they are hurt. If they can't recognize having been hurt, they won't be able to allow themselves to feel helpless and sad. We can think clearly only when we have felt and finished the emotional process, which is feeling hurt, feeling helpless, and generally feeling overwhelmed by our emotions. If you have felt these feelings, the emotion subsides and you can think about what you might say about the hurt. Above all remember your feeling is a very central part of you, something to be appreciated and understood. So, before you speak, you need to keep in mind several things:

- Consider of how important your feeling is, like whether it is something that you are compelled to communicate or whether it is just a passing emotion.
- Consider whether the other person is someone who has true interest in you and someone willing to allow you the "wide berth" you need to express your feelings.
- Consider whether there is sufficient time for you to express your feeling.
- Consider whether this is the right place to express your feeling.
- Keep in mind that your expression of feelings will likely generate feelings in your listener.

This process of determining when and how to express your feelings of hurt is all about thinking: knowing that you love something and knowing that you have lost something. Then you are prepared to actually talk about how you have felt hurt. Go forth with courage into talking about hurt just as we have discussed in Chapter 4 trying to abide by the Rules of Engagement, we outlined in Chapter 6. Remember, for instance, that your words will be imperfect and imprecise.

When you have spoken yourself, note the joys and sorrows that you have. You are happy that you got to say something. You might also be sad that you didn't say all that you wanted to say, or that you said some things poorly. Leave the conversation with some expression of appreciation for your listener. You might need to ask for some time to be alone with your feelings. You might notice that you are hurt less and healed more. We know that the program that we suggest for expressing feelings of hurt is replete with various dangers, but we believe you will get better at it as you wade through these murky waters of feelings. There is some danger of over-using the "hurt" word by some people, but a larger danger of under-utilizing the word with most of us. Furthermore, communicating feelings isn't just about hurt.

IT'S NOT ALL ABOUT HURT

How odd it must seem to end this chapter with what seems like a contradiction to the title of the chapter. It's all about hurt? It's not all about hurt? What are we trying to say? We're trying to say when we talk about "feelings," we are talking about more than hurt even though our main focus in this chapter has been on hurt. We would be remiss to suggest that all feelings are about hurt or that most feelings are about hurt, which they most certainly are not. Most feelings are not actually about hurt, but when we fail to recognize, govern, and appropriately express hurt, that hurt dominates our emotional functioning. Remember our feelings are reflections of our core selves, all which is good about us, all that we value and love. We feel hurt only because we have goodness inside, purity inside, and love inside. An important matter in expressing one's feelings is to speak of the many feelings that are positive and filled with gratitude. We began this chapter with an extensive examination of hurt, so let's close this chapter with a brief discussion of joy. Recall that joy and sadness are both generated by love. If you want to dramatically improve a relationship, you need to learn how to recognize and process the experience of love which always has the emotions of joy and sadness.

Sometimes joy is a simple, indescribable experience like we had the night before I wrote these words. We were at our cabin sitting on our dock in the waning dusk of the day and saw three loons pass in front of us just a few meters away, seemingly in complete disregard of our presence. We just watched as the three loons took turns diving into the water only to surface some further out in the lake barely within eyesight. This was one of those ineffable experiences that brought a sense of joy, peacefulness, a connection to nature, or perhaps it was simply gratitude. The moment passed but the memory stayed. It was a joyful moment and it remains a joyful memory. Sitting there watching the loons we both remained silent. Then later we both talked of the profound joy we each experienced. Experiences like these are important in a relationship. The joy we each experienced and then expressed wasn't discussed and figured out. It was simply experienced in silence, albeit side by side, and then later, expressed, each in our own way true to our natures.

The emotion of joy could come like it did to us last night, simple and wondrous, but it can come in many other forms, times, and places. When we find ourselves saying, "Oh, do you remember when…" and consequently find ourselves experiencing the joy that we previously felt, the joy isn't just a reflection of a past experience, it is a new joy built upon the recall. Joy is most easily recognized through one or more of our five senses. Whenever Ron and I hear Pachelbel's Cannon, we glance at the other and smile if not get up and embrace into a dance. Just hearing the Cannon bring us a mutual joy that is indescribable. It is easy to recognize joy when enhanced through our five senses but joy also comes through intuition, cognition and fantasy.

We originally wrote an entire chapter on the feeling of joy identifying the many possible joyful experiences that are available to us with our five senses, but we decided to defer that discussion until we can do a more exhaustive presentation on this wonderful and valuable topic. In recognition that joy is as much a part of ourselves as hurt, we want to briefly make note of the experience of joy that goes beyond our five senses, a level of joy we might simply call random joy or intuitive joy. Random joy can be the result of a particular anticipation, or simply an unidentifiable physical release or thrill. Whatever we call these times, we should make note that they can bring us great joy and great pleasure. We think that these moments are ones where we have an experience that does not lend itself exactly to a physical, emotion, cognitive, or active experience, although any or all of these can come into play. Rather, this type of experience seemingly transcends all of our four basic emotional expressions. It might be the "flow" that Csikszentmihalyi (1997) speaks of. We have come to use the term "spiritual" to describe feelings, and also prefer this term when we are talking about intuitional feeling. If you allow intuitive feelings to roam around your body and soul, you will come to trust the experience and then the expression of it. These types of joyful experiences are unique to you on a spiritual level. Like all our emotions, this form of joy is something that simply emits from our core as a reminder of our spiritual nature.

We encourage you to speak of all of your feelings however you do that best, namely physically, emotionally, cognitively, or actively. We also encourage you to speak about your intuitional feelings as often as possible and as often as it is wise to do so. If you have experienced what you determine to be an important intuitional feeling, it behooves you to express it because an intuitive experience that is joyful is an important part of you. The more you notice these intuitive experiences, the more you will recognize that they lead to the emotion of joy. As you allow yourself the freedom to feel these feelings, you will discover that they come in various experiences in life, some of which occur in regards to people, some with work, some with play, and some when you are alone. You can discover that all of these intuitional feelings have at their core a feeling of love that then leads to the emotion of joy. Indeed, some intuitional experiences should be kept private, but many times, it is very worth sharing them.

Our point here is that sharing your joy is just as important as sharing your hurt. Hurt, like joy, comes from your soul. Both joy and sadness are reflections of that most inner piece of you we call Core Self. We recognize that while this chapter is dedicated to helping you understand your hurt, we know that joy is just as important in communicating yourself.

SUMMARY:

1. Hurt is a universal human experience that cannot be avoided
2. Hurt originates in love. I am hurt when I lose something that I love
3. Very often, what is lost is a sense of self-regard, i.e. I feel hurt when I am criticized
4. Hurt causes a temporary feeling of helplessness: I cannot unhurt myself
5. Hurt almost always leads to the fear of being hurt more
6. Hurt often leads to anger
7. Sometimes hurt leads to hiding
8. Hurt is almost always unintentional; i.e. the person who hurt me did not intend to hurt me
9. We are hurt by different things because we value different things
10. Hurt unrecognized can turn to resentment
11. Hurts that occur in the present may also stir hurts that occurred in the past
12. Hurt is resolved by recognizing it and accepting the temporary feeling of helplessness
13. Some hurt needs to be expressed, but not all hurt should be expressed
14. The experience of hurt can be balanced by recognizing the joys of love and life
15. We all have an instinctive, intuitive feeling that becomes quite joyful

Chapter 8

Temperamental Conversations

WE HAVE BEEN EXAMINING the nature of feelings in the previous chapters, and have made note of the fact that feelings are so important that they can't be defined. They can, however, be observed and experienced. We have discussed the expressions of feelings that include physical sensations, emotions, cognition, and activity, all four of which emanate from feelings. We discussed the important nature of emotions, perhaps the most problematic element of feeling expression but have noted that emotions bring great joy in life. We discussed the importance of expressing feelings and the challenges of hearing feelings in light of the "rules of engagement" when we express feelings. We discussed some important personality differences that are displayed in the experience and expression of feelings. Finally, we discussed the centrality of hurt in the human experience. We have given a few examples of how people express feelings and how they hear feelings. We would now like to give a few examples of how people might engage one another with a deeper understanding of their feelings. From the very beginning of this discussion we admit that the experience of feeling is so personal and deeply internal that any expression of this feeling is imprecise at best. We adjure you to move forward into these murky waters of feeling expression noting particularly the emotions that are so important in feelings and the rules of engagement that we have proposed.

It is easiest for us to begin with a personal example noting how imprecise our own expression of feelings is, and yet how central our feelings are to each of us and then how important they are as we attempt to express these feelings to one another. As I write these words, I am looking out my office window at about 12 inches of snow that has recently fallen here in Wisconsin where we live. I thought I would take a break from my writing and do a little snow plowing. Physical work is a great break from the challenge of writing. I needed to pull Deb's car out of the garage that is in the lower section of our barn/office in order to get to the tractor. To do so, I had to carefully back the car out of the garage at an angle to make room for the tractor. But as I did so, I heard a crunch on the outside of the car. I felt something immediately. First, I felt a mild stomach agitation and then I felt scared. Hearing a crunch sound when you are driving a car suggests that you hit something, but regardless of what the "crunch" actually meant, I felt an immediate feeling of fear, just like the immediate fear we discussed in Chapter 5 when you hear a siren while driving. Notice that my first expression of feeling was physical quickly followed by an emotional feeling. Note that I didn't attend to my "stomach feeling" but raced into my emotional feeling which is usually the first experience that I recognize when I feel something. Skipping quickly past the cognitive expression of feelings, I put the brake on the car and drove forward. Then I got out of the car hoping to see some snow or ice that I had run over. No such luck. I saw that I had run into the brick wall in our parking lot. Then what did I feel, think, say, or do? After a brief guttural expression, I told Deb, who was shoveling some snow nearby, that I had just damaged her car. Then I put my head in my hands while I stooped down to the brick wall and just felt "awful." What does "awful" mean? It means that I felt sad. By the way, in between the seconds of seeing the damage to Deb's car and my feeling awful, I felt a tinge of fear. What was that about it? This fear was different in nature from the fear I felt with the original crunch because this fear was of Deb's hurt and anger. That fear was graciously assuaged by Deb coming over to me and putting her hand on my back while I had my head in my hand. And even more graciously, she soon said that she wasn't upset about the damage to the car, which seemed quite generous of her. Now, about two hours past this event, I still feel "something" in my stomach. So, what is this "something"?

It is most likely residue of the sadness that I yet feel about having damaged Deb's car, an example of the "love problem" that we discussed. What is the "love problem"? It is a combination of loves: I love Deb, certainly. I love the car to some degree, and love any kind of property being the caretaker I am by temperament. I love being careful when I drive. I love plowing snow. I love writing and then taking a break from writing to do something physical. So, in this whole process, I have felt this myriad of things…and yet feel some of those feelings, no longer any fear, but yet still some sadness. I will need to allow this sadness to "finish" as we discussed in order to have this incident be a part of my past and not a part of my present or my future.

So, what was the feeling that emanated from my core that erupted into my emotional reaction and my action? The feeling is one of valuing, namely valuing property and people, specifically Deb. Consider what might have happened if I had not allowed myself to feel sad upon damaging the car. Fear, yes. Then anger. Then, some kind of defense or explanation. Then, God forbid, some kind of anger at the car, the brick wall, or worse yet, anger at Deb. Underneath all these defensive reactions would be some kind of anger at myself. I didn't get angry at myself, except perhaps for just a moment. I did learn something in this process but only after allowing my emotions to run their course. I learned to be more careful when backing out the car when the tractor is still in the driveway. I can profit from this unfortunate experience only if I allow myself to feel, but the predominant feeling is emotion, and the predominant emotion is sadness. All experiences in life have feelings at their core and all feelings have emotional components to some degree. The key is to recognize the feelings that you have, note the emotional reaction that usually occurs with the feeling and allow the emotion to occur, govern this emotional reaction, and allow the emotion to come to rest. I have done defensive and reactive things in the past, but they didn't occur this time. I continue to work on keeping such secondary reactions apart from the real experience of feeling, which is loving something.

Let's consider some other examples of how feelings occur almost always with a predominant emotional element in other circumstances. We normally think of times when feelings get out of hand and turn to anger in some form. But as we have discussed in the previous chapter, it is equally important to note the two love-based emotions of joy and sadness that occur every day, and occasionally find time to express these emotions, which are always based on loving something.

ENCOUNTERS WITH LOVE-BASED EMOTIONS

When we have encounters with significant emotional elements, we are always dealing with love in some way. Recall that we discussed how all four basic emotions relate to love in some way: joy having something I love, sadness losing something I love, anger having lost something that I love, and fear potentially losing something that I love. We have suggested that the emotions of joy and sadness are "love-based emotions" while fear and anger are "defense-based" emotions, but more accurately, all four emotions have an underlying love element. We encourage people to express their feelings as frequently as possible but also as much as is socially responsible. We have also noted that it is unfortunate that "I need to tell you my feelings" has a negative ring to it suggesting that I want to tell you something wrong, usually wrong with what you said or did. Let's consider some ways you might express the love-based emotions of joy and sadness that occur daily.

> *Mary*: John, I gotta tell you about something that happened to me today. It was a great experience, but kinda weird.
>
> *John*: Mary, I'm all ears.
>
> *Mary*: I was doing my morning walk and had this odd feeling. I can't put my finger on it, but it was really good. Weird, huh?
>
> *John*: Weird perhaps, but good, huh? Tell me more.
>
> *Mary*: I was on my standard trek on Riddle Road when I felt the need to stop. So I stopped walking. I didn't know why I needed to stop, but something told me that I should just stop. Like, "stop and smell the roses," perhaps.

John: Sounds really interesting, Mary. Tell me more.

Mary: There isn't much more I can say except to note that I felt extremely peaceful. Perhaps it had something to do with the spring air or the noise of the tractor in the field, or something else. I just felt peaceful. Peaceful. Wow, it was just weird, but weird in a good way, understand?

John: I think I get the picture. Sounds wonderful. I wish I had been there with you.

Mary: You know, John, I think it might not have happened if you had been there. It seemed like, well, like uh, like some kind of a very personal feeling that didn't have to do with you or us. It didn't even seem to have to do with me. It was like I sometimes feel in meditation, like I was just at peace with everything and everyone.

John: Mary, I am truly happy for you. Thanks for sharing.

Mary: Thanks for listening. Weird, huh? Good, huh?

John: Yup, weird…good.

Oh, that people would allow themselves to have these moments. We think that everyone has such experiences but fail to take notice and take the minute to experience such things. Weird, yes. Good, yes. Feeling, yes. Special, personal experiences that Mary had may need to remain private, but they can be shared only if John is with her, not asking questions, not talking about his feelings, and not interrupting with his feelings. In fact, if people are able to recognize important personal positive emotional experiences, they might be better able to share positive interpersonal experiences. Similar good feelings can come when two people are together in some common activity, like enjoying a meal together.

John: This is just a great meal, isn't it, Mary?

Mary: Absolutely. What makes it great for you, John?

John: I don't know. It just feels great. Good food, of course. Good service, which is always important to me. Good setting. The wine, simple as it is, is good. You know how I like good simple wine.

Mary: I do know, John, but please tell me more. It's exciting to share your feelings.

John: You know, it just occurred to me that when I said what I liked about the meal I didn't include you in the topic. That seems odd, doesn't it?

Mary: I'm not offended, John. I am all ears about your feelings about the goodness of the meal. I know that I am a part of it, but this is your feeling, and I enjoy hearing anything you have to say about it.

John: Thanks, Mary. For a moment I was a bit scared that I might have offended you when I spoke of the service, the meal, the wine, but didn't mention you.

Mary: I'm good, John. We're good. But this moment is your moment, your experience, and your feeling. You're good.

John: Just sitting here, just seeing what we have at this moment: the meal, the service, the wine, and "thou." It all seems great. Just a great feeling.

Mary: Wonderful. Thanks for sharing. Please pour me another glass of Shiraz.

John: Yes, and (clink), to your health.

Sound too impossible to do. Not at all. The words are imprecise, but the feeling is perfect, and the core self underneath the feeling is pure. Granted, not all walks spur a peaceful experience, and not all meals are special, but there are a lot more times like this if you can just let yourself feel the peace and specialness. Consider another "John and Mary" interaction that is more interpersonal and replete with feelings:

Mary: John, I need to tell you my feelings.

John: I'm with you Mary. You know, when I used to hear, "I need to tell you my feelings," I was always prepared for being criticized. Sorry for that. My bad.

Mary: Not entirely your bad, John. I admit that I have often used the "F word", feelings, as a way of telling you something I didn't like about you. My bad there. Glad we're able to hear each other's feelings without that kind of attack and defense. Those were some difficult times.

John: Glad they're over. So, let me have it: tell me your feelings. I'm all ears.

Mary: I'll do my best, but I probably need to start with something that is bothering me.

John: Oddly, I am not scared. I know that this whole feeling business is about who we are individually, not about the other person. Go ahead.

Mary: I've had this weird feeling lately, John. You know about these "weird feelings" that happen from time to time with me.

John: I certainly do. And I have learned to attend to them. Weird away, Mary. When you go weird, things always turn out good.

Mary: You know how we have had some intense times together in all kinds of settings.

John: Yup. That's part of our life.

Mary: I'd like for us to talk to someone who could help us continue in this path that we've been on for some time now.

John: You mean like a therapist or something?

Mary: Yes, but the word "therapist" has a negative ring to it, like we have some kind of problem or issue. I don't think we have something wrong that needs attention. I would just like to continue to get better at communicating feelings the way we've been learning.

John: I don't think therapy is just for people with issues and problems. We don't have any relatives in the area, like a wise old grandfather or uncle. So maybe seeing someone professionally could help us make a good thing better.

Mary: Seems weird. Going to a therapist to make a good thing better.

John: We're weird, right? Well, at least you are weird.

Mary: I'll accept that as a complement.

John: Exactly.

These are but a few of the possibilities that could occur if you begin to think that "I want to tell you my feelings" doesn't have to be something wrong. It's a good way to start talking about feelings. It's a way to get the negative out of the feelings word. Consider what you might say if you just said how you felt good about something. It could be a movie you saw, a song you heard, a moment of personal reflection, a thought, a hope, a nostalgic memory. The more you work on saying something positive, something joyful to you, the more you will accustom yourself to speaking about your feelings in general, which will sometimes be joy, sometimes sad. The better you get at saying something that has a joyful element, the better you will get at saying something that has a sad element. You will find yourself noticing the frequency of both joy and sadness in your life and you will be freer to express both of these emotions as part of expressing feelings.

We have had many times together over the recent months reflecting on the loss of our daughter, times that we had alone, times that we had together, and serendipitous times that we have had, like the odd meeting yesterday, at a cobbler shop. We hadn't been to this shoe repair shop before, so when we were greeted by a young woman at the counter, we asked if she were the proprietor. No, she wasn't the owner, but then she noted that her boss, the owner, had just recently died, and then she immediately teared up saying that he had been a wonderful mentor to her. This led to our sharing that our daughter had died six months ago, which then led to Deb walking around the counter to hug her, both women crying, both comforting each other, while I explained to the next customer that we had both lost loved ones. He then told me that his son had lost a child recently. The whole scene was replete with feelings, with sadness, and also with joy, all of which was born of love.

Consider how our fictitious John and Mary might be free to express sadness in their daily lives:

> ***John:*** Mary, I need to tell you about something that happened today that had a significant emotional impact on me.
>
> ***Mary:*** What happened, John?

John: I was listening to the radio on my way to work and heard about another public shooting in San Antonio.

Mary: Really. I didn't know there was another one of these. What happened?

John: Mary, I'm not really sure what happened, who the perpetrator was, or why he did what he did. I do know that he shot and killed several of his family members.

Mary: Terrible. Tragic.

John: You know, of course, that we have had a spate of such things over the recent years and I sadly admit that I have become familiar with hearing such things. But this time it was quite different for me.

Mary: Please tell me about it, John.

John: I felt profoundly sad. I had to pull the car over to the side of the road because I was so overcome with grief. I just sat there with my head in my hands for a few minutes.

Mary: I am so sorry, John.

John: I don't know who these people are. I don't know anything else about the situation, the why's and such. I just felt profoundly sad. And I actually still feel sad.

Mary: John, you love people so deeply. It's a wonderful thing to see. You just love these unknown, faceless people. I like this part of you.

John: Thanks, Mary. I feel better. Still sad, but better.

This encounter between John and Mary can help them come together, understand each other better, and love each other better. Why is that? Because John is talking about something he loves and Mary understands the love that John has for these unknown people. It is good for John to feel sad, good for him to weep, and good for him to share his feelings. As a result of his sharing his feelings, replete with emotion, it is also good for Mary, and it is good for their relationship. They share in grief just as they have shared in joy.

Importantly, people love different things and hence derive joy from loving something and experience sorrow when losing something. Consider how John and Mary might face a loss of something that is important to Mary but not to John. Mary is a pet-lover and John is not, so how might they deal with the death of Mary's cat? A conversation might occur on the way home from the vet's office where Mary chose to euthanize her cat.

> *Mary*: It's very hard on me that I chose to put Gracie down, John. I can't believe I did that. I chose to take her life away. How could I do that to someone whom I have loved?
>
> *John*: Tell me more, Mary. I'm really interested.
>
> *Mary*: I loved Gracie for 20 years. I just can't live without her. It just seems horrible that she has died. It's like losing a member of the family. I know this must be silly to you.
>
> *John*: It's not silly at all, Mary. Gracie was a part of the family just as much as the kids and me. I understand that.
>
> *Mary*: But you don't feel that way about Gracie.
>
> *John*: No, I don't, Mary, but this is about your feelings not mine. I'm interested in you and in your feelings, and even more, I'm interested in what you love. You loved Gracie.
>
> *Mary*: I still do love here. It's like she is still here.

John: I stand corrected. Yes, you love her still. You still love her.

Mary: How can that be, that I love an animal as much as I love a human being.

John: I don't know, Mary, but you loved her, love her, and might always love her.

Mary: I still can't believe that I took life away from her today. I wouldn't do that with you or with the kids, or with any human being. How can I do that so easily?

John: It wasn't easy, Mary. It was hard. Really hard.

Mary: Unbelievably hard. How am I going to live this sadness and the guilt that I chose to kill someone…I mean some animal.

John: You love…love Gracie. That's what counts here.

Mary: It seems that I should love people more than animals.

John: I don't think there is any difference in what we love. We just love stuff, sometimes people, sometimes animals, sometimes things. I love cars. They're not even alive.

Mary: It has been hard for me to understand how you love cars. But I see what you mean. Do you love cars as much as people?

John: Sometimes. That must sound really weird. Weirder than loving an animal.

Mary: I feel better talking about this. I don't think most people would understand people loving animals and cars as much as people.

John: I don't understand how people love football teams, but I have come to believe that their love for the Green Bay Packers is just as valid as my love for cars and your love for cats.

Mary: I guess love is just weird sometimes.

John: Love is certainly weird.

Note that John first listens to Mary and tries hard to let her grieve for what she loves without making any judgment. Furthermore, he doesn't try to moderate her grief by giving platitudes like, "Well, Gracie is in kitty heaven," much less any denigrating of her love for her pet like, "Gracie was just an animal for goodness sake." Rather, he did his best to help Mary grieve for the loss of something that was very dear to her. He dared to make an example of how his love for cars was not something that most people have but was real to him. How difficult is it for us to understand what people love and why they love what they love. Very often, there is no "why" to loving; there is just loving something.

ENCOUNTERS WITH DEFENSE-BASED EMOTIONS

We try to help people increase the amount of love-based emotional expressions and decrease their defense-based expressions of fear and anger. We teach that joy and sorrow develop character, self-esteem, and social esteem whereas fear and anger usually do not. Yet we are cognizant that people get afraid and angry, often frequently, so to dismiss the importance of these defense-based emotions would be unrealistic. We try to help people start where they are emotionally regardless of the emotion that they feel. Indeed, we work to help people find the love that is always underneath fear and anger, but that is not always possible because people are so caught up in feeling these defensive emotions that they cannot actually see that they have a "love problem" as we say. Let's start this discussion by considering how John and Mary could migrate through the murky waters of their feelings, together with the emotions that are stirred up. First, a worst-case scenario:

> *Mary*: Well, thanks for the late anniversary card. I've got to tell you though; I was really hurt that you forgot our wedding anniversary yesterday. How could you forget such an important thing like that?
>
> *John*: Gosh, love, I don't think much about anniversaries. I am just glad your mom sent a Facebook notice wishing us a happy year. I went right out and got the card when she said that. You know, every time I see some LinkedIn notice of someone's job anniversary, I think, "Who cares?" Does it really matter how many years someone has been at a job or how long someone is married? Is the actual date of our wedding anniversary really important?
>
> *Mary*: It is to me. I wish it were for you.
>
> *John*: I'll try to remember it next year? So, hey, happy 14th anniversary, dear.
>
> *Mary*: 19 years, thank you very much. We've been married 19 years! I just want to cry that you don't know how many years we've been married, nor do you really care about it. I am really hurt about this.
>
> *John*: I don't understand why you are hurt about this.
>
> *Mary*: You really don't understand?
>
> *John*: Honestly, I don't understand the whole thing about "hurt." I hear the word from you a lot these days.

Mary: That's because you hurt me every single day. We need to talk.

John: We are talking. What do you mean "talk"? Talk about what?

Mary: Feelings.

John: What feelings do we need to talk about?

Mary: Hurt, for instance.

John: I'm not sure I have much to say about feelings, you know me: I don't "do feelings".

Mary: I do.

John: (Long audible sigh).

Mary: Let's just talk and we'll see where it goes.

John: Alright, but I got to tell you, that's a scary thought. I will try though.

The tone of this conversation is probably a frequent event in the lives of Mary and John. We know this because Mary indicates that John has hurt her many times in the past, and the missed anniversary is just the most recent time of hurt. Note the significant words in this discussion between John and Mary: *feelings, hurt,* and *"I don't understand."* This kind of conversation goes on in nearly every household between people who truly love each other. In this conversation John and Mary are at least talking with each other even though they are not on the same wavelength. It could have been worse, a lot worse actually. Things are worse when there have been years of living together without expressing feelings effectively.

Mary: I can't believe you forgot our anniversary yesterday! How could you forget such an important thing like that? I feel like you just don't care about me and that you don't care about us. You just go about your business doing what you want to do and don't care about me. How could you forget such an important day in our lives? What is your problem? What is wrong with you?

John: Why are you so upset about this one anniversary? It's the 14^{4th} or something. It's not like it is the 25th or anything. Isn't the 25th the golden anniversary? It's just a day like any other. Besides, I fixed that light in the kitchen you have been complaining about. Isn't it more important for me to fix the kitchen light than buy you some stupid six-dollar anniversary card?

Mary: You just don't get it, do you? No, it's not the 14th anniversary. It's the 19th, stupid. And the 25th isn't golden; that's the 50th. The 25th anniversary is silver, not that you would care. It doesn't look like we'll make it to the 25th, much less the 50th. And no, a light fixed is not an anniversary gift. I just wish the light in your head would come on!

John: Oh, come now, Mary, you know I am just not good at dates. Years blend into years. Why is the exact year important? We're married, aren't we?

Mary: We may not be for long if you continue to be so thoughtless. You're thoughtless about our anniversary and about everything else. How many times did I have to ask you to fix the kitchen light? When you finally did, all you did was grump about it and throw your tools around. You'd rather watch some stupid football game than make it so I can see things when I'm fixing dinner. You are just thoughtless!

John: What's thoughtless about fixing the kitchen light that you've been bitching about for months? I didn't want to spend all my weekends doing house stuff like fixing your kitchen lights. And yes, I watch a little football on the weekends. What's wrong with that? You watch all those stupid cooking shows that do us no good.

Mary: "Bitching," is that what you call it? And it's *my* kitchen, is it? What is yours? The garage? I think the dog house would be a better place for you. All you care about is yourself.

John: If all I cared about was myself, why would I go to work every day, work on another degree, and then come home to do every little chore you have for me?

Mary: You just don't get it, do you? You told me a long time ago we would talk about our feelings but that has never happened! I'm trying to tell you about my feelings now hoping that you will somehow understand, and all I get is your defensiveness. It is obvious, all you care about is yourself. Just forget it!

John: I guess I'll go to the garage since we don't have a dog house. Let me know when you've settled down.

Mary: Don't let the door slam when you leave.

The previous conversation was at least tolerable and lent some hope for improvement. This conversation is really negative and not much more than defensive attacking and potentially volatile. How might Mary express her feelings and have John understand these feelings if the two of them were more fluent with feelings and not dominated by anger? In the following conversation note how both John and Mary attend carefully to their feelings and reach beyond attacking and defending. Note also how both John and Mary use many of the Rules of Engagement.

Mary: John, I need to tell you about some important feelings.

John: Mary, please can you give me a few minutes. There are just a few minutes before the end of this basketball game on TV.

Mary: Certainly. I'm in no hurry.

(Time passes.)

John: Let's hear it. You said that you had something important to tell me?

Mary: Well, important to me, perhaps to you.

John: Doesn't have to be important to me. If it's important to you, I want to hear it.

Mary: That means a lot.

John: I've learned so much more about you since I have learned about feelings. What's up?

Mary: Here's the deal. Yesterday was our anniversary and I didn't hear anything from you about it. That hurt me.

John: Oh no, that's terrible! I'm sorry. I didn't remember.

Mary: I know that special dates are not very important to you.

John: That's true, but this is about your feelings, not mine. I am so sorry. Please, tell me more about this, Mary.

Mary: Special days are important to me, and maybe our wedding anniversary is the most important of all special days, even more than Christmas or birthdays.

John: I never knew that. Tell me more.

Mary: I don't think it occurred to me to tell you. I just thought that you and I had the same values, the same loves. Special days have always been important to me. Fun, exciting, even adventuresome. I sometimes count the days until Christmas, a birthday, or anniversary. It's fun to look forward to these days.

John: I'm beginning to understand, but it is still a stretch for me. Please go on, Mary. I need to learn about this part of your feelings.

Mary: I don't know what more I can say. Maybe I can just tell you a few days ahead of time that I am looking forward to a special day.

John: Then, maybe I can buy a present or a flower or something.

Mary: Thanks for that idea, but it is more important for me to have you understand my feeling than anything you might do. Yes, flowers or something would be nice, but this special day's thing is about how I feel, not about what you do.

John: I think I am beginning to get it. I still think it's a good idea for me to keep in mind your valuing special days. I am going to set a notice on my phone right now so that I don't forget the next one. Actually, maybe I have a bit more of that in me than I might think. I would never forget when

Super Bowl Sunday is… I will try better and recognize how important these special days are for you.

Mary: Thank you for hearing me on this, John. It means a lot to me.

Note again how Mary started and Mary ended with John adding little to the conversation with a primary focus on understanding Mary and her value system, which includes special days. There is no justification, no explanation, and little in the way of facts. It's all about feelings, primarily Mary's feelings. How easy would it be for Mary to indulge herself in anger or John to just be defensive?

This example of the anniversary is ripe with potential anger, but what about the other defense-based emotion of fear. When someone is afraid or anxious, it is even harder to express, communicate, and engender understanding in the other person who probably doesn't have the same fear, and might not have the same feeling underlying the fear. Recall that fear is our most basic emotion, something that keeps us alive. We all have fears, most of them seeming to be "irrational," but if we look closer at any fear, we can ultimately determine the origin of the fear and find a way to overcome it. Let's look at a couple of "John and Mary" interactions that have to do with fear, first examining an ungoverned emotional expression and an unresponsive reaction. Then we will look at how John and Mary might do better with communicating something that is anxiety-provoking without attack and defense.

John: Watch out, Mary! You almost hit that car pulling into the street. Do you know what you're doing?

Mary: I know perfectly well what I am doing. I saw that guy and I determined that he was going to stop.

John: You're driving is dangerous. You do things like this all the time.

Mary: There you go again, criticizing me. Do I do anything right in your eyes? You seem to think I'm stupid.

John: I think the way you don't watch where you're going is stupid.

Mary: If you don't like the way I drive, you can get out any time.

John: (Expletives).

What's happening in this scenario? Neither John nor Mary is using any of the "rules of engagement," most important of which, is staying with the "feeling" that someone has. Then we have the typical tit-for-tat, feeling-for feeling that often goes on between people when they feel different things and have different emotions. Mary is certainly not listening to John, but the more important thing is that John is not communicating his feeling, specifically the emotion that erupts from his feeling. Let's see if we can reconstruct this conversation in such a way that John can communicate his emotion first and perhaps then the feeling underneath so that Mary can understand him better, love him better, give to him some due, but not give into him.

John: I felt really scared when that guy pulled out of his driveway right in front of you.

Mary: I'm so sorry, John. I saw the guy pulling out. But more importantly, you are telling me about your feelings and I want to hear.

John: You know, we have had this conversation a number of times, but I haven't always told you how I feel. There are many times when you're driving when I feel scared. I don't think you're a bad driver, but you drive more aggressively than I do, and I end up being scared pretty frequently.

Mary: Again, I'm so sorry to scare you. Tell me more, John.

John: Thank you, Mary. I know you see different things than I see when you're driving, but it is important for me to tell you about being scared.

Mary: I understand scared, John, and I don't want to do anything that aggravates any kind of anxiety in you.

John: I feel kinda silly telling you about this fear thing. It doesn't feel very manly. But I know that it is real and I can't ignore it.

Mary: John, tell me every time you feel scared when I'm driving. I need to know when that happens. Perhaps I can manage my driving a bit more.

John: Honestly, Mary, I don't think it is so much about your driving as it is about driving in general. I need to think about this fear/driving matter a bit and figure it out.

Mary: Let me know if we need to talk more.

Note that, again, John's emotion was prominent in the discussion, not what Mary was doing or wasn't doing. John saying that he was "scared": allowed Mary to accommodate to his emotion. He didn't attack her and she didn't defend herself. How different is this conversation with people respecting the importance of the emotion of the situation, particularly when it is fear. This allows John to think about the fear and possibly do some psychological work on it, also possibly coming back to Mary later that night when he might talk about what the fear/driving thing is all about.

TEMPERAMENTAL CONVERSATIONS

We have discussed many aspects of how feelings are felt, expressed, and understood, but some of the most dramatic challenges that occur in feeling-based conversations has to with personality differences. In Chapter 3 we discussed a framework of personality temperament that we have found helpful in understanding people and how they experience and express feelings. Let's consider some examples of good, and not-so-good conversations that are reflections of the temperament differences that people have. First, consider that John and Mary are quite different in temperament, say, John is predominately a "lover" and secondarily a "player." Mary could be first an "analyst" and secondarily a "caretaker." A "temperamental" conversation might ensue something like this:

John: We don't have enough intimacy in our relationship.

Mary: You mean that we don't have enough sex, right?

John: Well, certainly, but intimacy is much more than sex. It's talking, getting together, being together, and enjoying each other's company.

Mary: Like snuggling on the couch watching a movie?

John: Well, that would be nice.

Mary: You know that I'm not a snuggler. Never have been.

John: Well, I am. I don't know what's wrong with you that you don't enjoy intimacy.

Mary: I enjoy intimacy, just not the snuggling sex-all-the-time kind of intimacy.

John: What else is there to intimacy? Being together, enjoying one another's presence, enjoying each other's bodies close to each other.

Mary: Lots. Like thinking, reading, talking, figuring things out. Maybe doing something that we both like.

John: That sounds like a class in philosophy.

Mary: My favorite classes in college.

John: Philosophy: sounds like a bunch of old German guys using long words.

Mary: Complex concepts require complex words.

John: I suppose those guys didn't need to have intimacy.

Mary: It's possible that they found intimacy in figuring out how the universe works.

John: So, let me be philosophical: are we going to have sex today or not?

Mary: Haven't thought about it.

John: It seems you never think about it.

Mary: You have no idea.

John: Right on that.

This conversation, if we even call it that, could go on for hours without any kind of resolution. Note how neither of these people is good at expressing feelings, and much worse at hearing feelings. Furthermore, they both seem bent on staying with how they see the world, John as a lover, which means a good deal of togetherness, connectedness, and physical intimacy. Mary has no idea of what John is talking about and hears his plea as primarily a sexual matter, whereas sex is but one part of his desire for connection. If either of them, preferably both of them, are aware of their temperaments, they might be able to communicate like this:

John: Mary, I need to tell you some feelings that seem quite important to me.

Mary: I'm all ears. Shoot.

John: You certainly know that I love you.

Mary: No doubt about that. I hear it from you every day, usually multiple times. I should be more appreciative. Many women do not hear such things.

John: Thanks. Glad you hear it; glad you believe it. My "feelings" has to do with this deep love I have for you.

Mary: I can't wait. You know, we've both been learning about how we can always get better at understanding each other by hearing each other's feelings.

John: Exactly. So, let me muddle through this feeling thing and see if I can successfully communicate my feelings. I'm still not good at it.

Mary: Muddle on. Feelings are murky waters. I will do my best to muddle with you.

John: This love thing, this "lover" temperament that I seem to have is talking to me a lot lately. My kind of love is one that is of connection, as you know, and this connection has a lot to do with being physically near you and physically connected to you.

Mary: You mean sex?

John: More than that. Sex is a part of this connection thing, and when we have sex, that is perhaps the best kind of connection. But "connection" is more than sex. It is union. Union of souls as we unify our bodies.

Mary: I hear the words, John, but I'm still a bit in the dark.

John: I know, and I'm sorry I can't be more concrete and specific. Let me say a bit more about this connection thing because it is at the heart of the feelings I have had lately.

Mary: Great, go on.

John: I think it comes down to this: I miss you. I miss being with you more, talking, snuggling, yes, having sex together, and just being together.

Mary: Help me with this John. It seems that we are together a lot. We talk a lot. We go out to dinner together. We have friends over for dinner. We go to plays and concerts. So, what is the "together" that you are talking about?

John: Yes, I know we do all that kind of togetherness, but there is another kind of connection that I seem to be missing. I think it has a lot to do with just being physically close, sometimes sexual, sometimes not, just physically close.

Mary: John, I really appreciate what you're saying here, talking about your feelings, but I need to hear more if I am to really understand.

John: I'll do my best but this is tough stuff.

Mary: I appreciate your work here, John. I'm still with you.

John: You know, Mary, maybe this is a good time to stop for a while. You've been really good hearing me and working to understand me, which I really appreciate. I seem to have run out of words even if I still have a lot of feelings. I think it would be best for me to stop for now and come back at this at another time. Perhaps I just need to think more about my feelings and see how I can better communicate them.

Mary: You just tell me when. I appreciate all that you have said and am glad to wait.

Now this is an example of several things, not the least of which is a lover trying to say how he feels about the lack of connection that he has with his partner. We also hear Mary working diligently to understand what John is saying but also admitting that she doesn't understand much about what he is feeling. John truly wants to communicate his feeling of lack of intimacy with Mary but he didn't use the term "intimacy" and only briefly the word sex. Rather, he did his best to say a bit of how he felt, and then when he didn't know what else to say, he wisely called a time out. Note that in this conversation we don't hear either of these parties attacking each other, insisting that the other person change, but rather we have two people working hard to speak, listen, and understand.

The feelings in this John and Mary conversation are related primarily to hurt and loneliness, namely John's feeling of not being connected to Mary. We might consider this conversation problem-centered even though the problem is a love problem: John wants to be able to love and be loved more by Mary in ways that are commensurate with his lover nature.

Consider a different "temperamental" conversation that isn't so much about a problem as it is about someone trying to communicate the nature of one's temperament and the needs that are different from the other person. Let's also take this next conversation out of the realm of marital-like relationships into friendship. Consider that Barb is a caretaker and her friend Sheila is a player. A difficult conversation between them might begin like this:

> ***Barb:*** Sheila, I just can't trust you. You said you were going to come over to watch our favorite movie and you didn't show. I waited all night, never even heard from you, and eventually just went to bed. How could you so irresponsible?
>
> ***Sheila:*** I forgot.
>
> ***Barb:*** Forgot? Is that it? Is that your answer? I thought we were good friends. I guess I'm wrong.
>
> ***Sheila:*** Of course, we're good friends. I consider you my best friend.
>
> ***Barb:*** Well, if I'm your best friend, please tell me how you could forget a date with me.
>
> ***Sheila:*** I can't really explain it. I just forgot.
>
> ***Barb:*** What did you do then last night that was so important that you forgot a date with your best friend?
>
> ***Sheila***: Well, I was at home watching TV. Truth is I just fell asleep watching some stupid movie.
>
> ***Barb:*** Ok, thanks a lot! So, watching some stupid movie on is TV is more important than being with me watching one of our favorite movies.

Sheila: Well, that is what I did. Sorry.

Barb: Let me know if you want to make it up to me sometime!

What's going on in this conversation? Hurt. We've just discussed the centrality of hurt in the last chapter. We see a perfect example of someone being hurt and immediately transferring that feeling of hurt into anger and then into criticism and resentment. Barb doesn't understand that her "best friend" is a player who is not one to necessarily plan, much less to remember plans that she has made. Many players are excited about something, make plans, but then find excitement about something else and forget…or neglect… their former plans. Sheila is not better in this conversation because she doesn't explain or take responsibility for her freedom-based, spontaneous nature that is so basic to players. She experiences life more than plans for it. How could they have done better?

Barb: Hey, Sheila. I missed you last night.

Sheila: What was last night?

Barb: I thought we had planned a movie night together.

Sheila: Barb, I'm terribly sorry. I completely forgot about it. Oh gosh, I don't even remember making the plans. But that's no excuse. Again, I'm really sorry for missing time with you. You are very important to me.

Barb: Thanks, Sheila. That means a lot to me. I was looking forward to watching our favorite chick flick and thought you would show up. Eventually, I assumed you just forgot. I know you aren't a planning person, but still it was difficult for me.

Sheila: Certainly, it was important. Again, I'm really sorry. You know, Barb, we are very different in many ways, and I think these differences make our relationship rich. But maybe it would be helpful for me to understand you a bit better. Like, the "on time thing" I know is important for you. I've always been an "on time is late" gal and that has not always been good.

Barb: Yes, I should tell you about this part of me. Simply put, planning and executing those plans is very important to me. It's like, I enjoy planning and executing. I enjoy the looking forward to something. I enjoy the doing, but it's, like, odd, because sometimes I think I enjoy the planning far more than the thing that I actually do. We talked about movie night, like, two or three weeks ago because we're both so busy, and I have been looking forward to seeing you and watching a couple of Meryl Streep movies.

Sheila: I am really sorry. Real sorry, Barb. Forgive me.

Barb: Thank you, Sheila. I know that you are not an irresponsible person. And I really love your freedom-loving, spontaneous nature. So, maybe I can remember this important part of you to understand you a bit better.

Sheila: For my part, Barb, I will keep in mind how important dates and times are. I think we'll both be better friends. I look forward to a long and fruitful friendship.

Barb: We're on it!

Here we see two emotionally mature people negotiating the important differences that are in their personalities. How long did it take Barb and Sheila to get to this maturity? Years of work. Years of practice. Many mistakes and misstatements. Now they can deal with hurt without hurting each other more and without defending themselves. Then hurt is finished, but the event is not forgotten. For Barb and Sheila, as well as for John and Mary, to really communicate, they will not be able to jump from defense-based emotions to love-based emotions in a day. But they can do it. You can do it.

We have presented conversations between people who love each other but have differences, some having to do with temperament, some to do with values. We have attempted to demonstrate how we can communicate ourselves better if we know ourselves, know our values, and know the feelings that erupt from our inner core, which is always pure and perfect even if our words are imperfect.

Chapter 9

Scripts for Successful Feeling Communication

WE HAVE ENDEAVORED TO make a small contribution to humanity regarding how people can communicate better with one another. We have made a case that good communication is based on understanding the centrality of *feelings*. We have discovered, however, that while "feelings" are central to communication as well as central to being human, they are not easy to communicate. In fact, communicating feelings is imprecise at best and often seemingly impossible. Yet it is the imprecise nature of feelings that makes them so enjoyable, and it is the imprecise nature of feelings that gives us an opportunity to grow as people as we grow in our ability to express our feelings. Throughout the preceding chapters we have frequently suggested how people might communicate with the central message always being the communication of feelings, however hard that is to accomplish. In this final chapter we return to that procedure of examining various opportunities that occur in what we might call a typical day.

Sometimes this typical day is fraught with challenges and disappointments, while some days are full of joys and success with other days a mixture of all kinds of emotions. In each of the examples we set forth note the centrality of feelings, how they are elusive, how they are central to our psychological existence, and how they can make for a successful day. We have noted how these feelings are not only a challenge and a joy to communicate, but there are times when it is best not to communicate these feelings. Finally, we have noted how difficult and how important it is to speak feelings and even more difficult to listen to feelings that others speak to us.

You will note that in the examples of having feelings and communicating feelings we have presented the physical and emotional experiences of feelings, the thoughts that result from noting the physical and emotional aspects of feelings, and finally the decision as to whether to speak about these feelings or keep them to yourself. While we have previously presented challenging conversations where the speakers and the listeners were not so good at the speaking and listening to feelings, in this chapter, we want to give some simple examples of how people might choose to express their feelings. Note the emotional maturity and social maturity in each of these examples, namely that people know how they feel, which is the central element in emotional maturity, and have a rudimentary understanding how other people feel, which is social maturity.

A good day at work

- Your internal reflections are
    - You had an especially successful day at work.
    - You notice that you feel better about your work than you have felt in a long time.
    - This gives you a feeling of excitement in your body.
- The know how you feel *emotionally* - happy (joyful)
    - You know that this joyful feeling has to do with love.
    - You know that you love to do good work and succeed at work.
- You *think* about your feeling having felt it physically and emotionally
    - You know that it will be difficult to communicate this feeling but it remains important for you.
    - You know that your partner also has had some sort of day, perhaps good, perhaps not so good.
    - You consider the importance of your joyful feeling for you and know that it might be good enough to just feel the joy.

- As you think further about the good day you have had, you think that it is imperative that you at least make an attempt to share your feelings about the day.
- You decide to *say* something about your feeling to your partner
  - You find the right time and place to speak about your good day.
  - You start by telling your partner that you want to tell him about your "feelings."
  - Your partner knows that he now has the opportunity to know you better so he can love you better, so he says that he is "all ears."
  - You start talking about how good you feel and what you did today, and without being prepared for it, you find yourself tearful. You know that these are tears of joy, which is to say that they are tears born of love.
  - You continue talking being unconcerned for the tears.
  - You partner listens, and listens, and listens while you speak using the imprecise words of feelings.
  - You feel understood. You feel finished. But you also know that you don't need to hear anything from your partner.
  - Your partner knows the same thing, and so the two of you simply look out the window and relish the moments when one person has spoken feelings and the other person has heard feelings. Both partners are better for it.
  - You decide you need to go for a walk not minding if it is alone or in the company of your partner.

A difficult day at work

- Your internal reflections include
  - This was one of those days when nothing goes right.
  - You are definitely worse for having had this day at work.
  - You are not in the best of shape.
- You note the *physical* sensations that you feel
  - You initially just feel like "something is not good."
  - You feel that "pit in your stomach" feeling.

- You feel uncomfortable in your skin, like having an itch that you can't scratch.
- You are able to identify the *emotions* that you have
  - You feel primarily sad, perhaps sad about the day, but perhaps also sad about other things.
  - You feel a bit of fear, like if the boss has noticed that you are not working efficiently. You even worry that you could lose your job.
  - You are able to quell the fear-based feelings by focusing on being sad at having a difficult day while also realizing that you may be sad about other things as well.
- You *think* about your feeling
  - You remember that you did not sleep well last night, some of having to do with thinking about the difficult tasks you had to do today.
  - You know that you have had a lot on your mind lately.
  - You know that you have some important decisions to make in the near future.
  - You know that your mind hasn't been on your work lately because of all the other thoughts you have had.
- You consider *saying* something or doing something
  - You decide that you need to feel more and think more before you say anything because your thoughts and emotions are not very clear.
  - You come home and tell your spouse simply and succinctly that you've had a difficult day and that you need some time alone.
  - You go for a walk.
  - You clear your head and allow yourself to feel sad.
  - You find yourself thinking more clearly and conclude that your feelings are a cluster of feelings, some about the current day, some about the future, and some about the past.
  - You come back home, tell your spouse that you feel better, but that you think it best that you sit on your thoughts for a while, but promise to get back to her in the near future.
  - Your spouse thanks you for telling a bit about your feelings and says that you can take all the time you need to sort out your feelings.

An appreciation

- You run into the grocery store on the way home to get the can of tomatoes your wife says that she needs for the chili. You're already late because of a last-minute meeting you had to attend at the office
    - You get to the cashier stall and see that there are two people ahead of you, both with grocery carts stocked for the next month. You get in line, a bit frustrated.
    - The woman in front of you offers that you get in front of her because you just have the one can of tomatoes. You accept graciously, but now you are still behind the guy with the other full grocery cart.
    - The guy sees you behind him and invites you to step in front of him to buy your tomatoes. You graciously accept. You pay for the tomatoes and go to the car.
- You get to the car and feel a huge inhale of *breath* followed by an equally huge exhale of breath coming out of your mouth
    - You feel your stomach making this funny movement almost like your digesting something.
    - You find your eyes are filling up with tears.
- You recognize that you are feeling a deep *emotion* that is hard to identify
    - You are crying, at least a little, and you don't exactly know why.
    - You feel some odd combination of joy and sorrow, but still don't know why.
    - You allow yourself the privilege of crying, and find your head starting to hang down a bit as you seem to need to cry more.
    - You let this happen without knowing much but the fact that you're crying.
    - You finish crying.
- You begin to *think* about what you've just experienced
    - You realize that you have just encountered not one but two people who were generous to you, gracious to you.
    - You realize that you didn't deserve their graciousness, but find it humbling that these people completely unknown to you showed this simple act of generosity.

- You think of all the times you have been angry at someone for their lack of courtesy, whether at the grocery store or on the highway. You see that all those times pale in comparison to these few recent moments when you were the recipient of someone's kindness.
- You wonder what you might *say or do* after this experience
  - You decide you have to run back in the store and buy some flowers for your wife.
  - You might also grab a couple of bad-for-you candy bars for the kids.
  - You can't wait to get home to tell your wife what just happened.
  - So, you tell her the story. She gets it. She hugs you, and you both shed a few tears together. The kids see you two crying and ask what's "wrong."
  - You explain to the kids that crying is about love, sometimes sadness, sometimes joy. You tell them about the joy you feel.
  - You can't wait to get back in a grocery store cashier line and do the same that was done to you.

A disappointment

- Your son has just brought his first quarter seventh grade report card home. His grades were mostly Ds, one C, an F in English, and an A in physical education
- You feel something in the pit of your *stomach*
  - This something, you know, could turn into anger, but you restrain that emotion in favor of "just feeling it."
  - In a few seconds the pit of the stomach "something" has changed to a kind of calm.
- You begin to feel a great deal of *emotion*
  - The first thing you note is the feeling anger and the desire to rail at Jack for his grades. You restrain this angry feeling.
  - You know that you need to feel emotionally through this event before you say something, so you go to the kitchen and grab a beer from the fridge, Unbeknownst to you your wife has just

stocked the beer in the fridge, and it is warm. No matter, you don't need a drink. You know that you just need to feel through this thing that seems like anger.
- You begin to feel sad.
- You remember the emotion of sadness is a "love problem," so you began to think about what or who you love that has made you sad.
- You note that you have to continue to govern the tendency to get angry at your son.
- You begin to *think* about what has made you sad
  - You ask yourself who and what you love.
  - You find the first thing is how much you love your son.
  - You see he has many gifts, among them are his very outgoing nature. Everybody likes him, adults and children.
  - You love his other gifts too, like his interest in athletics.
  - You then notice how you want the best for him, want him to succeed in life.
  - You realize that your sadness has to do with seeing the loss that your son has had in getting Ds and Fs. You feel the sadness that he might not be able to feel.
  - The more you allow yourself to feel sad, you recognize the sadness dissipates.
  - You think more and more about what a good kid your son is. You mind wanders around all his strengths and abilities.
- You begin to consider what to *do or say*
  - You decide to say nothing for a while, perhaps to give your son the opportunity to say something about his grades.
  - Two days pass and your son hasn't said anything about his grades.
  - You take an opportunity one morning to talk to him. You begin by telling him that when you saw his grades, you remembered the time when you got a 1.73 GPA one semester in college and how one D put you on academic probation. You tell him how you had joined a fraternity and all that goes with it. You also tell him that you never really liked reading, and it was not until after college that you began to enjoy reading.

- You tell him that you expect he was quite disappointed in his grades; perhaps like you were disappointed when you got the 1.73.
- You suggest that the two of you go out back and play catch.
- You feel a great love for your son. The matter of his grades seems not to be very important anymore.

A view of the future

- One morning you find yourself thinking about what you might do in the distant future
- You find yourself taking a deep *breath*
  - *You* allow yourself to take this breath, and then another one, and then another one.
  - It feels good to breathe.
  - You forget about your thoughts about the future for a moment.
- Then you find a certain *joy* erupting out of you
  - You can't put an exact name to it, or a reason for it, but you just find yourself feeling particularly good for some unknown reason.
  - You allow yourself to feel this "good feeling" and it stays with you.
  - You take another breath, and then another and this good feeling continues.
- You find yourself *thinking*
  - How good is it to be alive.
  - How good is it to simply breathe.
  - You think about how complex your body and brain are in order for you to breathe without thinking about it.
  - It feels like you will always be alive, but you realize that you most certainly won't always be alive.
  - So, you wonder what might happen in the hours or years that you might have yet to live.
  - You find yourself thinking about how you might want to fully use the hours and years you might have yet to live.
- You decide to *do* something with these feelings

- You write a list of the things that you would really like to finish, like finish the kitchen cupboards that still need to be stained and varnished.
- You look at the bookshelf of all those unread books and write down the ones that you would really like to read.
- You write a list of the things that you would really like to experience, like going to Alaska, going sky diving, and learning to play the flute.
- You have enjoyed making this list so much that you decide to write a blog about it.
- You can't wait to tell your spouse about what you have been feeling.

A *view* of the past

- Sometime during the last afternoon at work, you feel this "something" in your *chest*
  - You take a moment while at your desk and allow this feeling to be there.
  - The feeling continues to be there and seems to get "bigger."
  - You find yourself coming slightly to tears.
  - You don't know what this feeling is about, but you decide to allow it to be there.
  - You tell your officemate that you will be back in a minute or two, and so you take a brief walk outside.
- You find yourself feeling a deep sense of *emotion* that begins to fill your chest
  - This emotion seems to be a combination of joy and sadness.
  - You know that joy and sadness both have to do with love, so you allow yourself a moment to just feel this emotion as it seems to wander back and forth between joy and sadness.
  - You still don't know what this emotion is about, but you allow it to be there.
- You find yourself *thinking* about all the joys and sorrows that you have had in your life

- You think alternatively about what you have done and what you wish you had done.
- You remember a time when you were nine playing cowboys and Indians with your friend Jackson Smith. You remember throwing your gun at him thinking that this was something that you do when you play cowboys and Indians because you had seen it on old westerns. You regret having hurt Jackson.
- This memory of having hurt your best friend leads you to think about other things that you regret having done.
- You know that you don't have time to think much about these regrets, so you decide to delay further thinking about regrets until you have some time alone.
- You go back to work still feeling alternatively joyful and sad but thinking primarily about the regrets you have about your past life.

- You still have the thoughts of regrets on your mind when you get home but by this time you have decided what to *do*
  - You have lots of things that have to be done at home, so you decide to postpone thinking anymore about your past, and go about doing the necessary duties.
  - You tell your family that you need to be alone for an hour or so, grab your laptop, and go to the den.
  - You decide it might be a good thing to write out a list of the things you regret having done. This leads to writing down things that you regret having said, and then things that you regret not having done, and things that you regret not having said. It turns out to be a long list.
  - You feel lots of sadness as you write the list of regrets, but you remember that sadness is about love…and loss.

- These thoughts of regrets, sadness, and love lead you to another feeling, first in your chest and then in your eyes
  - These tears seem to be more tears of joy than of sorrow.
  - You start to remember the successes you have had in your life.
  - You notice that you have moved from physical feelings to emotional feelings and then to cognitive feelings.

- So, you decide to finish the process of feelings and do something about these joyful feelings. You decide to write a different list, this time about the successes in life.
- (This is an example of one feeling leading to another feeling, In this case a feeling of past failures to a feeling of past successes.)

A conversation

- The situation: you are having a performance review with a subordinate at work
  - You feel pretty good entering this conversation because you have looked over this employee's resume and her work over the past year.
  - You have thought about the importance of making positive statements as well as making suggestions for improvement.
  - The conversation begins easily as you share a cup of coffee together and talk about her interest in professional skating.
  - But then "something" happens that changes the tone of the conversation. You don't know what has just happened but you know…
- That you feel queasy in your *stomach*
  - You simply notice the queasy feeling and let it be there for a moment.
  - The stomach feeling seems to get larger for a moment, and you find it necessary to take a deep breath as if you need to fill your lungs with air for some reason.
  - You allow these physical sensations to exist without commenting on them.
- Your physical sensations begin to lessen, but then you begin to feel some kind of *anxiety or fear*
  - You know best to simply allow the emotion to exist without trying to figure it out or change it.
  - The feeling of anxiety seems to have migrated from your original stomach feeling to a feeling in your chest.
  - You know that fear and anxiety are emotions representing a need to defend yourself. You don't know why your brain is telling you

that you need to defend yourself, but you allow this emotion to be there without judgment.
  - As you allow your anxiety to be represented in your chest experience, you note that the emotion changes from fear to a kind of sadness. You know that sadness has to do with something that is loved that has been lost.
- You begin to *think* about what might have been lost in this conversation
  - You consider that the feeling of sadness you have could be that your subordinate might feel some kind of loss that you have picked up on.
  - You consider that your emotion could be that you have lost a connection with the employee in this conversation.
  - You consider that something else might be going on with your employee than the content of the conversation.
- You begin to think, just to yourself, of something that you could *say or do*
  - You could just allow this fear-come-sadness to be there without comment.
  - You could ask the employee a question with a subtle reference to the emotion that seems to be in the room.
  - You could state your own emotion being careful not to intrude on your employee's personal feelings and personal life.
  - You decide to say nothing and see how the conversation flows and how you feel.
  - Your emotions subside, and you are able to get back to the matter at hand.
  - (In this case you have allowed the physical, emotional, and cognitive elements of your feeling to run their course and lead to action. The "action" you eventually have taken is to not say anything.

A moment that is too private to share

- The situation: you had a pleasant sexual encounter with your partner last night, but this morning you found yourself remembering your very first sexual experience many years ago that occurred with a different person

- Remembering this original sexual experience, you feel a bit of an erotic reaction in your *body*
  - You allow this erotic feeling to exist without judgment.
  - The memory you have and the physical feeling you have are pleasant.
- You find yourself being a bit *nostalgic* about this sexual experience that occurred many years ago
  - You remember this original partner and you together, and how pleasant it was.
  - The memory brings a true sense of joy to you in the present.
  - You have no thoughts about this original experience but simply the pleasant feeling that comes with the memory.
  - You are alone, so it is possible for you to just allow this joy to run its course together with the memory of this joyful experience many years ago.
  - Both the joy and the erotic feeling pass after a minute or two.
- You *think* about what you might say or do with this memory
  - You could say nothing.
  - You could talk to your partner about your experience.
  - You could try to engage in some kind of sexual experience similar to what you had with your first love.
- You decide to *say or do* nothing
  - The sexual encounter you had with your partner was good.
  - Your sexual encounter with your former partner was also good.
  - It is good enough to have both of these memories.
  - You decide that it is best for you, and for your current love, to simply have these two memories: one recent, one many years ago.

A moment that is too important to keep private

- You have been enjoying doing genealogical research and make contact with a distant relative who proceeds to inform you that your father is apparently not your biological father.

- When you read the email that contains this information, you are overwhelmed. You feel all kinds of things *physically* including the pit in your stomach, tingling in your fingers and toes, and for a moment, a feeling like you can't breathe
  - You allow these physical sensations to run their course.
  - Your body seems to be screaming from every cell. You allow it to scream.
  - You start to feel angry and start to think of what you can say or do, but you think better of it, and just allow the physical screaming to subside.
- When your body settles down, you return to the mixture of *emotions* that you had
  - You feel angry, and want to say something, but you think better of it. Better to just feel angry, you say to yourself.
  - You feel scared, wondering who this unknown sperm donor was but, once again, keep yourself from thinking too much. "Just feel," you tell yourself.
  - You feel sad. You have lost the person you thought was your father for all your 42 years, and you have lost any kind of relationship with your biological father. You have lost trust in your mother for having deceived you, and you wonder if the person you have known as Dad knew that you weren't his biological son. You are aware of all kinds of losses.
  - You feel like you can't trust anyone in your family. Is your sister really your sister, or is she a step-sister, half-sister, or biological sister? As these thoughts run through your mind, you realize that these are not thoughts, but simply words associated with your strong emotions.
  - You finally find yourself settling down emotionally, and take a good breath.
- Now you are able to *think*, at least a little
  - You wonder if the random thoughts you've had for years about being adopted might have had some measure of truth in them.
  - Having recovered from your initial anger and sadness a bit, you think that your Mom is a good person.

- You think there is some good explanation for your true biological heritage.
  - You think that your "father," the man who raised you, is also a good person, and there is no good reason to start calling him Eric instead of Dad.
  - You think hard about what to ask your parents about this. Is it possible that Dad doesn't know that he isn't your biological father?
  - You find yourself thinking more and more about your paternal biological heritage and think that it would be good to find out more of this heritage. Are you Swedish on both sides of the family as you have always thought, or does your black hair suggest that you have some southern European in heritage?
- Having felt through this difficult situation and thought through various things and options for what you might do, you construct a rational *plan*
  - You will contact the ancestry company and see if you can get more information.
  - You will not discuss this situation with your parents at this time.
  - You will talk to your wife about this so that she knows what you're dealing with and help you decide if and when to talk to your parents.
  - You talk to your wife and find that she is all ears. She doesn't have any of the anger, fear, and sadness that you have had. She doesn't have any suggestion as to what you can do. She listens to your thoughts and emotions and begins to understand this important feeling.
  - You feel better, have some plans and have some uncertainties. You are able to live with it.

The thoughts, feelings, and words that occur with all thoughts and feelings are varied as we have attempted to portray. We could fill many pages with other illustrations, but we hope you get the point: know how you feel, feel it, and then decide what to say or do…including nothing. You can see that any conversation that might erupt because of your feelings displays some of the important ingredients we have discussed in this book: speaking, listening, one person speaking feelings at a time, patience, acknowledgement of hurt as central, understanding that hurt is rarely intentional, and other "rules of engagement." It is hard to express feelings, and it is harder yet to hear feelings. It is hardest to have feelings that are a result of spoken feelings, but this is the hallmark of a mature person, a person who is emotionally mature, who then become socially mature. Let's consider one more situation before we close this chapter and this book. And this is an example of just having fun with feelings.

A giddy feeling for no apparent reason

- The situation: You're going about your day doing a bit of this or that. Things are going well for the most part and you seem to meet the challenges and the unexpected pretty easily. Then, all of a sudden, while sitting at your desk chair, you have this giddy feeling. It just comes over you with no warning
- You have an immediate *whole-body* experience
  - You would like to stand up, raise your hands and yell like you were part of a group of college students at a football game after the home team makes a touchdown.
  - You could just yell something, maybe even some curse word in exclamation.
  - You are laughing but for no apparent reason.
  - You are unable to keep from moving, but you are content to tap your feet under your desk.
- You immediately realize that you are feeling *joy*, just joy, just unmitigated joy
  - So, you allow yourself to feel this joy.
  - You dare to get up, go over to your office mate, and ask him to dance. There is some soft rock in the background, but it is not good enough. You wish it were salsa or rock. Nevertheless. You do your best. Your officemate is generous enough to give you a few steps, but then needs to retire.

- So, you go back to your desk and just bask in the sunlight, the artificial sunlight, by the way, of the overhead florescent lights.
    - You're good.
- You *think* a bit, but it doesn't take much thinking
    - You do think of all the things you appreciate in life, like work, family, kids, and your old classic car.
    - You can't wait to go home to tell your husband about your giddy time.
    - You don't waste too much time figuring it out because figuring out isn't necessary.
- You decide to *do* something about this giddy feeling
    - You write in your journal.
    - You do, indeed, talk to you husband.
    - You put this giddy feeling into your memory to recall at a later time.
    - You are really good.

We think that you can have giddy feelings like these and find ways to fill your life with them. In order to do this, you have to know all of your feelings, become safe with them, and appropriately expressive of them. We encourage you to trust the feeling process and feel more, love more and live more.

About the Authors

Ron Johnson and Deb Brock, husband and wife, are co-directors of Midlands Psychological Associates where they have logged a combined 100 years of work in the field of psychology. They have been together for 40 years, raised children, managed grandchildren, lived in Iowa and Newfoundland, Canada before coming to Wisconsin, and travel frequently and widely. They have similarities and differences in personality and have found ways of utilizing these differences to better understand one another and enhance their individual lives and their life together. Deb and Ron share a common philosophy regarding humanity that affects how they think and how they feel in their daily lives, and what they do in their work with people. They believe it is of utmost importance that people understand themselves, namely what they think, feel, and value so that they can successfully engage the world of work, relationships, and personal fulfillment. Instead of finding out what is *wrong* with people with one or more psychiatric diagnoses, Deb and Ron prefer to examine what is *right* with them. They have jointly developed a system of psychological analysis that includes personality type, personality temperament, cultural development, emotional development, social development, and the various elements of intelligence. From this broad base of assessment, they then proceed to assist individuals in their challenges with self-esteem, relationships, vocational adjustment, and general life adjustment working from a basis of strengths and abilities rather than weaknesses and limitations. In the process of facing people's life difficulties it is usual that Deb and Ron encounter the central phenomenon of "hurt" that is so central to life and central to this current book.

Deb began her academic career with a B.A. in Deaf Ministries at Mid-Atlantic Christian University, followed by a B.S. at Bellevue University in psychology, an M.A. in Counseling Psychology at Vermont College, doctoral work in women's studies at Trinity College and Theological Seminary, and a PhD in clinical psychology from Breyer State University. Deb works almost exclusively with women who look to understand themselves and enhance their lives. Her professional interests include the integration of spirituality and psychology through in-depth individual psychotherapy, personal mentoring, gender-related matters and teaching a client to "braid" her body, mind, and spirit into an integrated whole. In addition to her passion for her personal mentoring and psychotherapeutic work Deb experiences her spirituality primarily through nature. She loves gardening and hiking both locally on the Wisconsin Ice Age Trails and afar in the southern Utah canyons. She reads widely in psychological-spiritual integration, feminism, poetry, and enjoys perusing maps and world atlases. Ron and she savor frequent weekends at their cabin in Northern Wisconsin.

Ron finished his B.S. in history at the University of Wisconsin-Madison before entering seminary at Western Baptist Seminary and finishing his M.Div. at Denver Seminary. He then completed an M.A.in counseling psychology and a PhD in clinical psychology at the University of Iowa. He has a regular blog site devoted to his current thinking, which then often leads towards creating books. Ron plays basketball three times a week in order to keep fit but more to just have fun. He enjoys time at the cabin with Deb, reads extensively in history, theology, and psychology. His individual practice is devoted primarily to helping men find themselves, communicate effectively, and become leaders in their lives. He also conducts a substantial number of neuropsychological evaluations always based on understanding what is right about people.

Beyond their formal education and degrees both Deb and Ron have logged thousands of hours of advanced training, mostly in the field of psychology but also in theology, spiritual-psychological integration, and body-mind integration. They have also spent many hundred hours in self-examination, often with the help of various mentors and trusted colleagues. Ron and Deb have conducted many seminars, lectures, and workshops, have written extensively in professional journals, and have contributed chapters to psychology-related books. Their joint-authored book, *The Positive Power of Sadness*: *How Good Grief Prevents and Cures Anxiety, Depression, and Anger* was published by Praeger in 2017. They are also self-publishing *Friendly Diagnosis, Watch Your Temperament, Mantalk: How Men Communicate Their Feelings, The 4-8-12 Child, Seen and not Heard,* and *Balls: Men Finding Courage.* They are currently working on *Good for Me; Good for You.*

Annotated References

Barrett, L.F. (2017). *How emotions are made: the secret life of the brain.* New York: Houghton Mifflin.
    The author, a neuropsychologist, believes that emotions are "made", or "constructed" as a necessity of survival and understanding how to engage the world, particularly the social world. She suggests that we are born with an innate ability to do this "construction." She challenges the more traditional view that emotions erupt naturally out of a need for physical survival and pleasure.

Bennett, M.I. and Bennett, S. (2015). *F*ck feelings: one shrink's practical advice for managing all life's impossible problems.* New York: Simon & Schuster.
    A simple and irreverent look at the difficulties people have in life. The title reflects the primary author's belief that people need to get away from attending to how they feel and face their abilities and limitations. He advises accepting what you can't change, including one's propensity to various mental illnesses like anxiety and depression. He is against understanding and resolving traumata and in favor of doing what you can to go on with life, which is often unfair.

Bloom, P. (2016). *Against empathy: the case for rational compassion.* New York: HarperCollins.
    Makes a case for distinguishing "emotional empathy," i.e. feeling what someone else feels, and "cognitive empathy," understanding what someone

else feels. He notes the dangers of emotional empathy, you can't empathize with more than one person at a time, and distinguishes compassion from empathy. Recommends cognitive empathy because of the danger of meeting immediate wants but not long-term needs, whether individually or societally. Some neuropsychology related to empathy.

Brock, D. and Johnson, R. (2011). Narcissism as evil. In *Explaining evil: definitions and Development*, J. H. Ellens, Ed. Santa Barbara, CA: Praeger.

We review the current understanding of narcissism including the fact that young children all have "natural narcissism" as a means of understanding how they are a part of the world, which then becomes one's core self if properly engaged. Narcissism in adults is perceived as a developmental lag that is largely caused by a combination of neglect, indulgence, and shame.

Buckingham, M. and Clifton, D. (2001). *Now, discover your strengths*. New York: Free Press.

Buckingham and Clifton, principals at the Gallup foundation have developed a system of identifying strengths that people call the StrengthsFinder, used primarily in business. They find 34 "themes" as strengths.

Chapman, G. (1992). *The five love languages*: How to express heartfelt commitment to your mate. Chicago: Northfield Publishing.

This very popular book suggests that there are five "love languages," namely ways that people express love and want love expressed to them: Words of appreciation; Physical touch; Receiving gifts; Quality time; and Acts of service. There are, of course, combinations of these gifts, but the larger value is knowing that we do not love the same, nor do we want to be loved the same.

Claus, D.B. (1981). *Toward the soul: an inquiry into the meaning of psyche before Plato*. New Haven, CN: Yale University Press.

The author gives an exhaustive examination of this very early word, *psyche*, which how early Greeks conceived of what we call "core self" rendering a translation of "inner self." He also examines seven other words related to psyche that reflect various aspects of selfhood including words related to passion, heart, thought, emotion and nature. A tough read but immensely valuable for the student of etymology.

Csikszentmihalyi, M. (1997). *Finding flow: the psychology of engagement with everyday life*. New York: Basic Books.
In this and other books the author proposes the experience of "flow" as central to human existence, the heart of emotion and feeling, and important in human relationships, flow being the optimal daily experience when life moves forward positively. Consciousness is composed of emotions, intentions, and thought, and his preference is for "concentration," which is essentially thinking ahead. Flow occurs when a person faces the future with forethought based on experience but not governed by emotions but by using "arousal and control." Happiness results when one can look back with pleasure on one's hard work and success.

Damasio, A. (1996). *Descartes's error: emotion, reason, and the human brain*. New York: G.P. Putnam's Sons.
His first of two books espousing mind = brain challenging Descartes's understanding of a physical body and a spiritual mind/soul/spirit which led to a "Cartesian" view that body and mind were separate but connected, sometimes called dualistic. Begins with the well-known Phineas Gage traumatic brain injury and other contemporary impaired patients. A good deal of basic neuropsychology. The "mind" is how the brain makes sense of sensory input. Emotions erupt from drives that protect us.

Damasio, A. (1999). *The feeling of what happens: body and emotion in the making of consciousness*. NY: Harcourt Brace.
Deals with consciousness, again suggesting a biological substrate to it. He notes that consciousness and emotion are not separable, and that emotions are an integral part of reasoning. Discusses "core consciousness", which is primary, and extended consciousness, which is learned. Sense of self emerges from core consciousness. He distinguishes emotion and feeling,

which is the "private mental experience." Believes there are 6 primary emotions (joy, sadness, fear, anger, surprise, and disgust).

Damasio, A. (2003). *Looking for Spinoza: joy, sorrow and the feeling brain.*
The author looks at emotions as essentially neurological functions, which then become "feelings" as they are processed intellectually and become the stuff of what makes a person uniquely human. Feeling = thinking. Mind is brain. "Primary emotions" (fear and anger) erupt as a protective mechanism to perceived danger and reaction to pain, whereas "social emotions" (joy and sorrow among others) erupt later in the evolution of humankind and later in individual development.

Davidson, R.J. (2012). *The emotional life of the brain.* New York: Hudson Street Press.
A neuroscientist proposes that there are multiple "emotional styles," resilience, outlook, social intuition, self-awareness, sensitivity to context, and attention. He discusses both personality and pathology dimensions with each of these. Reflects much on the PFC as perhaps more the center of emotion than the limbic system (amygdala, etc.). An important focus is particularly on self-awareness, and he has much experience and sees much value in meditation along with its neurological substrate.

DeBenedet, A.T. (2018). *Playful intelligence: the power of living lightly in a serious world.* Solana Beach, CA: Santa Monica Press.
A study, largely with people examples of what the author proposes are various qualities of play: imagination, sociability, humor, spontaneity, and wonder.

Ekman, P. (2003). *Emotions revealed: recognizing faces and feelings to improve communication and emotion life.* New York: Henry Holt.
Ekman is known mostly for studying faces and the feelings that are represented in faces. He identifies the basic emotions as joy, sadness, fear, and anger that we see as basic, but adds disgust, surprise. He advises emotional awareness to prevent premature expression or action based on emotions.

He also studies other emotional experiences such as resentment and hatred erupting out of anger. He notes that fear always precedes anger. The feeling of joy can lead to contentment, excitement, relief, amusement, or wonder.

Forman, R.K.C. (1999). *Mysticism, mind, consciousness.* New York: State University of New York Press.
    The author is a unique combination of a true scholar and someone who works hard at explaining the phenomena of mysticism, particularly PCE's (pure consciousness events) that occur during certain forms of meditation and alternate states of consciousness. He makes a point of distinguishing knowledge that is "knowledge-by acquaintance", "knowledge about" and "knowledge by experience," the latter typified in deeply meditative states.

Gazzaniga, M.S. (2018). *The consciousness instinct: unraveling the mystery of how the brain makes the mind.* New York: Farrar, Straus and Giroux.
    A well-respected neuroscientist examines the brain/mind complex trying to find a way to avoid a mechanistic brain-only view and a dualistic view. He suggests the answer lies in the "complementary, which holds that a single thing can have two kinds of descriptions and reality." This view suggests that there is an "inescapable separation of the measurer and the object," which then leads to the creation of the mind.

Goldberg, E. (2001). *The executive brain: frontal lobes and the civilized mind.* New York: Oxford Press.
    The author deals primarily with normal and abnormal brain functions related to the two hemispheres noting that the right hemisphere is good at processing information and the left at processing familiar information. Noting that western civilization has increasingly focused on left brain operations, which are not "actor-centered" and adaptive leaving people to acquire such activities without instruction or enhancement. He examines evidence of gender differences in hemispheric operations, particularly the "context-dependent nature of males cf. the context-independent strategy more typical of females.

Herbert, N. (1993). *The elemental mind*. New York: Dutton.
>Examines consciousness from several perspectives. Considers that consciousness is "about me" while much of life is about others. Admits that a sense of self is impossible to quantify. The contents of consciousness are sensation, action, memory, emotion, and cognition. "Human spirit enters matter in some unknown way…." Notes that existence may be related to perception. Deals with the possibility principle and the random hypothesis to understand how this happens. A bit of study of minds connected in some way.

Hillman, J. (1960/1992). *Emotion: a comprehensive phenomenology of theories and their meanings for therapy*. Evanston, IL: Northwestern University Press.
>An older volume with 50-year dated references by one of the best known Jungians presents a comprehensive view of emotions including emotion as many things including: a distinct entity, accompaniment, energy, quantity, totality, situation, signification, conflict, disorder, creativity, and spirit. His last chapter, Integration is superb where he suggests that emotion is closest to the human core.

Hillman. J. (1971). *The feeling function*. Dallas TX: Spring Publications.
>Perhaps the best examination of Carl Jung's feeling function. The author reviews the earliest recorded understanding of feeling beginning with a quote from Moses Mendelsohn (1776): "We no longer feel as soon as we think." Our feelings are closest to our sense of self or soul, but they are stirred by the physical and social environment. "Self-realization is feeling realization." Feeling is related to the other Jungian functions of sensing, thinking, and intuition, but also related to physical sensation and emotion. For instance, we may feel our thoughts, and feeling often leads to emotion (or affect). The feeling function needs to develop in order to be useful in life. "Above all feeling provides the order and logic for love."

Jasanoff, A. (2018). *The biological mind*. New York: Basic Books.
>A focus on the neurological substrate of the mind. Author makes a point of noting the interplay of biology, brain, and environment to create the

"mind." Some interesting notes regarding other elements of the body beyond the brain, and how physical environmental and social influences affect the mind.

Johnson, R. (1994). *Watch your temperament!* Madison, WI: Midlands Associates.
A study of the four temperaments: player, caretaker, lover, and analyst

Johnson, R. (1996). *Friendly diagnosis.* Madison, WI: Midlands Associates
A review of personality type, temperament, intelligences, and development in an attempt to replace a pathological diagnosis with a "friendly one," then approach the problems of life with a life-enhancing approach rather than a problem-fixing approach.

Johnson, R. and Brock, D. (2017). *The positive power of sadness: how good grief prevents and cures depression, anxiety, and anger.* Santa Barbara, CA: Praeger.
In this volume we discuss the centrality of the emotion and feeling of sadness. We suggest that sadness is the most important feeling we have because we lose everything we love. Understanding sadness and allowing its process prevents (or cures) depression, anxiety, and anger.

Jung, C.J. (1970). *Psychological Types.* Princeton, NJ: Bollingen Publishing.
Jung is without a doubt the central figure in understanding much about personality factors, which he referred to as psychological types. He focused on differences in energy (introversion and extraversion) and how we gather and process information (objectively or subjectively). It is the subjective element that we are studying in this book, which would include both perception and judgment.

Keirsey, D. and Bates, M. (1984). *Please understand me: character and temperament types.* Del Mar, CA: Prometheus Nemesis Book Company.
A wildly popular book among followers of personality type out of the MBTI tradition. Proposes temperament as combinations of some of the elements of the MBTI perspective.

Lazoni, S. (2018). *Empathy: a history*. Newhaven CN: Yale University Press.
  A good history of the term, its origins, and its development starting primarily with the German Einfühlung, meaning "feeling into", with some early references, then Jung, Otto Rank, Theodor Lipps, Theodore Reik, Jesse Taft, Kohut, Gendlin, and mirror neurons.

LeDoux, J. (1996). *The emotional brain: the mysterious underpinnings of emotional life*. New York: Simon and Schuster.
  A foundational and classic book on the neurological components of emotions, e.g. the thalamus, hypothalamus, the amygdala, the hippocampus, and the prefrontal cortex. His basic message is that emotions have evolved and are necessary for our survival and thoroughly physical/neurological. There is no "mind" apart from the brain, nor does he distinguish feelings from emotions. External stimuli cause "arousal," which in then causes cognition, then emotion, and then action. Fear is the basic emotion for survival. Much in common with Damasio.

Lowen, A. (1967). *The betrayal of the body*. New York: Collier.
  One of several books by the author who follows W. Reich and others in the pursuit of biological-medical connections.

Lutz, T. (1999). *Crying: the natural and cultural history of tears*. New York: Norton.
  A fine summary of the history, chemistry, biology, neurology, frequency, personal, and interpersonal elements related to crying. The author notes "the more loving we are, the more prone to tears." Crying occurs not at the peak of an emotional experience but at some point after the peak during the return to a "sense of self." He reviews the "cathartic therapies", gender differences, and cultural differences in crying.

McGilchrist, I. (2019). *The master and his emissary: The divided brain and the making of the western world*. New Haven, CN: Yale University Press.
  The author provides a well-researched document regarding many aspects of the differences in the two brain hemispheres with many references

to neuroscientists, philosophers, and fiction writers. His point is that the Western world, and much of science, has been dominated by a belief that the left hemisphere is the "dominant" hemisphere. He makes a good case for understanding the right hemisphere as the housing for one's core self and "feelings." Read the extensive Chapter 2 and skim the rest where he departs into too much of a diatribe against left hemisphere dominance.

Myers, I.B. (1992), *Gifts differing*. Palo Alto CA: Consulting Psychologists Press.
This is one of the foundational books describing the Myers-Briggs understanding of personality type, namely the "16 personality types" composed of the four psychological operations. Particularly relevant to our discussion of is the "judging" dimension of "feeling and thinking" first described by Carl Jung.

Pillard, N. (2015). *Jung and intuition*. London: Karnac.
An in-depth analysis of intuition as understood and presented in the works of Carl Jung. The author notes the intrinsic connection between feeling and intuition. Intuition starts with instinct, then moves into the unconscious, then into the "underconscious," and then appears in thought or feeling. He notes the difference between concrete and abstract intuition depending on one's personality. He discusses empathy, inspiration, imagination as related to intuition, and then touches on trauma as it relates to the discussion.

Narramore, S.B. (1984). *No condemnation*. Grand Rapids, MI: Zondervan.
This author views the matter of guilt from a distinctively Christian orientation, hence dealing with theological/biblical matters related to guilt. He discusses "constructive sorrow," as what we might real guilt and artificial guilt, namely fear of judgment.

Orstein, R. (1997). *The right mind: making sense of the hemispheres*. New York: Harcourt Brace & Company.
The author's primary purpose is to suggest that humans need to fully utilize both hemispheres, an idea running counter to much of education,

which focuses largely on the left. He highlights some of the strengths of the right hemisphere, such as emotional and social development as well as music, but also notes the "global" perspective of the right side. Yet he notes how important it is for the two hemispheres to work together in all spheres of life. While the left hemisphere houses language, reading, math, and most cognitive capacities, the right side "makes sense" of things that can lead to meaningful action.

Perls, G., Hefferline, R.F., and Goodman, P. (1977). *Gestalt therapy*. New York: Bantam Books
 The founder of gestalt therapy discusses the technique that includes observation of physical manifestations of emotional reactions and emotional disturbance.

Pert, C.B. (1997). *Molecules of emotion: why you feel the way you feel*. New York: Scribner.
 This is largely a story of how the author, a neuroscientist, came to see how certain chemicals in the body, specifically neuropeptides cause and affect emotional life. These chemicals "join the brain, glands, and the immune system in a network of communication between brain and body." She reviews and applauds many paramedical procedures as helpful in emotional and physical health.

Power, J (1969). *Why am I afraid to tell you who I am?* Allen TX: Tabor Publishing.
 An older, simple, largely Christian take on the apparent fact that people are quite simply afraid to reveal their thoughts and feelings. The author's suggestion is that there is a deep need in all humans to be "known" but a related fear of being judged. He suggests that self-knowledge and self-acceptance are enhanced in self-revelation. Furthermore, self-revelation enhances both self-love and love of others. He also deals somewhat with (emotional) hurt and suggests that awareness of emotions does not always suggest that they should be expressed or acted upon.

Rafalski, Monika (2018). *Empfinden, Intuieren, Fühlen, Denken: die Vier psychischen Grundfunktionen in Psychotherapie und Individuation.* Translation by Boris Matthews. Stuttgart: Verlag W. Kohlhammer.

A recent addition to C.J. Jung's understanding of psychological type with a focus on the feeling function. Note the physical and emotional components of feelings.

Reich, W. (1961). *The function of the orgasm.* New York: Farrar, Straus, and Giroux.

This author was perhaps the first modern psychologists to examine biological-emotional connections. This book focuses not only on orgasm but eating, sleeping, etc.

Riso, D.R. and Hudson, R. (2003). *Discovering your personality type.* New York: Houghton Mifflin.

One of many books on the Enneagram.

Rohm, R.A. (2005). *Positive personality profiles: D-I-S-C-over: personality insights to understand yourself and others.* Emeryville, CA: Alibris Publishing.

One of many books on the DISC identifying four personality types: Dominance, Influence, Conscientiousness, and Steadfastness. Used frequently in business settings.

Schore, A.N. (1994). *Affect regulation and the origin of the self: the neurobiology of emotional development.* Hillsdale, NJ: Lawrence Erlbaum Associates.

This is a well-researched (2300 references) study of early infancy emotional development from a researcher familiar with neuropsychology, developmental psychology, psychoanalysis, and some psychotherapy. Particular attention is paid to mother-infant bonding, normal infantile narcissism, "moral" development, and play. Frequent references to the value and disvalue of shame as well as the importance of the PFC in the lateralization of emotions, the learning of control/inhibition, the ultimate development of self, and some examination of resultant psychopathology.

Schutz, W.C. (1967). *Joy: expanding human awareness.* New York: Grove Press.
An author central to the experience-based psychotherapy of the 1960's and 1970's, his ideas, while dated and limited are marked by a body-based understanding of feelings. Somewhat a student of Alexander Lowen, he proposed that creativity is the essence of joy beginning with experience, then association with other experiences and information, followed by expression, evaluation, and production. He seems not to distinguish feeling from emotion.

Schwartz, J.M. and Begley, S. (2002). *The mind and the brain: neuroplasticity and the power of the mental force.* New York: HarperCollins.
The author describes the neuroplasticity of the brain, i.e. the ability the brain has to re-wire itself. Examples from impaired individuals and normal development in childhood and adolescence. Does not adhere to the mind equals brain as with Damasio and LeDoux and is willing to allow the mind to exist without exact definition. He suggests that the noncorporeal mind is as fundamental to the universe as is matter. He challenges Damasio and others' "brain only" materialism, and yet examines extant neuropsychological phenomena. Examines mindfulness and Buddhist psychology. Uses the concept of neuroplasticity as a means of healing the brain by use of the mind through "mental force," something akin to will.

Seligman, M.E.P. (2002). *Authentic happiness: using the new positive psychology to realize your potential for lasting fulfillment.* New York: The Free Press.
The author is the co-founder of "Positive Psychology", which emphasized "what is right about people" rather than what is wrong with them. A number of strengths are examined, like optimism and hope that are well studied in the psychological community but also includes the philosophical "virtues" of wisdom, courage, love, justice, temperance, and spirituality that are less well studied but ones that the author believes lead to happiness. He deals with gratitude and forgiveness that are more relational in nature. His is essentially a cognitive approach to life, particularity to adversity. He compares the "pleasures of the emotions" to the gratification that comes

with utilizing one's strengths and virtues, but ventures into the realms of love, work, and relationships.

Stotland, E. (1969). *The psychology of hope.* San Francisco, CA: Jossey-Bass, Inc. Publishers.
An early work that is a thorough review of extant literature on hope until 1969, yet valuable as hope and resilience became central themes in positive psychology. He suggests that hope is the antithesis of anxiety, i.e. looking forward with fear or positive expectation, as well as the opposite of "learned helplessness" in depression. He also notes the importance of thoughtful planning, recovering from failures with a "schema," the value of social support. He examines hope and lack of hope in psychopathology.

Tangney, J.P. and Dearing, R.L (2002). *Shame and guilt.* New York: Guilford
The principal author, Tangney, developed the Test of Self-Conscious Affect, a very valuable instrument that distinguishes guilt and shame among other feelings. She has done extensive research in the area. This is perhaps the most valuable view of guilt and shame available.

Tournier, P. (1958). *Guilt and grace.* New York: Harper and Row.
A "Christian psychiatrist" early in the field writes eloquently about "false guilt" and "real guilt," the former being guilt as we see it, the latter as shame as we see it. A bit rambling, but a valuable distinction of guilt and shame.

Van der Kolk, B. (2004). *The body keeps the score: brain, mind, and the healing of trauma.* New York: Viking Press.
The classic neuropsychological understanding of trauma with a focus on the effects on the right hemisphere, the primary housing for emotions.

West, M. (2007). *Feeling, being, and the sense of self: a new perspective on identity, affect, and narcissistic disorders.* London: Karnac.
Perhaps the best contemporary understanding of feeling and its cognates. He distinguishes a "sense of I" and a "sense of being," the former being

the subjective sense of being, the latter an equally subjective sense of experience. The author relates these two elements of feeling into a right hemisphere, largely emotional, experience relating to the world and a left hemisphere, largely intellectual, experience of self separate from the world. He refers to this as the "identity-affect" model of feelings. One's sense of being tends to lead to subjective judgment of "sameness and difference," but prefers sameness and can lead to narcissism. Maturing comes from "affect regulation" without losing affect.

Wolf, F.A. (2002). *Matter into feeling: a new alchemy of science and spirit.* Portsmouth, NH: Moment Point Press.

    The author's basic tenet is shared by many other authors, some scientists, some psychologists, and some philosophical theorists, namely that the universe is founded not so much on matter as it is on feeling and thinking, which through perception creates matter as we know it. Love is at the heart of the universe. Much of his ensuing argument is related to how individuals connect with one another and the universe at large, which the author believes to be essential in successful life. "Ego arises as a spirit/matter interface." Feelings erupt into emotions, which in turn create somatic sensations. He proposes a continuing interaction of Jung's four functions.